Adam
Schaff
Language
and
Cognition

Adam Schaff

Language and Cognition

introduction by
Noam Chomsky

Edited by
ROBERT S. COHEN
Boston University

Based on a translation by
OLGIERD WOJTASIEWICZ

McGraw-Hill Book Company

New York   •   St. Louis   •   San Francisco   •   Düsseldorf

Mexico   •   Montreal   •   Panama   •   São Paulo   •   Toronto

Language and Cognition

Translation copyright © 1973 by McGraw-Hill, Inc. All rights reserved. Printed in the United States of America. No part of this publication may be reproduced, stored in a retrieval system, or transmitted, in any form or by any means, electronic, mechanical, photocopying, recording, or otherwise, without the prior written permission of the publisher.

Copyright © 1964 by Panstwowe Wydawnictwo Naukowe, Warszawa.

Formerly published as Jezyk a Poznanie by Panstwowe Wydawnictwo Naukowe, Warsaw, Poland

Library of Congress Catalog Card

Schaff, Adam.
    Language and cognition.

    Translation of Jezyk a poznanie.
    Bibliography: p.
    1. Languages—Philosophy. I. Title.
P106.S2513   401   73-4621
ISBN 0-07-055080-8
ISBN 0-07-055081-6 (pbk.)

1 2 3 4 5 6 7 8 9   MU MU   7 9 8 7 6 5 4 3

Introduction

The questions raised in this book are classical ones; that is to say, they are fascinating, tantalizing, and endlessly frustrating. These are problems that seem to fade from view as soon as attention is carefully focused on them. Is it the case, for example, that humans necessarily think in language? Obvious counter-examples immediately come to mind. Our only evidence of any substance is introspective, and introspection surely tells me that when I think about a trip to Paris or a camping expedition in the Rockies, the few scraps of internal monologue that may be detected hardly convey, or even suggest the content of my thought. In struggling with a mathematical problem, one is often aware of the role of a physical, geometrical intuition that is hardly expressible in words, even with effort and attention—I am not persuaded that Schaff's discussion of van der Waerden really touches the point of his argument. But are these counter-examples sufficient? Perhaps this is not "thinking," in the intended sense; perhaps the term "language" should be extended to other symbolic processes; perhaps introspection does not reveal the full extent to which the mind is speaking to itself. All of these suggestions are plausible, but they raise doubts as to the possibility of constructing a thesis concerning thought and language that is neither a tautology nor a fairly transparent falsehood. It is precisely when we find ourselves in such intellectual straits as these that philosophical analysis is called for, as a preliminary to any meaningful empirical study. We can be grateful to Adam Schaff for offering some new perspectives, both historical and substantive, regarding this and related problems on the borderlines of science and philosophy.

Schaff approaches the problem of language and thought, of the active role of the mind in cognition and of language in determining the activity of the mind, within the framework of a controversy between materialism and idealism. He presents a very useful historical summary of the treatment of these topics in modern thought, within this framework. This summary raises questions which will certainly continue to occupy scholars. Thus, to mention only two examples from the very recent past, there is quite a leap from Cassirer's assertion that "cognition never is *simply* a copy" (italics mine) to the conclusion that Cassirer defends the thesis "that cognition *creates* the world of objects," in its entirety (I take it that this is what is implied by Schaff's critique). Similarly, it is far from apparent that Carnap's "principle of tolerance" commits him to the view that the origins of natural language are to be found in arbitrary choice or convention. I would personally be interested in a somewhat tighter argument to establish these, and many other conclusions. Or, to mention a question that carries us back much further, it seems to me less than obvious that Humboldt's concept of form is strictly Aristotelian. I think an argument can be given that his characterization of the form of language as a fixed structure that underlies the generative activity of mind adds new dimensions to the classical concept of form. Nevertheless, one of the merits of this book is to call critical attention to some valuable earlier work that is too often neglected, or referred to in a purely ritualistic way, and to do so within a coherent and comprehensible framework.

Intertwined with the discussion of the materialism-idealism controversy is the issue of monism and dualism. Care must be taken to separate several strands in this discussion. Thus Schaff occasionally uses the term "dualism" to refer to the view that thought and language are not identical, that we do not necessarily think in language, a view which, he argues, has been refuted by empirical studies. This sense of "dualism" must be sharply distinguished from the sense in which "dualism" refers to the view that mind and body are separate substances. The issues are quite independent. These two senses of "dualism" define four possible positions, each of which seems internally consistent. Similarly, I think that one should refrain from falling into the easy assumption that a strictly materialist view requires, or is in any way associated with, the claim that "verbal language developed genetically, from animal cries which expressed emotion and served the purpose of emotionally 'contagious' experience," or from any assumption whatsoever about a possible "continuity of the evolution of ways of communication," including human language. Schaff accepts this conclusion too uncritically, in my opinion. It is true that in the past it has often been those who were concerned to demonstrate the divine origin of language who argued for strict discontinuity between animal communication and human language (e.g., Süssmilch), but this is a matter that has no bearing on the correctness of the hypothesis. I see, in fact, no reason to suppose, on known biological or linguistic grounds, or on grounds of general plausibility, that human language falls along any significant evolutionary dimension that relates it to systems of animal communication. But whatever the facts may indicate, it is clear, surely, that there is no logical connection between a consistent materialist view and any particular evolutionary assumptions.

Quite separate from the question of monism and dualism and the question of identity of thought and language is the matter of the activity of the mind in cognition. Again, this is an independent issue. The hypothesis that there is a subjective element in elementary sensory and perceptual processes can consistently be maintained by one who denies any influence of language on perception. And all of these questions must be distinguished from the question of "linguistic relativity," the issue whether a "world-view" or "the structure of sensory perception" is dependent on "the categories imposed upon cognition by language" in varying ways, determined by differences among languages. Again, it is conceivable that possession of language may affect cognition in significant ways without there being any actual or even possible difference among human languages in this respect. (I refer not to "logical possibility," of course, but to possibility with respect to the variety of potential languages accessible to the innate human language faculty.) The actual range of true linguistic universals—those that hold not by historical accident but that are, rather, essential to human language, given the fixed character of human mental processes—is unknown. Many would argue—I certainly would—that we have so far come nowhere near specifying the rich system of constraints that determine the form of language. There is surely nothing in such a conclusion to surprise anyone who holds that the mind is a device of a specific sort, the character and behavior of which is susceptible to physical explanation. About all of these matters, this book has many things to say, and raises many questions that have no simple answers.

The hypothesis of linguistic relativity as formulated particularly by Whorf, discussed here at some length, is one that has given rise to much interesting thought and speculation. Many of the inadequacies in Whorf's formulation are sketched here; there are others that deserve more prominence than they have received. Whorf argues that the structure of language plays a role in determining a "world-view," and supports his argument by contrasting the "world-view" characteristic of speakers of Standard Average European (SAE) with that of speakers of various American Indian languages. As Schaff notes, the hypothesis practically rests on the treatment of the categories of time and space in Hopi. The category of space is similar in Hopi to SAE, but the Hopi, Whorf argues, do not have our "intuition of *time* as a smooth flowing continuum," with a past, present, and future, in our sense. The basis for this distinct "world-view" is provided by the categories of their language, which does not formally provide the past-present-future analysis of verbal forms, as in SAE. Against this it has been argued that Whorf gives no evidence for a difference in cognitive modes corresponding to the difference in linguistic structure, but, rather, begs the question by postulating the difference on the basis of the difference in the formal structure of Hopi and SAE. Here, then, is a point where further research might reasonably be proposed, perhaps along the lines that Schaff suggests, to bridge the gap in the argument.

But there is, after all, a much more fundamental defect in Whorf's argument, namely, that his description of SAE is incorrect. In English, for example, there is no structural basis for the past-present-future "world-view" that Whorf attributes, quite correctly, to SAE speakers. Rather, a formal analysis of English structure would show a past-present distinction, a set of aspects (perfect and progressive), and a class of modals, one of which happens to be used to express future tense (among other devices that serve this purpose). Approaching English from a Whorfian point of view we would conclude that an English speaker has no concept of time as a doubly infinite line, he himself occupying the position of a point moving constantly from past to future, but rather he conceives of time in terms of a basic dichotomy between what is past and what is not yet past, in terms of an aspectual system of a subtle sort, and in terms of a superimposed and independent system of modalities involving possibility, permission, ability, necessity, obligation, future (the latter not being distinguished in any special way). The conclusion is absurd, which simply goes to show that our concept of time is not determined by the linguistic categories, in any detectable way, but is rather quite independent of them. If this is true of speakers of English, why not of speakers of Hopi?

From consideration of these matters one is led to several conclusions. First, the investigation of linguistic relativity presupposes an exact analysis of linguistic structure of a sort that is not available for SAE, let alone for American Indian languages. This is no quibble over tenth-order effects. Even an excellent linguist like Whorf was able to misconceive the nature of such a basic part of English structure as the system of verbal auxiliaries. What is more, it might yet turn out that Whorf's quite naive conclusion about English was actually correct. That is, further research might, in fact, show that at a deeper level of analysis than can be realized today, there is a past-present-future system underlying the formal structure outlined in the preceding paragraph. I see no indication that this is true, but it would not be a very great surprise. If it turned out that Whorf was correct, this would further substantiate my feeling that studies of linguistic relativity are entirely premature, since his correct guess would have been based on no evidence of substance and no defensible formal analysis of English structure.

When we turn to languages that are not well-studied, the premature character of the research proposal that Schaff outlines seems to me much clearer still. My impression is that Schaff vastly over-estimates the quality of the material that ethnolinguistics can provide. It sheds no discredit on the anthropological linguist, who is faced with problems of vast complexity and scope, to point out that the evidence that he can provide is of an altogether superficial sort. It has been suggested, quite plausibly, I believe, that an almost native command of a language is required before any substantial insight can be achieved into its structure. Short of this, the facts are simply not available to the investigator. This is, fundamentally, a no more surprising proposal than the conclusion, to which no one would take exception, that a biologist would be well-advised to immerse himself in factual material relevant to his theoretical concerns. The conclusion is somewhat controversial, in the case of language, only because of certain methodological scruples, borrowed from a poorly understood positivism, that seem to me quite indefensible. A fortiori, the student of "cognitive structure," in a cross-cultural context, is not very likely to arrive at very deep or convincing experimental results. In this area, one barely knows what questions to ask even in a familiar culture. For such reasons as these, I would tend to be extremely skeptical about the possibility of empirical research that will have serious bearing on the problems of "linguistic relativity." Quite apart from this, the initial plausibility of the thesis does not seem very great, to me, at least. The sources of the view that languages and cultures can exhibit almost limitless variety would make an interesting study; the arguments and evidence that can be adduced in support of such a view, even qualitatively, are not overly impressive.

In general, I think that one must take a rather skeptical attitude towards the available data regarding language and cognition and their interrelations, whether it comes from the study of normal adults, from pathology, or from developmental studies. It is rather misleading to speak of "demonstrations," "proofs" and "refutations" in these domains. There is, for example, no doubt that mental disability is a consequence of not having acquired a language, but one can hardly conclude from this that thought and language are to be associated in the manner that Schaff suggests. Other data suggest that deaf children with no language are not significantly different from normal children in performance on tasks that do not specifically require knowledge of language; cf. the work of H. Furth, for example. But the issues are obscure, and the experimental studies inconclusive. Caution is certainly very much in order, as well as a fair amount of skepticism about what the near future is likely to provide.

These are some of the thoughts that come to mind in reading this most timely and suggestive book.

Noam Chomsky
Massachusetts Institute of Technology
Cambridge, Mass.

Contents

Introduction

> The chief defect of all previous materialism (including that of Feuerbach) is that things, reality, the sensible world, are conceived only in the form of *objects of observation,* but not as *human sense activity,* not as *practical activity,* not subjectively. Hence, in opposition to materialism, the *active* side was developed abstractly by idealism, which of course does not know real sense activity as such.
>
> Karl Marx, *Theses on Feuerbach, Thesis I*

In establishing their philosophical lineage, Marx and Engels invoked the idealist tradition as well as the materialist one, even mentioning Kant as one of their predecessors. Moreover they admitted the superiority of dialectical idealism to mechanistic materialism in specific realms, especially in the realm which Marx termed the "active aspect."

Marx was quite young when he set forth his *Theses on Feuerbach.* He formulated them in a period different from our own, when philosophers generally felt neither constrained by nor interested in the rigor of precise thinking and careful articulation. Nowadays such rigor is exercised as a matter of course.

Marx's language is metaphorical. Almost every one of his phrases and expressions requires explanation and interpretation. The epigraph above is hardly a paragon of precision or unambivalent formulation. Yet it contains a profound idea which helps us understand many issues in the history of philosophy. I have in mind above all the evaluation of pre-Marxian materialism and idealism in the light of the problem of the "active aspect," which Marx identified with the subjective aspect of the process of cognition.

It was in fact the idealists (or primarily the idealists, at least) who developed the notion of the active aspect and the concomitant notion of "human practice" in pre-Marxian philosophy. For that reason Marx proceeded from analyses made by idealists (after having turned them right side up), especially those of Kant and Fichte, and not from an exclusively materialist tradition, once he had selected "practice" to be the foundation of his epistemology. All the more interesting, then, is the fact of the continuation of such procedure in the post-Marxian period (clearly confirming Marx's diagnosis). Thus, when we study, for example, the problem of the active role of language in the process of cognition, a problem of topical interest in contemporary philosophy, we find that it has been studied mainly by idealists and not materialists.

Why is this the case? Must it continue to be so? This is an important theoretical and methodological question.

A philosopher's approach to any problem is conditioned by a number of factors which affect his consciousness, and one of these is the philosophical school to which he belongs, a matter of immense importance.

Every philosophical school is shaped through its clashes with rival schools of thought. We cannot understand a certain stage in the development of materialism without considering its struggle with idealism, and vice versa. In its struggle with idealism, materialism is naturally inclined to bring out whatever is objective in the human picture of the world, whereas idealism tries to bring out what is subjective and connected with the creativity of the subject. This is a result of the basic conflict between these two *Weltanschauungen*. Idealism is more intimately connected with the problem of the active aspect only because it has been forced to be so in its ideological struggle with the rival trend.

This phenomenon assumes the proportions of a general law. But its manifestations are diverse and vary with the state of human knowledge and hence the constellation of philosophical problems, as well as with the determinate form which the conflict between materialism and idealism assumes at any given time.

But must it be so? Must the active aspect remain the prerogative of idealism? In principle, of course not. Nothing prevents a philosopher from both cultivating materialism and taking into account the role of the active aspect, or, in other words, subjective element in the process of cognition. In practice, nothing prevents this except one powerful factor—the one-sided approach, which eliminates a certain aspect of the problem only because it has been traditionally dominated and exploited by the opponent.

The problem of the active role of language in the process of cognition may serve as illustration.

Marxist philosophers have known for a long time that the process of cognition is the unity of the objective and subjective factors. That knowledge has enabled us to disassociate ourselves in epistemological research from both idealism and mechanistic materialism. In practice, however, this has not prevented us from transforming the copy theory of cognition into a mechanistic theory.

It is one thing to declare that the process of cognition, and hence of copying, includes the subjective element; it is another thing to make use of this factor in concrete analyses of the cognition process. Just what mechanisms are involved here? We are talking about the influences of the physiological apparatus of perception and the social conditioning of individual cognition. What do we mean by conditioning? What role does language play in this conditioning? Unfortunately, we Marxists have had little to say about this problem which has become one of the main problems of contemporary non-Marxist philosophy.

I think our relative silence is no mere coincidence, but regardless of how we evaluate this, there can be no doubt that the problem itself deserves closer examination by Marxists. In this way we can increase our knowledge of the role of the subjective factor in the process of cognition and further develop our theory of cognition; and we can also more effectively counter various idealist trends. And also we can better evaluate the non-Marxist stand on these issues. This is why the present work has been undertaken.

The problems discussed here have a long and respectable tradition, but this work is not a historical treatise and we need not concern ourselves with the whole of that tradition. However, the opinions at the root of contemporary philosophy interest us—as Marxists and as philosophers—not only as history. First and foremost, they help us put the contemporary period into perspective. Historical opinions are discussed in the two chapters of Part 1. The first chapter is primarily devoted to the philosophy of language from Herder and Wilhelm von Humboldt to present-day neo-Humboldtism, called "field theory." The second is primarily devoted to the elaboration of the philosophy of language by philosophical schools *sensu stricto,* and in particular to the trends best representative of contemporary non-Marxist philosophy: Cassirer's philosophy of symbolic forms, conventionalism, and logical positivism.

The linguistic and philosophical interpretation of the philosophy of language forms the background for the problems which interest us. The philosophy of language has recently acquired certain still fragile empirical foundations which are based on the conclusions and generalizations of ethnolinguistic research. This is indeed a promising prospect because it foreshadows the possibility of breaking through the magic circle of philosophical speculations and of formulating a larger number of verifiable assertions. These matters are discussed in Part 2 of the book.

The problems we are interested in here may produce statements capable of empirical verification only in the future, since the research conducted so far has not even approximately complied with our requirements. This makes the organization of new research a necessity. It must be based on a foundation that will guarantee adequately grounded, decisive conclusions. Philosophy can help build such a foundation by explaining and qualifying the problems and by analyzing the categories which are to form the basis of future research. This task is a semantic one only, but it may affect the trend and success of empirical research considerably. It is discussed in Part 3 of the book. The first chapter deals with the issue of language-thinking, the second with the relationship between language-thinking and reality, and the third with the influence of language-thinking upon human behavior.

This, in outline, is the structure of our present work. The work is, of course, based on certain assumptions, but it also suggests a program of research—and this, in my opinion, is its most important quality.

Part 1

The History of the Problem

Chapter 1

Linguistics: From Herder to the Theory of the 'Linguistic Field'

Habent sua fata libelli. One of the most interesting methodological problems is the analysis of the adaptation and reworking of earlier scientific insights under new historical conditions. An idea which developed in a certain period and a specific milieu and which corresponded to specific conditions and requirements of scientific development may reappear in a new period and in a new milieu but then it adapts itself to the new conditions and requirements. In one sense it is the continuation of the older idea which was provoked by the initial problem and became what Ludwik Krzywicki once called a "travelling idea" in time and space. But at the same time, it is a new idea, for its content and its entire intellectual and social context are new.

Obviously this travelling idea, having become less important or having fallen into complete oblivion after its initial success, will reappear in the history of human thought when the development of society or science makes its problem context important.

The problem of how a system of language shapes a system of thinking presents a typical and interesting example of the rebirth of old ideas in new conditions and their reinterpretation in the light of new needs of science. The problem was first formulated by Herder, and German linguistics from Wilhelm von Humboldt to the contemporary linguistic field theory has treated it continuously. But this is not the most interesting aspect of the contemporary rebirth of Herder's old idea. The main thing is that his idea develops in many different ways, often without any connection with Herder's basic problems. In raising the issue of the active, shaping role of language in the process of human cognition, the philosophic theory of conventionalism drew inspiration from sources in no way connected with the Herderian tradition. (The case of the adoption of conventionalism by the logical-positivist philosophy of language was different.) In the case of modern ethnolinguistics, this problem is treated differently once again. On the basis of empirical data on the languages of peoples from remote cultures, ethnolinguistics is drifting toward hypotheses which very much resemble Herder's ideas despite differences in philosophical assumptions. Now that the role of linguistic problems is increasing in epistemological research, that renascence of Herderian issues, often quite unexpected, is highly significant. It forces us to consider the present-day aspects and implications of these issues and to remind the contemporary reader of the history of the problems in question. Once he has taken into account what was discussed and analyzed before, he need neither repeat old errors nor discover issues long since discovered.

In his *Von den Kräften der deutschen Sprache,* a work of fundamental importance for linguistic field theory, Leo Weisgerber pointed explicitly to Herder as the forerunner of the idea of the active role of one's native language in the shaping of one's *Weltanschauung* (vol. 3: *Die Muttersprache im Aufbau unserer Kultur,* chap. 1, "Herders Entdeckung").

In 1757 the Berlin Academy of Sciences announced a prize for the best work on the question, *"Quelle est l' influence réciproque des opinions du peuple sur le langage et du langage sur les opinions?"* In 1759 the prize was awarded to J. D. Michaelis, professor in Göttingen University, and in 1762 his work was published. That paper, which the young Herder read in 1766 (and which disappointed him completely), provoked Herder's interest in the problem and gave rise to the opinions formulated in the second edition of *Fragmente über die neuere deutsche Literatur* (1768), in *Journal meiner Reise im Jahre 1769,* and in his work *Über den Ursprung der Sprache,* awarded an Academy prize in 1770. The idea which Herder developed at that time and which later came to influence some trends in the philosophy of language included the thesis that the system of the language spoken by a given nation shapes the *Weltanschauung* of the members of that nation.

Unfortunately, Herder's fate was similar to the one Lessing once prophesied for Klopstock: Who will not praise Herder, but who will read him? No one. And that is a pity. For when we do read the two-hundred-year-old-work of the twenty-five-year-old Herder, we must admire his brilliant insight into the evaluation of the role of language in the process of cognition. We realize that he was a forerunner of many ideas now considered the latest achievements of science. We find notions on semiotic, or the general theory of signs, an ideal language of philosophy based on a one-one relation holding between expressions and their *designata*; the organic unity of thinking and language; the semantic field of language; and many other linguistic problems in his works.

Herder's idea can be summarized as follows: Language is not only an instrument; it is also a treasure house and a form of thinking. It is a treasure house because the experience and knowledge of generations are accumulated in language, and it is a form of thinking because these are transmitted through language to the next generations in the process of upbringing. We think not only *in* some language but also *through the intermediary* of some language; that is what we mean by saying that language is a form of our thinking. Hence the point is that language molds and, in a way, restricts the mental process. The mold consists of the native language, which is an accumulation of the knowledge of a given nation, knowledge that corresponds to that nation's experience, living conditions, and character. Language is "a form of science, a form not only in which but also in accordance with which, thoughts are shaped."[1] In the process of upbringing we come to know ideas through the intermediary of words. We think in a language. Thinking is nothing but speaking. Hence every nation speaks the way it thinks and thinks the way it speaks. The language of a nation fixes its experience and the various truths and falsehoods which the language transmits to coming generations, and thus the language molds their vision of the world. "The three goddesses of human knowledge—truth, beauty, and virtue— have become as national as language."[2]

Language is therefore not only the instrument and content of science but also, in a sense, its pattern (*Zuschnitt*),[3] its "shaping maker"; language "determines the boundary and the outline of all human cognition."[4]

In outlining a program of research on the German language, Herder raised a question which often reappeared in the subsequent German literature on the subject: "To what extent is the language of the Germans in harmony with their way of thinking?" The continuators of Herder's idea and his method of approaching the problem raised the same question in connection with the problem of the 'spirit of the nation' (*Volksgeist*) and the related idealist mysticism. In Herder's works *Volksgeist*—as far as I know—does not occur. Of course his statements include formulations which connect the linguistic system with the national character, but these formulations are made in a spirit of rationalism free of Romantic speculations, Hegelianism, and the historical school of law.

> To what extent is the language of the Germans in harmony with their way of thinking? To what extent has that language influenced the form of their literature? How can one detect from the elements, pronunciation, and syllabic measure, from the whole nature of their speech, that it was shaped under the German sky for Germans who lived and worked under it?
> How can one refer in language to the world of situations and events, so that the proper content of the language may be deduced from the way of thinking and living [of the Germans]? What—beginning with the etymology of the individual words and ending with the structure of the style—can be explained by reference to the specifically German way of looking at things, so that the rules of linguistics should run parallel to the basic character traits of the Germans, and the entire great secret of the specific properties of the German language should prove the mirror of that nation?[5]

The spirit of the nation is interpreted here in terms of a "mirror" of the nation, but even this interpretation by Herder is remote from the interpretation given by his epigoni as proponents of objective idealism.

The concept of the spirit of the nation is as old as Montesquieu, but its mystifying form is connected with the German tradition, in particular with the traditions of classical German philosophy. *Volksgeist* and *Weltgeist* got into the ideological luggage of the nineteenth century through various channels and through the intermediary of various carriers. The concepts characteristic of Romanticism and of the historical school of law (Savigny and Puchta) had important influence, but the decisive part was played by classical German philosophy, and in particular by its quintessence, the Hegelian system. Those aspects of human communities constituted and organized by history which one usually interpreted sociologically or psychologically, Hegel made into absolutes and presented in the form of spirits of various levels. Whereas in Hegel's system that mystifying aspect of objective idealism is compensated by the genius of its founder, his epigoni usually lack that genius and leave only pure mystification. As a rule all epigoni who make use of the prefix 'neo-', in order to join some school recognized as classical, adopt the most backward elements of the classical systems and meticulously remove every manifestation of its true greatness. So it was with Kant's epigoni, and so with the various epigoni of Hegel. In these cases, the return to tradition was conditioned socially by reactionary groups that used the authority of historical greatness to oppose new social forces and transformations. It is obvious that the authors selected just those elements from tradition which suited their purpose best— elements which might serve reactionary intentions. A classical example was provided by the fate of Hegelian idealism, and especially the 'spirit of the nation', in the German humanistic studies of the nineteenth century.

Linguistics was influenced by Wilhelm von Humboldt's views rather than by Herder's philosophy of language. Humboldt's philosophical views were a mixture of the opinions of Kant, Herder, and Hegel. But on the problem now under consideration—the role of language in shaping a *Weltanschauung*—the similarity to Herder's idea is striking.[6]

The central idea in Humboldt's philosophy of language is the concept of the formative function of language in man's spiritual processes. That concept becomes a theory of the philosophical function and the inner form of language.

The problem of the *Weltanschauung* inherent in every linguistic system and the corresponding role of the native language as a creative force molding the way of thinking of the members of a given language community, i.e., a nation, is clearly of Herderian origin. In Humboldt's case, however, the connection with the idea of the 'spirit of the nation' is stronger.[7]

Humboldt considered the problem of the *Weltanschauung*-forming function of language so significant as to be *the* subject matter of linguistics. He thought that the opinion that different languages use different signs to denote the same objectively existing objects was a result of prescientific reflection on language.

The variety of languages is for him [for man] merely a variety of sounds, which man, interested in things themselves, only treats as a means of establishing contact with them. This view is detrimental to linguistics. It is a view which hinders any spreading of the knowledge of language and makes existing knowledge dead and sterile. *The true significance of research on language consists in studying the share of language in the making of ideas.* This includes everything, since the sum of those ideas constitutes man.[8]

The idea of a *Weltanschauung* inherent in language is closely associated by Humboldt with the idea of the role of language as a factor which transforms the world. He asserts that language is *Weltanschauung* not only because it is extensionally equal to the world but also because spirit can only comprehend the unity of the world thanks to the transformation of reality by language.[9] Earlier in the passage quoted above, he says that the essential importance of linguistic studies consists in revealing the role of language in making ideas. The concept of the role of language as a factor which transforms, or rather *creates,* the human world is combined with the methodologically fruitful thesis that language is not *ergon* but *energeia*; thus it should be studied dynamically, genetically, not as a ready-made and petrified product.

The same concept is also connected with the idea of an 'inner form' of language, the creative and transforming force inherent in language; but this idea was never formulated by Humboldt with sufficient precision, and consequently there were endless controversies over its proper interpretation. It seems that Humboldt used the term 'form' in the Aristotelian sense as the shaping factor. Since Humboldt moreover did not explain the relationship between the creative force which he rather vaguely called the 'inner form' and the *Weltanschauung* inherent in language, nor the difference between them, this issue gave rise to additional confusion and controversies. In my opinion the concept of the inner form of language which makes it some kind of intermediary between the world and man is closely connected with a belief in a specific force inherent in the nation. Unfortunately this notion is similar to the *Volksgeist,* a fact which was never mentioned in those controversies. This closes the circle of Humboldt's ideas on the cognitive role of language.[10]

Thus language is a nation-forming force and is also the force which plays a decisive role in shaping the attitudes of individuals. But language is also a product of the nation, of the spiritual forces inherent in the nation.[11]

Humboldt formulated that idea still more distinctly elsewhere:

> The peculiarity of the spirit and the structure of the language of a nation are so intertwined internally that if we have one we can deduce the other from it. *Language is also an external manifestation of the spirit of nations. Language is their spirit, and their spirit is their language. Their identity can never be sufficiently expressed.*[12]

The Herderian concept of the *Weltanschauung*-forming role of language thus found a consistent presentation in Humboldt's ideas. Through Humboldt it influenced the German philosophy of language in the nineteenth and twentieth centuries and gained entrance to the works of various scholars outside Germany. (For instance, in Russia A. Potebnia took over the idea of the inner form of language with all its implications, and in Poland in 1929 Jan Baudouin de Courtenay, known for quite different views, wrote a paper entitled *Einfluss der Sprache auf Weltanschauung und Stimmung,* which clearly echoed the opinions of Wilhelm von Humboldt.

The advocates of a linguistic field theory eventually accepted the ideas of Herder and Humboldt completely and tried to develop them, and on the road to field theory many works were written which testified to the vitality of those ideas and to their continuation in the German humanistic studies. True, there was not a full and direct continuation. Different aspects were accentuated (especially as concern the problem of the creative factor in language and the reflection in language of the spirit of a nation), but there *was* a continuation.

In 1899 Franz Nikolaus Finck published his lectures in a book entitled *Der deutsche Sprachbau als Ausdruck deutscher Weltanschauung;* in 1905 the principal ideas of those lectures were repeated in *Die Aufgabe und Gliederung der Sprachwissenschaft.* The old ideas of Herder and Humboldt of the *Weltanschauung* inherent in language and of the inner form of language (decisive for its active role in cognition) reappear. Finck, however, reduced the peculiarities of language to differences in the temper and character of various individuals.

The same idea was taken up within the context of the doctrine that the spirit of the nation is reflected in the nation's language by Wilhelm Wundt in his *Völkerpsychologie* (1900), the first part of which is devoted to language.

The connection between language and the spirit of the nation was more sharply accentuated in the works of Karl Vossler, following Croce's conception but at the same time continuing the tradition of German idealism. Vossler's ideas expounded in 1904 in *Positivismus und Idealismus in der Sprachwissenschaft* can also be found in his later works (*Frankreichs Kultur im Spiegel seiner Sprachentwicklung*, 1913; *Gesammelte Aufsätze zur Sprachphilosophie*, 1923; *Geist und Kultur in der Sprache*, 1925).

The tradition of Herder and Humboldt was also continued in *Die Sprache als Bildnerin der Völker* by Georg Schmidt-Rohr, where we read:

> Languages are not only products of the national soul and forms of the spirit of nations, but are for the individual completely the very spirit of the nation, as a living, forming, and shaping force, a force molded in a specific manner and having its own direction and specific personality. *Language is the very living, powerfully fertile and creative spirit* of the nation, in which mankind has been flourishing and from *which it has developed in the various nations.*[13]

'Neo-Humboldtism' and 'field theory' are ambiguous terms which stand for different trends and different shades of linguistic thought.[14] But if we set aside the differences between the various trends of field theory (above all, the trend represented by Trier and Weisgerber and the rival conceptions of Porzig, Ipsen, Jolles, and others) a linguistic-philosophical background remains, common to all. It is this linguistic-philosophical background which is the subject matter of our considerations. That is why we may reduce theories and standpoints which otherwise differ from one another to this common denominator.

Field theory is directly connected with the problem of the active role of language in the process of cognition. Its authors (this is at least clear in the case of Trier and Weisgerber) have taken over Humboldt's fundamental ideas: the 'world outlook' (*Weltansicht*), supposedly inherent in language; the 'inner form' of language, which shapes our perception of the world; a linguistic 'intermediary world' (*Zwischen-welt*), which acts as an intermediary between speech sounds and the world of things; and the 'spirit' (*Geist*), which manifests itself in language as the nation-forming factor. These do not pertain to the individual words of a language, treated as independent and mutually isolated units, but to specific wholes, linguistic 'blocks', which are called by some 'conceptual fields', and by others 'semantic fields'. This, too, goes back to Wilhelm von Humboldt, although its modern form has certainly been influenced by de Saussure's concepts of synchronic systems.[15]

Here we are only indirectly interested in field theory as a theory of meaning. Hence we need not examine the intricate details of that theory.[16] We need only examine its general idea, and that only as necessary for the proper description of those opinions directly connected with our topic.

Jost Trier begins his *magnum opus* with a terse and clear presentation of the idea of the 'conceptual field'.

> Simple observation of one's own speaking and hearing makes us realize clearly that a given word spoken in a sentence obtains its meaning *not only* from its connections with that sentence, and that that sentence is not the *only* reality which imparts life to a dead single word. A much greater role is played by another reality, the system of the whole objective conceptual field which is conveyed to and present for speaker and hearer alike. . . . A word is comprehended only in connection with that whole. The field of a verbal sign is to be comprehended, and it will be comprehended, only in connection with the whole. The field of a verbal sign must be present if a single verbal sign is to be comprehended, and it will be comprehended only *depending on the degree* of the presence of the field. It "means" only within that whole and thanks to that whole. Outside the whole field meaning cannot appear at all. The general theory of meaning will have to take this into account much more than it has so far. . . . It is not a single sign which *says* something, but a system of the totality of signs which may say something *in view* of single signs. In this way a word is combined with the remaining words of the same conceptual field into a whole governed by its own laws, and receives the scope of its meaning from that very whole. The

proper meaning of a word becomes known only when we delimit
it from the meanings of neighboring and opposing words. It has a
meaning only as part of a whole, since meaning occurs only
within a field.[17]

The philosophical foundations of the field theory in the context of
the general theory of signs were expounded by Karl Bühler in his
Sprachtheorie (1934). We have the advocates of the field theory to
thank for the theoretical and practical applications of the theory of
signs in linguistics. Their initial notion was simple: contrary to
appearances it is not single, isolated words, but their sets, or 'blocks',
as Trier called them, which carry meaning; and within each set the
various words form a mosaic and are semantically defined by the other
elements of the whole in the space of the field. The meaning of each
element varies according to the number of words and their order in the
structure of the whole. The movement of one element—as in the case of
a move of a pawn on the chessboard—suffices to change the structure of
the whole. True, the followers of field theory differ among themselves
as to the wholes into which language, in their opinion, is divided (Trier
interprets a conceptual field as a system of words within a single
category, e.g., the category of reason, while Porzig forms wholes from
verbs and their corresponding subjects or subjective complements, e.g.,
"the dog ... barks," and Jolles forms them of antonyms of the type
"right–left," etc.),[18] but their common idea is quite clear. Despite all
the objections raised from various quarters, the idea is a fruitful one
and should not be simply rejected without being tested practically, in
linguistic analysis. From the philosophical point of view, the idea that
meanings of words in larger conceptual wholes are conditioned by the
system to which they belong seems convincing and dialectical.

But, as indicated above, this is not the most important point here.
The issue can only be settled by linguists, on the basis of theoretical
considerations and the application of theory to practice. We are
interested in the issue because of its connections with Humboldt's
theory that language determines human cognition. To pursue this, let us
return to the book by Jost Trier quoted above.

> In making the subject matter of research the dismemberment of
> the field (*Feldaufgliederung*) and its variability, we raise an issue
> from the sphere of problems which underlies the notion of the inner

form of language. We see the ordering inner form of language in a new light now. For the order resulting from the inner form of language is manifested above all in the co-occurrence of words which belong to the same block and form a closed sheath of signs, and also in the way in which these words differ from one another in meaning. When this becomes known, the image of the world as provided by a given language is revealed to us. ... To study the division of the [linguistic] field is the same as to study a given fragment of the inner form of language, namely the ordering inner form of language in which ... the *Weltanschauung* provided by a given language is manifested at a given moment and in a manner which provokes no misunderstandings. The division of a given field permits us to come to know a fragment of a linguistic image of the world.[19]

The same idea is expounded by Weisgerber, both when he defines the field and when he asserts that the *Weltanschauung* provided by one's mother tongue is shaped by two laws, the law of signs and the law of linguistic field.

Essential to Humboldt's theory was the assertion that *Weltanschauung* is inherent in language and that this *Weltanschauung*, which he called 'the intermediary world of a language' (*sprachliche Zwischenwelt*), spiritually transforms the world (*geistiges Umschaffen der Welt in das Eigentum des Geistes*). These ideas return indirectly in the field theory, but as usual they return more strongly emphasized, and hence simplified. I have mentioned that epigoni try to simplify matters. This seemingly removes vagueness from the ideas of the master, but in fact it impoverishes them, in most cases, by continuing their least remarkable and most retrogressive aspects. Compared with the markedly idealist and chauvinist conceptions of his epigoni, Humboldt's conception is plastic, rich, and dialectical. This is the result of those "inconsistencies" of which it was later so radically purified.

A simple comparison of two texts, the first by Humboldt and the second by Trier, on the relationship of language, thinking, and reality will be very illuminating in this respect.

Owing to the interdependence of thinking and speech it is obvious that languages are not only the proper means of presenting truth already known, but also help reveal truths yet unknown. Their variety is not a variety of sounds and signs, but a variety of *Weltanschauungen*. Here is both the foundation and the ultimate goal of all research on language. *The sum of that which is knowable, as the field cultivated by human spirit, is situated between all languages and independently of them. Man cannot approach that purely objective territory except in a manner proper to his cognition and experiencing, and hence in a subjective manner.* ... But the subjectivity of all mankind is once again something objective in itself. The original agreement between the world and man, on which the possibility of any cognition of truth is based, is acquired by following the footsteps of the phenomenon, step by step, gradually.[20]

There are elements here of Kantian idealism, of which Humboldt is an adherent, and of the Kantian hesitation expressed in the concept of the 'thing-in-itself'. But there is also an interesting idea about the dialectic of the objective and subjective factors in the *process* of cognition. For cognition is interpreted by Humboldt as a process. Even if we do not agree with Humboldt's philosophy, we can not deny the profoundity of this idea and its importance for epistemology. Weisgerber quite correctly points this out in his comment on the above passage.

Let us compare the passage with a statement which may be considered typical of the field theory:

We cast a net of words on what we have a vague and obscure feeling about, in order to order it and to contain it in fixed concepts. The formation of concepts by means of words is a structuring process of explaining from the position of *the whole*. In doing so, language *does not reflect* real being, but *creates* intellectual symbols. Being itself, that is, the being given to us, is not independent of the kind and composition of linguistic symbolic structures.[21]

These two standpoints are so closely related and yet so different! Humboldt clearly finds it difficult to adjust his thesis of the *Weltanschauungen* inherent in language and conditioning human cognition to the thesis of the objective nature of the world in itself (*an sich*) as the object of cognition. He is as inconsistent as Kant is, but like Kant he is brilliant and profound. That is why his ideas on the subjective factor and on the role of linguistic system in the process of thinking are stimulating to this day, even for those who reject his philosophy.

Trier is consistent in his idealism; he does not experience the difficulties Humboldt felt, nor does he show Humboldt's hesitations. But at the same time he loses what was profound and intellectually stimulating in Humboldt's works, the dialectic of the objective and the subjective factors in cognition. The attitude of the neo-Kantians toward Kant is analogous to the attitude of Trier, Weisgerber, *et al.* toward Humboldt. The former 'purified' Kant of his materialistic inconsistencies: by eliminating (actually or as a result of interpretation) the thing-in-itself, they arrived at pure subjective idealism. The representatives of the field theory have done the same to Humboldt: of his original views only a peculiar amalgamation of objective and subjective idealism remains.

For Humboldt the problem whether language does or does not reflect reality was an intricate problem involving the dialectic of the objective and subjective factors in cognition. For Trier this problem is quite simple: language does *not reflect* reality; on the contrary, it *creates* symbols and thereby creates reality. True, Trier says he means that reality which is *given* to us, which is not independent of the system of symbols, but he does not mention that *other* reality, independent of man, to which Humboldt refers. In this respect there is a striking analogy between the field theory and conventionalism, especially in its radical version. The same refers also to the idea of casting a net of words (concepts) onto the world, by which we turn something amorphous into our articulated world, and we see that it becomes *our* product.

There is no doubt that Humboldt follows in the footsteps of Kant, in both the materialistic 'inconsistencies', and the nativistic idealism inherent in the Kantian *a priori* approach. In the case of Humboldt the *a priori* which makes cognition a subjective construction is the *Weltanschauung* inherent in language and the 'inner form' of language which makes it possible to transform the world into man's spiritual property, that is, to transform the world "in-itself," an unknowable noumenon, into the world "for us," an epistemological construction. Is this transformation subjective? Yes and no. In the case of Kant, nativism determined the clearly subjective-idealist nature of the construction of the world of phenomena. In the case of Humboldt, it is, of course, the individual who comes to know, and hence *creates* the world, but the creative force of language is conveyed to him socially through upbringing. Language is a nation-forming force and also an external manifestation of the spirit (*Geist*). This objective though ideal being was borrowed from Hegel, and was certainly quite alien to the Kantian tradition.

For his epigoni, the *a priori* nature of language was the most attractive element in Humboldt's opinions. It is easy to realize why this was so: it made it possible to 'purify' his views of materialistic inconsistencies and vacillations and make the whole theory serve the purpose of German chauvinism (since nothing serves that purpose better than all the variations of the concept of the 'spirit of the nation').

This specific use of the Kantian concept of *a priori* in linguistic philosophy can be found in the neo-Kantian Ernst Cassirer. His philosophy has considerably influenced adherents of the field theory, as the quotation from Trier indicated. Together with a clear admixture of the Hegelian spirit of the nation it forms the philosophical substratum of the field theory.

It is evident that the idea of the spirit of the nation, which underlies the concept of the active role of language in cognition, plays a larger role in Trier and Weisgerber than in Humboldt, influencing the entire conception more clearly and more strongly. But this should not surprise us. After all, a different period of history is involved, one in which the notion of *Volksgeist* was deliriously successful.

Of all the field theorists, Weisgerber is the most philosophically minded. In his works *Geist* appears in many variations, but its fundamental role for the entire conception is always beyond doubt.

> The sum of the results we have obtained will thus permit us fully to comprehend what we have obtained in investigating the image of the world provided by the German language, as *the reality of the spirit structured in language.*[22]

In another place we learn about the reality of *Sprachgeist*.[23] And in the conclusion of the work we read:

> If we want to define the source and linking of all our perceptions in a word, then we must say that the possibility of indicating the *traces of the shaping spirit in*

its linguistic form was growing in an ever increasing degree. And when in concluding our considerations we want to express our essential intent again, we shall say that we have tried briefly to sum up the data we have obtained on the subject of the existence, mode, and activity of the shaping spirit of the native tongue.[24]

True, Weisgerber thought it necessary to dedicate the final chapter of his work, which bears the significant title "Das Reich des gestaltenden Geistes" ("The Realm of the Creative Spirit"), to an explanation of the concept of *Geist* in its various uses, but those explanations only make it clear to the reader how vague the entire issue is. However, that issue does not concern us here. *Geist* plays only an auxiliary role in Weisgerber's construction of the concept of 'the spiritual transformation of the world' (*das geistige Umschaffen der Welt in das Eigentum des Geistes*).

The mechanism of that transformation is as follows: The *Geist* inherent in language (*Sprachgeist*), the meaning and origin of which are extremely vague, conditions the reality of the *Weltanschauung* characteristic of every language (*das sprachliche Weltbild*). That *Weltanschauung,* which also owes its origin to Humboldt, combines Humboldt's concept of *Weltansicht* (the world outlook, which is the sum of the results of cognition inherent in language, that is, something static— *ergon*) with the *innere Sprachform* (the inner form which is a dynamic force in the spiritual transformation of the world, that is, *energeia*).[25] What is of basic epistemological importance is the fact that language not only serves to communicate the results of cognition but also shapes that cognition by transforming the chaos which we call 'the world' into an ordered product of the spirit. Language becomes the maker, the *demiurge* of the only world that is accessible to us; and this is the world constructed by language. This is a truly Kantian concept, but applied to the sphere of linguistic categories rather than to the sphere of *a priori* categories. Weisgerber's subjectivization of cognition is, by the way, much broader than Kant's, since it covers not only the categories of time, space, and the causal nexus but everything given in cognition.

The concept of the transformation of the world by language may be interpreted in two ways:

1. As the acceptance of the role of the subjective factor in cognition: a definite system of language affects the process of

cognition and performs a specific function in it;

2. As the concept of 'creating' an image of the world (beyond which, however, nothing can be given in cognition) by a given system of language.

The first interpretation is rational; the second is mystical and idealist. I have emphasized that Humboldt's works were written in the spirit of the rational interpretation. Such interpretation can also be found in the work of representatives of the field theory (though much more rarely and indirectly). Were it not for that, it would make no sense to spend time studying the history of the problem. The point of such an investigation consists in the possibility of discovering, in the past, problems which are of topical interest today, problems which have been, or can be, solved rationally.

Yet in the cases both of Humboldt and of his present-day continuators we find indications (incomparably more frequently in the latter case) that the second interpretation is in no way an invention of ours. One indication, for instance, is Weisgerber's interpretation of language as a 'spiritual intermediate world' (*geistige Zwischenwelt*) which is the world outlook (*Weltansicht*) inherent in language.[26]

What we have noted here should and must be expounded in a generalized form. Essentially, for Weisgerber, *the intermediate world, inherent in native language, is associated with the forms of sounds of native language.* In other words, language signs have their counterparts neither in direct factual data of the external world nor in spiritual images of some other provenance, but in the specific mental world of the native language, which is associated with them from the very origin. Yet those language signs are, as it turns out, linked inseparably with that world, since they and that world seem to be *two aspects of the same whole.* This means that phonetic language signs are language primarily because they interact with the intermediate world of the native language. And that spiritual intermediate world derives its existence in turn primarily from the fact that the world of signs of a given language possesses strength and durability.[27]

It is not surprising that in such an interpretation of the linguistic *Weltanschauung* the transformation of the world by language acquires not only idealist but even mystical traits. Weisgerber is not alone in his opinion, which is in perfect agreement with Trier's view, quoted above, on the role of the net of words which *creates* our world out of chaos.

The natural consequence of the assertion that language *creates* reality is the categorical rejection of the copy theory of cognition.

> *The native language as a transformation of the world*: in this respect too this is no *ergon* or simple copy, but in its very essence an intervention (*Zugriff*) by man, a spiritual humanization of being.[28]
>
> No linguistic instrument is an ordinary reflection of being. A *spiritually shaped being* lives in each of them. The definiteness of linguistic instruments does not come from the aspect of "things" or "objects," but, to a far greater degree, from the transformation of "objects" by men.[29]

A detailed presentation of the idealist, mystifying aspect of the field theory is necessary for its proper understanding. This is particularly important in Poland, where the positivist tradition often underestimates the influence of irrationalism and mysticism in contemporary bourgeois philosophy. But the rejection of the idealist, mystifying aspect of the doctrine does not eliminate the research problems which have been mystified. The field theorists are not only speculative philosophers but, first and foremost, experts in the various specialized disciplines. This fact accounts for the double aspect of their views and the real problems emerging from the fog of mysticism and irrationalism.

One such problem which deserves attention is the active role of language as part of the subjective aspect of the process of cognition.

This problem was clearly brought out by Humboldt. In the field theory we find its rational form in analyses concerned with the influence of language systems upon the perception of reality and on the way we see the world when we think in a given language. This is a real problem which is raised not only by the field theory today; the results of its investigations may be interesting regardless of stratified idealist interpretation. We shall consider them in the concluding part of the present book, where I offer my own analysis of the active role of language in the process of cognition. Field theory analyzed the conditioning of the perception of the world by the various language systems using such examples as kinship systems, the ways of seeing constellations, classifications of plants, and the perception of colors and tastes. One idea underlay all those analyses and the results they yielded: when dealing with a definite class of objects (material things, relationships, etc.), we conceive of it in classification systems provided by the language in which we think.

Kinship systems are of particular interest in this respect, especially as regards possible future investigations on the relation of language to thinking. Kinship systems are differentiated according to the culture pattern of the milieu under investigation, and there is a wealth of research data to be generalized and given a synthetic explanation. Weisgerber describes those relationships by examples drawn from German and Latin.[30] Despite the meager comparative material, the results are obvious: in view of the differences in the systems of terms—much more developed in Latin than in German, because of difference in family systems—certain terms are not translatable, and the interpretation of the relationships for which these terms stand must be different in the two societies. If we were to take into account the Chinese language, the languages of American Indians, the Eskimo languages, the languages of Australian aborigines, etc., this phenomenon would be even more obvious.

Let us reject the idealistic speculations, which make Weisgerber see mystic 'spiritual objects' from the sphere of the 'linguistic intermediary world' (*geistige Zwischenwelt*) everywhere. Instead of engaging in mysticism, let us attempt a reliable analysis of the societies in question and the structure of the family within these societies. This will yield a clear and rational explanation of the differences in family structure as reflected in the vocabulary of German and Latin. But in rejecting mysticism for science, we should not reject Weisgerber's fundamental observation that linguistic differences are differences in classifications of the objects encountered in the world around us, which in the last analysis affect our vision of that world. It may seem of no practical importance that we cannot find a single equivalent of the German *Onkel* in Latin and that in Latin we must distinguish patrilineal and matrilineal kinship terms (*patruus* and *avunculus*, respectively) just as in the case of *Tante, Vetter, Neffe*, etc.).

Another variation of the problem is offered by a comparative analysis of the terms used in the various languages for constellations.[31] Again, we must reject speculation and engage in empirical social and cultural analysis (which Weisgerber provides to a certain extent) if we want to understand the various ways of seeing and classifying heavenly bodies in different cultural spheres (Weisgerber compares Graeco-

Roman and Chinese cultures). It is undeniable that the vocabulary of a given language affects the way people brought up in the group using that language see segments of reality.

Still another variation of the same problem is the way a person's perception of colors varies with the terminology for colors in his language. That field of research is now extensively exploited in developmental psychology, psychopathology, ethnolinguistics, and several other disciplines. The data accumulated so far and the resulting opportunities for a synthesis make this and similar issues of especial interest to philosophers. The picture becomes more comprehensive once we add data on the perception of tastes, valuations, and classifications of various objects (e.g., plants).

Let it be stressed that regardless of all mystifications and misleading philosophical interpretations, these data point to a real problem: the role of language as a component part of the subjective factor in the process of cognition. Epistemology is deeply interested in the solution of that problem. For Marxist epistemology its solution, and even its clear formulation, is valuable for at least two reasons:

1. It will help us to make the (Marxist) copy theory more precise. An insufficient explanation of the role of the subjective factor in cognition has been an embarrassing gap.
2. It will make possible an effective criticism of idealistic philosophy, which, especially over the last few decades, has focused its attention precisely on these issues.

We shall return to these issues in Part 3 of the present book.

Chapter 2

Philosophy: Neo-Kantianism, Conventionalism, Logical Positivism

The problem of the role of language in the process of cognition is essentially philosophical though its connections with linguistics cannot be denied. The philosophy of language is marginal to the science of linguistics, especially to contemporary linguistics. On the other hand, many issues traditionally part of the philosophy of language are, so to speak, the daily bread of the philosophers, especially of epistemologists, who are concerned professionally with the analysis of the process of cognition and who therefore may not ignore the function of language in that process. The process of cognition is always verbalized; to a certain extent this is admitted even by those who see the possibility of some 'true' nonverbal cognition. That is why philosophy has been concerned with the question of language and truth from its very inception and has offered various and often controversial solutions. A detailed history of the difficulty involved in understanding the role of language in the process of cognition would be a valuable contribution to a problem-oriented history of epistemology. Such a work is, however, still waiting for its author (though its beginnings are to be found in vol. 1 of Ernst Cassirer's *The Philosophy of Symbolic Forms*).

It would be important for its historical value (it would contribute much to the reconstruction of a general history of ideas) and also for the practical needs of contemporary students of the problem of cognition. In contradistinction to the pure sciences, the development of the humanities—and this is especially true of the abstract discipline of philosophy—has followed tortuous paths, where progress does not consist in simple summation of the various fragmentary relative truths and rejection of what has proved evidently false in the light of experience (in the broad sense of that term). In philosophy, the demonstration of truth and falsehood is extremely complicated, if at all achievable in a final and universally acceptable manner. Thus the development of the humanities, and of philosophy in particular, takes the form of a clash of opinions. Autonomous filiation of ideas is much stronger in philosophy than in other disciplines; the entire process is, accordingly, much slower, and in the course of analysis the grains of truth are much more difficult to separate from the chaff of verbal speculation. As a result philosophical problems live much longer and stay in circulation longer than is the case in other fields of human knowledge. The age of opinions is not a criterion of their being or not being of topical interest. Sometimes we find ultramodern ideas in remote epochs and we often realize that opinions of classical authorities satisfy all the requirements of modernity. Hence knowledge of the history of those problems which often fall into oblivion, misunderstood and underestimated by contemporaneous or later generations of investigators, is of particular importance. How many revelations have we witnessed by discovering important truths under the dust of age-old oblivion! Since the problem of the role of language in the process of cognition has a long and respectable past, there is no doubt that we might learn much by reviewing the opinions of the many generations of our predecessors, opinions lost on the long road of historical development. This is the principal meaning and the significance of the history of the problem.

But it is not my intention here to undertake that strenuous, extremely important and useful task. I realize the historical connections and parentage of the problem we are concerned with, but I prefer critically to examine modern views in order to become familiar with the philosophical climate and background of the theories involved. Of course, this implies a conscious selection, based on some criterion of evaluating what is important and which deserves to be brought to the fore.

In my opinion, the three most important philosophical trends in the twentieth century have been the philosophy of symbolic forms, connected with neo-Kantianism; conventionalism; and logical positivism. They differ from one another in many respects and in some respects even contradict one another (neo-Kantianism and logical positivism), but there is at least one factor in common: they each hold that language *creates* an image of reality; they reject the claim that our views of reality are a *reflection* of an order of things independent of us. In doing so, each of these philosophies starts from its own assumptions and justifies its standpoint in its own way: the philosophy of symbolic forms by a certain spiritual energy, conventionalism by an arbitrary agreement, and logical positivism by the consequences of the choice of a given system. But for all these differences they share aversion to the copy theory of cognition and accept an interpretation which makes language the maker of the image of reality. This alone would suffice to explain why we will analyze these theories jointly. But these theories have been chosen because of the undeniable weight and influence of their philosophical ideas upon the modern philosophy of language and, in particular, upon the formulation and resolution of the problem of the active role of language in the process of cognition.

To approach that fascinating problem from a new point of view, we must first consider the linguistic aspect of these theories in detail and then analyze them critically.

The Philosophy of Symbolic Forms

In one of his summaries of the function of language in the process of cognition, an article bearing the significant title *Le language et la construction du monde des objets* (Language and the Construction of the World of Objects), Ernst Cassirer explained the essence of the controversy which prompted his theory of symbolic forms with extraordinary clarity and succinctness.

> When we consider integrally the functions, the connections and intertwining of which determine the structure of our moral and intellectual reality, we have to choose two ways of theoretically interpreting those functions. We can see in them, above all, a copy, a secondary fact, or the original, a primary fact. In the former case the starting point is the assumption that the world, "that which is real," that to which those functions refer as their object, is given in a form ready as to its existence and as to its structure. The role of the human mind would then consist merely in taking hold of that given reality. ... The world is reflected in consciousness as in a mirror. ...[1]

Cassirer opposes this version of the copy theory by starting from statements connected with the 'Copernican revolution' characteristic of Kant's theory of cognition. According to that theory, cognition is a construction of the human mind, which (through a spontaneous act of synthesis) contributes to the perception of a given object those characteristics which we ascribe to it. Starting from this point, Cassirer continues his offensive against the concept of cognition as a copy of objectively existing reality. It is necessary to understand, he says, that what is given in cognition not only depends on the object of cognition but on the nature of the cognizing subject as well, that cognition

> . . . .does not reproduce a pattern already given in an object, but implies an original act which created that pattern. Hence cognition never is simply a copy, but always expresses the original creative force. The intellectual images of the world, which we get in cognition, in art, or in language, are, to use Leibniz's words, "living mirrors of the world." They are not simple receptions and passive recordings, but acts of the mind, and each of these original acts draws a specific and new image for us and outlines the horizon of the objective world.[2]

Cassirer's statement is interesting for two reasons: first, because it decamouflages the main elements of Cassirer's opinion, and secondly, because it raises issues common to all the defenders of the assertion that language creates an image of reality. This significantly clarifies the theoretical aspects of the case, which the esoteric language of elitist philosophers and the notorious vagueness and obscurity of formulations by renowned thinkers often make difficult to decipher.

Let us begin with Cassirer himself. He belonged to the Marburg school of neo-Kantian philosophy and agreed with its other members, and in particular with Natorp and Hermann Cohen completely. The problem of Cassirer's attitude as representative of neo-Kantianism toward the classical opinions of Kant himself (a problem important for pinpointing the specific characteristics of neo-Kantianism) will appear later in our discussion.

As a neo-Kantian, Cassirer came out *against* Kant's dualism. While Kant considered cognition to be a construction of the mind, he accepted the existence of a world of things-in-themselves, objective and external to cognition. That dualism led to the dualism of sensory perception and the *a priori Anschauung*. In accordance with a tendency observable since Fichte, neo-Kantianism strives to eliminate that dualism and thus be rid of Kant's inconsistency. Idealist positions are deliberately adopted and openly admitted. The offensive against the concept of things-in-themselves and an objectively existing object external to cognition ends in firm rejection of the copy theory of cognition. It rejects not just a vulgarized, mechanistic version of the copy theory, but all those ideas, whether empiricist or intuitionist, which claim that the object of cognition exists independently of that cognition.

Thus Cassirer comes out against the thesis that cognition mirrors the world of objects and defends the thesis that cognition *creates* the world of objects. He finds support in the old Kantian concept of the *a priori* nature of cognition, although Cassirer's theory of symbolic forms greatly emphasizes the *a priori* nature of the Kantian forms of sensory *Anschauung* and the categories of the intellect.[3] Starting from such assumptions, Cassirer can deny our right to speak of the existence of things-in-themselves: "The question, what is being-in-itself, apart from the forms of *Anschauung* and *Anschaubar-machen,* and what is its essence, must now be dismissed."[4] In general, one should confine oneself to the world of forms and reject the world of matter *as a useless metaphor.*[5]

Cassirer's frequent criticism of the copy theory, based on these assumptions, is the negative side of his thesis on the constitutive function of cognition, the thesis that cognition creates its own object.[6] That thesis leads us directly to the problem of the active role of language in the process of cognition.

According to Cassirer, Kant's 'Copernican revolution' consists in having taken cognition—not the world—as his starting point. Kant really was inconsistent, for he left the object as a self-existing thing-in-itself as an unknowable x. But Cassirer states in dozens of places that the mind does not *reproduce its object but creates it.*[7] By 'object' Cassirer means "intentional object"; thus the neo-Kantian concept comes close to that of Brentano and Husserl. This is only one of the ways in which the neo-Kantians tried to liberate themselves from the Kantian tradition of objective things-in-themselves.

At higher levels of contemplation it [thinking] is more or less clearly aware that it only possesses its object in so far as it relates itself to that object in a special way. What ultimately guarantees objectivity itself is the way in which it is approached, the specific direction that the mind gives itself in relation to a proposed objective context.[8]

An object is never 'given' to the knower; it is always 'made' (*gesetzt*) for it is always a construction, a product of mind.[9] Of course, the neo-Kantians mean an *object of science,* and not an object in the everyday sense of the word, i.e., a thing. Both Cohen and Natorp—and Cassirer follows them in this respect—emphasize the methodological nature of their analyses. They do not deny the existence of objects in the everyday sense of the word, and Cassirer even vigorously attacks Berkeley's thesis *esse est percipi* for its subjective idealism. The neo-Kantians do not talk about the world, but about the (scientific) *image* of the world, at least in their methodological declarations. It must be stated though, that contrary to their declarations, they did not go beyond the image of the world, beyond this construction of the mind. Moreover, they do in fact think it necessary to combat Kantian dualism, especially the concept of thing-in-itself. In their 'world' not only is nothing left which is not an image constructed by the mind, but the very possibility of something being left is combated vigorously and vehemently. Thus their procedures do not follow their declarations, something which has happened not just once in the history of ideas and is not the sin only of neo-Kantians. What is left is an idealist construction that may be interpreted either subjectively or objectively. Subjectively, the individual cognizing mind is considered to be the 'constructor' against which the neo-Kantians would protest vigorously; objectively, the construction is interpreted as a manifestation of objective spirit, in other words, when the logical, and not psychological, interpretation of Kant's *a priori* philosophy is adopted.

The key to Cassirer's philosophy is also to be found in the *a priori*. For Cassirer substantiates his opinion that the object is a *product* of consciousness and describes the mechanism of the *creation* of the world of objects by consciousness by means of 'a priorism', but in its modified version, not in its classical form, Cassirer introduces 'symbolic forms', which are forms of the creation by the mind of the world of objects. Symbolic forms also are *a priori* in nature, but in many points they deviate from Kant's classical view. (This results from the rejection of the concept of things-in-themselves.)

To Kant forms of sensory appearance, *Anschauung*, and categories of intellect, such as time, space, and causal nexus, were interpreted as constant, universal, and inborn in every mind (a specific kind of nativism). Their function was confined to *cognition,* to science. Cassirer rejected nativism (though it is not always clear whether his choice of the objective interpretation, in the spirit of Hegelian phenomenology, is the only one and the final one), and he refused to limit the forms to cognition and science. He claimed they were constitutive of all manifestations of mental life. What are Cassirer's symbolic forms and what is their function?

We learn only that symbolic forms are a special mental energy and that their function consists in creating our image of the world.[10]

Husserl took the scholastic doctrine of 'intentional act' and 'intentional object' from Brentano. An object is constituted by intention which imparts meaning to judgments; an object is that upon which intention is directed. What that mysterious intention is if it is not a psychological act and in what it consists are not explained by Husserl. Cassirer introduces something no less mysterious (although he en- deavors to explain that 'something'), namely the 'symbolic form' thanks to which cognition establishes the object of consciousness. A symbolic form is also not a psychological act, but is, we are told, mental energy of an *a priori* nature (but not inborn, as the nativists would interpret it), the function of which is the *creation* of the world of objects (of course, in the sense of objects of consciousness). This idea is no clearer than in Husserl, although the idea's intent is evident. It intends to announce that the world of objects is a construction and to reject the thing-in-itself and the reflection theory of cognition completely. Without the concept of symbolic forms it is impossible to postulate a world of objects constructed by consciousness, a world covering all 'reality', a correlate not only of cognition, but also of religious, aesthetic, and other cultural experiences.

> The Copernican revolution which Kant began, takes on a new and amplified meaning. It refers no longer solely to the function of logical judgment but extends with equal justification and right to every trend and every principle by which the human spirit gives form to reality.[11]

Thus analysis should not start from 'reality', reduced to some common element existing 'outside' consciousness; the point of departure should be the forms of consciousness and their *unity*. Hence again, as was the case with Kant, the 'Copernican revolution' remains clearly idealistic in nature.

Symbolic forms produce an image of the world, not arbitrarily, but lawfully. The philosophy of symbolic forms, which contrasts the world of signs to the world of objects, is concerned with the discovery and formulation of that law.

There are various symbolic forms, various forms of spiritual energy that produce the various images of the world. These forms include language, myth, art, and scientific cognition, and they differ from one another. This is not in accord with the Kantian thesis of the uniformity and invariance of the forms of sensory *Anschauung* and the categories of intellect. They are universal and cover all the manifestations of spiritual life, and hence are not restricted like the *a priori* to the sphere of cognition.

In this way language, the fundamental symbolic form (since it is used both by myth and by science) is interpreted as certain spiritual energy which *creates* the image of the world *a priori*. This interpretation of the problem both links Cassirer's conception with Kant's and Humboldt's conceptions and distinguishes it from them. An analysis of the similarities and differences may help to clarify Cassirer's opinions and standpoint.

Cassirer took two principal theses from Kant: that cognition is a construction of the cognizing mind and that the mind performs that construction thanks to definite categories given to it *a priori*. But like the neo-Kantians of the Marburg school he differs from Kant in important ways.

First of all it should be mentioned again how the neo-Kantians overcome the dualism of the Kantian philosophy and the materialistic 'inconsistency' of that philosophy by a radical rejection of the thing-in-itself. In his *Prolegomena* Kant explicitly disclaimed idealism and had reasons for doing so.[12] Cassirer, on the contrary, explicitly emphasizes his idealistic standpoint, and in precisely that sphere in which Kant thought it proper to protest idealism. Like other neo-Kantians, Cassirer 'purifies' Kantianism of the existence of objective things and transforms things into specific intentional objects.

It is only after such a 'purification' that Cassirer can raise his *a priori* forms to the rank of *makers* of the image of the world. He ascribes to them logical properties, universal properties (in the sense of covering all the products of the spiritual life), and variable properties (since different forms yield different images of the world). These properties differ essentially from Kant's original idea. Their purpose is to eliminate the Kantian dualism completely.

This departure from Kant also affects Cassirer's attitude to Wilhelm von Humboldt's opinions.

In a sense we are witness to a direct continuation, a point often emphasized by Cassirer in his works. The philosophy of symbolic forms is the best transition from linguistic opinions of the philosophy of language to philosophical opinions *sensu stricto*. These include, first, the notion that language creates a *Weltanschauung,* which implies that different language systems create different *Weltanschauungen*; and secondly, the idea of language as *energeia,* the 'inner form' of which makes a given *Weltanschauung.* It is easy to see a direct connection between the 'symbolic form', interpreted in a specific way, and the 'inner form', and between both of these and the 'form of *a priori Anschauung*'.

What separates Cassirer from Humboldt once again is the problem of the thing-in-itself. Humboldt is closer to Kant. He accepts the existence of the *world of things* and makes language an *intermediate world* between cognition and the world of things. For Cassirer, language is no intermediate world. There is no need of an intermediary. Language is just the *maker* of the image of the world that appears in consciousness.

Hence Cassirer was a radical idealist; the issue is indisputably clear. We might only question whether the idealism is objective or subjective. Moreover, as already noted, Cassirer is proud of his idealism. But does this make his opinions less problematic? Not in the least. The problem that remains is quite real and essential: does a given system of language affect a given manner of perceiving and cognizing, and if so, to what extent?

Let us leave, for the moment, the mystifications and obvious admixture of philosophical speculation; the subtle but nevertheless clear denial of a reality which is external to consciousness and hence objective; the clearly idealist interpretation of the world as an image of the world; the resulting denial of the copy theory, not in the sense of a definite theory of cognition, but in the sense of a definite ontological theory. I agree with the assertion of Susanne Langer, an advocate of Cassirer's philosophy, that the problems raised by Cassirer are not intrinsically linked with idealist philosophy[13] (though apart from this I agree neither with her reasoning nor with her formulations).

As Marxists, we accept the principles of philosophical materialism and hence we begin with the principles that the world of material things exists objectively and that cognition is always a definite relation between subject and object; and thus we start from assumptions contrary to Cassirer's. Nevertheless, we have to face a number of problems which make up the rational core in Humboldt's and Cassirer's argument. Is man's manner of perceiving the world independent of his manner of thinking and hence of the given system of language *in which* he thinks? Do 'raw facts' (*faits bruts*) of experience exist? Are sense data independent of other factors of mental life and in particular independent of language? Is the manner of seeing the structure of reality independent of language? By adopting such a hypothesis, do we not commit the mistake of naive realism, which states that things are always the way they seem to us and that sensory qualities are inherent in things themselves? Do we not run the risk of vulgarizing the copy theory by adopting the thesis that the faculty of perception is given to man in an invariable form? And if we assume that language affects the manner of man's perceiving the world, what accounts for the ways language-thinking shapes things? Does it not follow from the thesis that language affects perception (and the process of cognition as a whole) that different linguistic systems shape the process of cognition in different ways? Will this differentiate the natural *Weltanschauung* which man receives from society as he learns to speak? Can all this be verified in some way, or are we dealing with merely philosophical speculations?

These and similar questions are implicit in Cassirer's philosophy. I do not mean that all of them were formulated by him nor that any one of them was formulated in the form given above. The problems they represent *are* inherent, however, in his philosophy beyond all doubt.

Such problems are real and important. Their formulation, which includes a modicum of interpretation, depends on the philosophical system in which they are raised, and false interpretation and mystification may enter. But a problem does not vanish just because it is falsely interpreted and mystified; in such a case a materialistically minded philosopher need only reject its mystified form.

That requirement deserves to be kept in mind when we follow the roads and blind alleys of conventionalism and logical positivism, the second great trend which contributed so much to shaping contemporary philosophy of language. Such an excursion will enable us to perceive the problems more easily but will also add some ballast of mystification. We must therefore be on the alert not to confuse real problems with their mystified forms. Above all, we must see to it that genuine scientific problems are not lost in the process of clearing up the matter, a mistake it is much easier to make in philosophy than in other disciplines.

The Philosophy of Convention: From Moderate to Radical Conventionalism

The Vienna Circle positivists often mentioned conventionalism among the philosophical sources of their own movement, generally called 'logical positivism'. This is fully justified, especially as far as the positivist philosophy of language is concerned. Strictly speaking conventionalism did not create its own philosophy of language, but created a theoretical substratum of a definite variation of such a philosophy.

One of the essential causes of the rise of logical positivism was the crisis in natural science and the ensuing methodological reflections at the turn of the nineteenth century. This proved to be the breeding ground for conventionalism and neo-Kantian fictionalism (as in Vaihinger). It also was a factor in linking otherwise different philosophical trends, which interacted and developed certain notions jointly.

An issue in conventionalism was the objective nature of the laws of science. The starting point, which may not be disregarded, was the observation made by naturalists and mathematicians (the principal representatives of conventionalism) on the role of idealization in science. In the case of mathematics or the deductive disciplines in general, this was a matter of the role of simplicity and economy, i.e., what mathematicians call 'elegance' in the construction of a system. The decisive factors were accordingly not only observation and experience but the contribution of the researcher's mind as well. The scientist, guided by considerations of simplicity, idealizes a given system.

In such cases, usually one step separates correct detailed observations from an incorrect generalization. Idealization certainly plays an interesting role in the formulation of laws of science, and elegance plays an equally important role in mathematical reasoning. It is also true that the human mind performs an active function in the formulation of laws of science. But the next step, which leads to the generalization: "The human mind *produces* laws of science in an *arbitrary* way," is false. Only radical idealists would deny that. But they have to accept the consequences of their philosophical standpoint, consequences which both common sense and the logic of science consider destructive. Such was the fate of conventionalism.[14]

Conventionalism formulated the problem of the relation between reality and the laws of science in various ways and gradually laid more and more stress on idealist and voluntarist elements. While Boutroux confined himself to negation of the necessary and universal nature of the laws of science and Poincaré introduced the category of *convention* (meaning simplicity of description and its convenience from the point of view of human activity), Le Roy and Duhem saw in the laws of science a *product* of the cognizing mind exclusively, and an *arbitrary* product at that. This was more strongly emphasized in Hugo Dingler's voluntaristic writings.

The evolution of conventionalism was connected not only with the radicalization of thought that took place as that trend liberated itself from certain traditions but also with the 'metaphysical genealogy' of the various representatives of the doctrine. As militant Roman Catholics, Le Roy and Duhem combined their philosophical and methodological views with their religion and with an open declaration of war upon materialism and the category of necessity. In their interpretation conventionalism became radically subjective. This provoked Poincaré's half-hearted reaction. Poincaré introduced the category of convention, and Le Roy the concept of universal arbitrary convention, as the foundation of science. It was Le Roy who classified facts into "raw" (*bruts*) and "scientific" (*scientifiques*) and asserted that the human mind *makes* not only scientific facts (which Poincaré in fact accepted) but raw facts as well (which Poincaré disputed). Le Roy claimed that even the simplest observation is conditioned by the existence of previously accepted laws, that is, the existence of definite conventions on the strength of which those observations are made. For all their differences, the conventionalists are united by the idea (emphasized to a varying degree) that the laws of science comprise an arbitrary construction, and the image of the world is a construction based on convention. In fact, the representatives of radical conventionalism subjectivize the world itself.

All this is only indirectly connected with the issue of the role of language in the formation of the image of the world. But conventionalism leads us in that direction, since it emphasizes the link between convention and the *choice of language*.

The idea of such choice originates with Poincaré, who reduced the laws of science to the status of analytic statements and maintained that they were *definitions*. Here again only one step separates such an idea (especially if it is combined with the notion of the arbitrary character of convention) from the assertion that these definitions depend on an arbitrary choice of language. That step was taken by Le Roy, who made the conventionalist doctrine a radical one, linked it with the philosophy of language, and paved the way for new trends of that philosophy within the framework of logical positivism. Le Roy was probably the first to claim that the choice of a given theory depends on the choice of language.

> Theories can be varied in a thousand ways, [and] are for that reason *multiple for one and the same subject matter*: "infinite numbers of solutions of an indefinite problem." Need we quote the well-known fact of the coexistence of the elastic and the electromagnetic theory of light, in support of that assertion? These are different languages, translatable into one another. But each of these languages is marked by its own genius and has its particular advantages. May the scientist not choose between them according to his personal likes or his purpose? ... Are all these modes of expression not equally legitimate? More than this. Each of them ought to persist, since it defines a point of view from which the world has an aspect *sui generis,* and it would be undesirable to neglect such an aspect.[15]

The choice of language is not free—there are always some reasons which account for it (the prevailing opinion, the consequences of conventions adopted previously, individual motives, etc.)—but it is free in so far as the scientist may assert whatever he likes once he accepts certain theoretical complications.

> Does this mean that the spirit may decree results according to whim? Of course it may, if it is ready to introduce infinite complications into its language: there is in fact an infinite number of ways of evading logical contradiction.[16]

In a later period, Kazimierz Ajdukiewicz explicitly emphasized the debt radical conventionalism owed to Le Roy. But the issue is much broader. It concerns the connection between the radical conventionalism of Le Roy and the positivist concept of language in general. Logical positivism adopted certain conventionalist ideas. It accepted the image of the world as a product of language and the arbitrary nature of every image of the world (the choice of the system of language is arbitrary and a given image of the world is a product of a language). The document formulating the program of the Vienna Circle did not specify the character of the genetic links between logical positivism and conventionalism, but it did correctly point to their existence. They came to play an important part in the development of logical positivism, and in particular of its philosophy of language.

Thus radical conventionalism, as Ajdukiewicz himself admitted, was in a sense a continuation of traditional conventionalism. But it is comprehensible only in the context of logical positivism and its philosophy of language. It is therefore a convenient starting point for an analysis of the inner coherence of the development from conventionalism to logical positivism and for an analysis of the relationship between that development and the development from Humboldt to neo-Kantianism.

According to its author's formulation, radical conventionalism differs from traditional conventionalism. It resorts to arbitrary conventions as instruments of cognition not only in some cases, as Poincaré had suggested, but in *all* judgments. Consequently, our image of the world becomes a totally arbitrary product of our mind, and the philosophical doctrine which expounds such views proves—for all its reservations—to be radically subjective and relativistic.[17]

I shall abstain from detailed exposition of the views of radical conventionalism; I have presented this elsewhere (see *endnote 14* of this chapter). I only want to bring out what directly refers to the philosophy of language.

Ajdukiewicz drew far-reaching conclusions from his assumptions:

> We thus reach the principal thesis of the present paper. Empirical data do not impose upon us any articulate judgment in an absolute way. Yes, empirical data force us to accept certain judgments if we accept a given conceptual apparatus, but if that conceptual apparatus is changed we may, despite the presence of the same empirical data, abstain from the acceptance of those judgments.[18]

The thesis that the image of the world depends on an *arbitrary* choice of the conceptual apparatus, i.e., language, is formulated explicitly here. In radical conventionalism, that thesis is made still more radical by the concept of 'coherent languages' (including, for instance, the language of physics, which is part of more comprehensive languages). Coherent languages are unconnected and hence mutually untranslatable. This is genuinely a radical concept, since it states not only that we may arbitrarily make a choice of language but also that we may not even speak of truth and falsehood without adopting the system of reference of a *given* language. We become inaccessible to any arguments 'from the outside', since either a person adopts our language, together with its 'truth', or he fails to reach us, since our language is closed and hence untranslatable. Should these philosophical speculations be taken literally, we would have to conclude that statements of a madman and scientific statements, which both satisfy the formal requirements of coherent languages, are equally 'legitimate'.

Radical conventionalism was a paradoxical doctrine which it was impossible to defend. Hence it was abandoned even by its author. But the doctrine was a product of a definite intellectual climate and played a specific role in subsequent reflection on the function of language in the process of cognition. It should be examined for two reasons: (1) to establish the rational elements which it contained, i.e., the real problem behind the mystified form; (2) to clarify the intellectual climate of logical positivism, which made its formulation possible.

The real problem which is reflected in radical conventionalism in its simple formulation seems trivial: how does language affect the way of thinking and how do the modifications of the system of language affect the modifications of the way of thinking? In such a general formulation the problem not only looks trivial but is certainly not specific to conventionalism. We have previously examined its history within neo-Kantianism. It might easily be absorbed and developed by material-ist philosophy. It is an ordinary fact in science that the same real problems happen to be included in different systems of interpretation.

To the general question, common to various philosophical trends, of the influence of language upon the way of thinking, the radical conventionalists added another one: do not differences between the various language systems determine the way in which we grasp reality and the problems which we perceive in it, and will an appropriate *selection of these problems* not modify our perspective of the world? This is an interesting question that deserves examination, once it is freed of mystifying, idealist admixtures.

This question is certainly contained in Ajdukiewicz's notion[19] and enables its adherents to disclaim subjectivism. But the fact that the radical conventionalists notice the problem at the roots of their doctrine does not in the least change the speculative, paradoxical character of that doctrine. It was more than ten years ago that I engaged in a discussion with radical conventionalism. In the meantime, my standpoint has changed in many respects, but I cannot change my strongly negative appraisal of that doctrine. This is speculation, but like all speculation it has its own philosophical basis. Similar causes and similar facts gave birth to strikingly different interpretations: to Cassirer's symbolism and Ajdukiewicz's radical conventionalism. It is worth examining what paths and assumptions led to radical convention-alism.

Logical Positivism and Conventionalism

The general tradition of conventionalism and the resulting intellec-tual stimuli undoubtedly worked in that direction, but as indicated above the radical form of that doctrine did not develop until after the advent of logical positivism.

The positivist philosophy of language was an organic part of immanent empiricism, and can be fully comprehended only in the light of that doctrine.[20] Only the epistemological thesis that empirical knowledge, which exhausts the cognition of reality, is reducible to protocols of the 'given', i.e., 'given in inner experience', could give birth to the distinction between meaningful (empirical or tautological) and meaningless (metaphysical) statements on the strength of a formal analysis of the language of science. In logical positivism the two theses were genetically connected. Later the thesis that language is the *only* object of philosophy became autonomous and was applied, as in the case of radical conventionalism, without any direct connection with logical empiricism. Yet it would be impossible to understand its origins and nature without that connection.

In its epistemology, logical positivism, or logical empiricism as it is sometimes called, was just a subjective-idealist variation of positivism. It was a direct continuation of Mach's empirio-criticism and admitted as much. The path which led scientists, struggling with metaphysics and irrationalism, to the metaphysics of subjective idealism, the path which led from the laudable call for the victory of empirical knowledge to immanent empiricism, might be a fascinating object of research for sociologists and psychologists of science. Nowadays it is generally admitted that contrary to their fine and noble intentions the participants in the antimetaphysical crusade strayed into metaphysics of a very poor quality. This is admitted even by such former adherents of logical positivism as A. J. Ayer. But only a combination of the antimetaphysical crusade with the assumption that language is the principal, if not the only, object of philosophical research, could occasion the positivist philosophy of language.

Logical empiricism was clearly marked by subjective idealism, and so was the corresponding philosophy of language. The discovery of antinomies in the foundations of mathematics (primarily in set theory), a discovery which also affected logic, and the difficult problems that came to face natural science following its revolutionary changes at the turn of the nineteenth century (in particular such new developments in physics as the theory of relativity and quantum mechanics) pointed to the danger of errors resulting from an improper use of language, including, among other things, the ambiguity of linguistic expressions. This suggested the notion that language is not only an instrument but also an object of study. This was a very important idea, which intensified interest in language and advanced the various forms of research on language; consequently, language has become one of the principal objects of research by contemporary philosophy. But to assert that language is an object of research and to claim that it is the *sole* object of philosophical thought are two different things. Logical positivism passed from the former, moderate thesis to the latter, radical one and moved in the direction of idealism.

Those who assert that the investigation of extralinguistic reality is metaphysics, i.e., nonsense, a pseudoproblem (to use the logical-positivist terminology), and that the only legitimate subject matter of philosophy is the analysis of the language of science replace objective reality with a subjective product of the mind—whether they mean to or not. And the logical positivists claimed in express terms that language is an arbitrary product and that the choice of a language system is an arbitrary one. This was pure idealism of the subjective type, which fits perfectly the immanent empiricism of their doctrine.

The logical positivists' concept of language contained an element of conventionalism from the very beginning. Logical positivism not only asserted that linguistic analysis enables us to distinguish between meaningful and meaningless (metaphysical) statements and that language is therefore the only subject matter of philosophy (this was considered the turning point in the interpretation of its subject matter of philosophy); it also asserted that language is an arbitrary product of man and hence that the choice of language is arbitrary. Such is precisely the sense of the *'principle of tolerance'* formulated by Carnap in his programmatic work.[21] The radical views of Ajdukiewicz and Hempel[22] were merely a logical conclusion drawn from that principle. An illustration of that standpoint was the logical-positivist doctrine of physicalism as the unity of science achieved through the choice of a definite language.

In logical positivism, the conventionalist element had its peculiar function within the context of the epistemology of immanent empiricism and the methodological solipsism assumed by the logical-positivist philosophy of language. The adherents of logical positivism prefer to forget this embarrassing fact, but we need only consider Wittgenstein's *Tractatus Logico-Philosophicus,* which played an important role in the development of logical positivism, or Carnap's early works, such as *Der logische Aufbau der Welt,* to realize that it is so.

The following formulations by Wittgenstein (cited from the *Tractatus*) must be well comprehended: "*The limits of my language* mean the limits of my world" (5.6); "That the world is *my* world, shows itself in the fact that the limits of the language (*the* language which I understand) mean the limits of *my* world" (5.62); if we want to comprehend his reflections on solipsism: "In fact what solipsism *means*, is quite correct, only it cannot be *said*, but it shows itself" (5.62).

It is only against that background that Wittgenstein's further theses, which form the essential content of logical positivism, and have been expanded and commented on by its representatives, acquire clarity and come out in full relief: "The object of philosophy is the logical clarification of thoughts" (4.112); "All philosophy is 'critique of language'. . ." (4.0031); "In logical syntax the meaning of a sign ought never to play a role. . ." (3.33); "Most propositions and questions, that have been written about philosophical matters, are not false, but senseless" (4.003).

Wittgenstein's linguistic solipsism was continued by Carnap in his early and basic theories of the 'constitution' of knowledge and of 'methodological solipsism' worked out mainly in *Der logische Aufbau der Welt.*

What may account for the fact that thinkers who represented a sober approach to science and were guided by the noble impulse to combat metaphysics and irrationalism could formulate such a concept of language, so burdened with idealism? The answer which first suggests itself is that it was a mistake to generalize conclusions drawn from the field of the 'language' of the theory of deduction and from the field of the 'languages' (the various formalisms and codes) formed in an arbitrary manner, though on the substratum of a natural language, to serve some special purpose of communication. It was obviously incorrect to apply a generalization made on the basis of the study of artificial languages to language in general (and hence to natural languages also). I think that such an error held particularly grave consequences for the authors of the logical-positivist concept of language.

After this short sally into the history of logical positivism, we return to the analysis of radical conventionalism with a different attitude. We notice not only the constitutive element, conventionalism, but also the idea of an autonomous language which forms our perspective of cognition. Without this idea, closely linked with immanent empiricism and with the subjective idealism typical of immanent empiricism, the thesis that language is the sole subject matter of philosophy would be incomprehensible. But the conventionalism of this doctrine only becomes comprehensible in the context of the general theory of language.

When we compare the logical-positivist solution of the problem of the active role of language in the process of cognition with the traditional conventionalist solution, we not only see a connection between them but realize that one is a continuation of the other. Logical positivism is a radical conventionalism. Not only are certain notions formulated more radically, but also certain implicit theses are made explicit. The theory gains in completeness and coherence, though not in reasonableness. There is also no doubt that conventionalism and logical positivism represent one and the same trend of development in linguistic philosophy and suggest subjective-idealist solutions to its problems.

We need only compare that trend with the trend of other post-Kantian philosophies reflecting Kant's ideas (Humboldt, neo-Humboldtism, and neo-Kantianism) to discover the differences and similarities. The fundamental theses that language *creates* the image of the world and that a change of language results in a change of the image of the world are similar. In some cases not only the essence of opinions but the details of formulations are similar (for instance, both radical conventionalism and the field theory speak of casting a net of concepts, which forms our perspective of the world). The main difference lies in the types of idealism: in the post-Kantian trend we note the influence of the Hegelian concept of an objective spirit which is manifested in our image of the world through the intermediary of language. Such an approach is more mystic, though not more striking, than linguistic solipsism, but it is difficult to estimate the degrees of philosophical oddity. Not only for a materialist but for any reasonable thinker who does not treat his apparatus of positive knowledge as a springboard into the realm of dizzy philosophical speculations both radical concepts are equally unacceptable. In both he can find stimulating ideas, problems, and partial solutions. But all this must always be appraised in a concrete manner. This idea has probably never been formulated in a finer and more authoritative manner (in view of his connections with logical positivism) than by Bertrand Russell, whose words, pinpointing the gist of the issue, will conclude these considerations:

When I say "the sun is shining," I do not mean that this is one of a number of sentences between which there is no contradiction; I mean something which is not verbal, and for the sake of which such words as "sun" and "shining" were invented. The purpose of words, though philosophers seem to forget this simple fact, is to deal with matters other than words. If I go into a restaurant and order my dinner, I do not want my words to fit into a system with other words, but to bring about the presence of food. I could have managed without words, by taking what I want, but this would have been less convenient. The verbalist theories of some modern philosophers forget the homely practical purposes of everyday words, and lose themselves in neo-neo-Platonic mysticism. I seem to hear them saying "in the beginning was the Word," not "in the beginning was what the word means." It is remarkable that this reversion to ancient metaphysics should have occurred in the attempt to be ultra-empirical.[23]

Part 2

The Empirical Background

Chapter 3

Ethnolinguistics: The Sapir-Whorf Hypothesis

The longevity of philosophical problems is due to the difficulties which ensue during their solution. Their degree of abstraction means that every philosophical generalization has some reasons to justify it and that none can be refuted finally and totally without adopting identical assumptions. Some system of values underlies every philosophical theory and *Weltanschauung*. I deliberately use the term "choice," since the factors affecting the decisions made are different from, and more complicated than, those determining the value system of the natural sciences or mathematics.

Is the sum of the angles in a triangle 180°? Is light corpuscular in nature? Is the world knowable? Each of these questions differs from the others, and the ways and chances of answering each of them differ in each case. Scientific statements must always indicate the conditions in which they can be verified, i.e., confirmed or refuted by experiment, computation, and the like. Philosophy knows no such univocal conditions. Indirect argumentation makes philosophical theses more or less probable, but this always leaves opponents room for argument. Only a madman would oppose the multiplication table or the laws of mechanics, but a genius may defend both the latest advances in natural science and a spiritualist standpoint in philosophy at the same time. Once a philosophical thesis changes its nature as a result of scientific progress and can then be univocally formulated and univocally verified, it ceases to be a philosophical thesis and becomes a theorem of one of the specialized disciplines. Russell was correct in formulating that law.

But he was wrong in considering philosophy inferior to science. The theses of philosophy and those of the specialized disciplines differ in character. Also, philosophy and the specialized disciplines differ in status. Philosophy is not the queen of sciences it once was, nor is it one of the specialized disciplines. But this does not lessen the value of philosophy, for the value of a given field of study is determined by its utility and place in the entire system of human knowledge. Philosophy is indispensable for the construction of an integrated image of reality (*Weltanschauung*) and for the elaboration of a general methodology. No wonder, then, that attempts to eliminate it artificially (as with logical positivism) end in failure. The real task is to apply a method of generalization that keeps philosophical theses from contradicting science and makes them follow from the science. Only such a philosophy may claim the status of a scientific philosophy.

Thus a thesis is not depreciated by merely being philosophical. But even this qualification does not help settle disputes between conflicting philosophical views, and the problem of the active role of language in the process of cognition is no exception. Some trends treat language as the maker of the image of reality; others support some form of the copy theory. Some trends assert that changes in the system of language result in changes in the image of the world; others assert that all men have passed through the same biological evolution, hence that the image of the world formed in the process of that evolution is the same, and hence that common linguistic elements may be found in all languages.

Similar controversies have been going on in philosophy for millennia, and may continue for a very long time. That is why it would be interesting to find empirical proofs to substantiate one of the opinions; to confront the general theses with the bare facts in order to verify or falsify the hypotheses involved. Some aspects of the problem can be settled empirically, but in order to do this we must descend from the heights of philosophy to the level of ethnolinguistic research.

Theses describing the links between language and thinking, and between language and reality, are typical philosophical generalizations, and it would be wrong to expect, at least at the current level of knowledge, empirical solutions to the problems they present. At the most we can demonstrate that what we learn about these matters from the various specialized disciplines speaks in favor of this or that standpoint, although it may not refute the argumentation of opponents directly and univocally. This holds *a fortiori* in all cases which require proof of the nonexistence of some assumed beings (as in the case of the various formulations of the theory of objective spirit); such a proof is impossible.

But there are other, more hopeful situations. The assertions of the philosophy of language that language makes the image of reality and hence that a change in the system of language results in a change in the image of reality are verifiable. Since people use *different language systems,* often differing in morphology, syntax, and historical and cultural context, we can analyze various language systems to see whether they imply different images of the world. We can investigate, empirically, the hypothesis that language includes certain constant elements (linguistic universals) despite differences in morphology, syntax, and the like and that the identical biological inheritance of all mankind is reflected in these universals. That is why this type of assertion is valuable for our discussion of the philosophy of language.

Any partial solution to the problem we are concerned with would start a chain reaction. Should it turn out that differences between the various language systems *do not result* in differences in the image of the world (and this can be tested), the thesis that the image of the world is formed by language would be undermined. It would lose more ground should the theory of linguistic universals prove true.

But should empirical studies show that the system of language really implies a *Weltanschauung* and that differences in language systems coincide with differences in *Weltanschauungen,* the idealist thesis that language forms the image of the world in an arbitrary manner would not necessarily have to be accepted. Only a modification of the copy theory of cognition would be required. We would have to formulate the function of the subjective factor in the process of cognition more precisely.

In any case, empirical studies can play an important role in verifying these hypotheses and in contributing, indirectly, to the solution of wider problems. The opportunity for such studies exists primarily in the field of ethnolinguistics. Ethnolinguists study the languages and ways of thinking of those peoples who have retained archaic traits in their cultures due to arrested development and who belong to spheres of culture remote and fairly isolated from our own. The latter condition is of primary importance. We can only bring out the differences between world-images when there are essential differences between the language systems (of the world) implied by different languages. Nobody has ever undertaken such research with a philosophical end in view. And for that reason we must glean the material for such an effort from the work of ethnolinguists and social anthropologists who have come into contact, in one way or another, with the languages of primitive peoples. The case is interesting, since such contacts developed spontaneously and the philosophical standpoints of the investigators had little to do with their conclusions.

The problem of the linguistic context of the culture of primitive peoples was examined long ago in connection with other studies. Particular attention is due the works of Lucien Lévy-Bruhl and Bronislaw Malinowski.

Lucien Lévy-Bruhl was not an ethnologist, yet he must be credited with the formulation of the problem of the specific nature of the languages of primitive peoples. We may reject his theories of 'prelogicism' and 'participation'. He later abandoned them himself.[1] But we have to take into account his constructive achievements, namely, his observations of the concrete nature of the languages of primitive peoples, based on an analysis of the numerical systems of these peoples.[2]

Bronislaw Malinowski studied the languages of the inhabitants of the Trobriand Islands as one element of their entire culture. He concluded that those languages are not literally translatable into European languages and that they must be interpreted in the context of the culture situation of those who use them. Although he was not directly concerned with the problems we are pursuing, his observations are very valuable and contribute to their solution. These remarks are to be found in such fundamental works as *Coral Gardens and Their Magic* (1935; vol. 2 is dedicated entirely to the problems of language), *Argonauts of the Western Pacific* (1922), and the brilliant study *The Problem of Meaning in Primitive Languages,* included as a supplement to the well-known book by C. K. Ogden and I. A. Richards, *The Meaning of Meaning* (1923). Malinowski formulated general theses on language as an instrument of *action* and on the need to understand the languages of primitive peoples within their entire culture context. He also confirmed Lévy-Bruhl's theses on the concrete nature of those languages.

The anthropological studies that have been made of the family and kinship systems among primitive peoples are also worth mentioning. Such studies usually cover a language and its classification of kinship relations, and may help to settle the issues we are investigating.

But our problem first emerged explicitly and in full bloom in the anthropological literature in the formulation, and attempted verification, of the Sapir-Whorf hypothesis.

The ideas inherent in the Sapir-Whorf hypothesis coincide with the main idea of Humboldt's linguistic theory. This is particularly interesting because it is a matter of congeniality, not of a simple continuation of otherwise known ideas, and because the old idea reemerges as a result of a generalization of empirical data. (Whether that generalization is valid or not is a different issue.) Whorf probably did not know Humboldt's views; Sapir did, but Sapir's ideas on the role of language in the process of cognition did not have any genetic connection with Humboldt's opinions, or in any case, there is no proof of such. The term "neo-Humboldtism," as often used to cover both field theory and ethnolinguistics, is an after-the-fact construction and merely obscures matters.

The Sapir-Whorf hypothesis is directly connected with ethnolinguistic research of the American school of anthropology. Anthropologists and linguists became interested in the life of American Indians in part because of the social problems caused by the existence of the various Indian communities in the United States. The languages of American Indians were recorded and studied. This practical base bred a school of anthropology, that of Franz Boas, and the data collected inspired theoretical generalizations now known as the Sapir-Whorf hypothesis.

The fundamental ideas of that hypothesis developed in the 1920s and 1930s (Sapir died in 1939, and Whorf in 1941), but only became popular in the late 1940s. It stimulated further research and publications in the next decade. Like any new and stimulating idea, the Sapir-Whorf hypothesis has won a considerable number of determined and enthusiastic supporters and many determined opponents and critics. Its supporters are mostly general social anthropologists and ethnolinguists, students of the languages of Indian tribes (such as Harry Hoijer, George L. Trager, Charles F. Voegelin, Floyd Lounsbury,

Dorothy Lee, Dell H. Hymes, and others), while its opponents are mostly philosophers (Max Black, Charles Landesman, Lewis S. Feuer, and others). Even supporters admit that there are still insufficient grounds to prove the hypothesis (though, let it be added, not enough to disprove it). So far only the hypothesis itself has been discussed. Systematic study of its foundations and implications has been neglected. That is why, despite recent attempts to refute the hypothesis, people constantly return to the ideas it contains. Nobody has declared himself in favor of the hypothesis as a whole. Nobody claims to be an orthodox "Whorfist." Instead, people have tried to bring out the rational elements and stimulating ideas in the hypothesis, by rejecting hasty generalizations, casual admixtures, and metaphysical assumptions.

In my opinion this is the only possible initial scientific approach. But the basic ideas of the hypothesis must be carefully and critically analyzed on the basis of empirical data. Even if the immanent analysis of the hypothesis does not reveal any inner contradictions, its final acceptance or rejection must be postponed until sufficient empirical data are collected to settle the issue. This is binding for a Marxist philosopher, as for all other scholars. But except for sporadic cases, the Sapir-Whorf hypothesis has not been an object of study by Marxist philosophers. To date, there exist no profound Marxist studies on the subject, although one might expect the topic to have fascinated Marxist philosophers, if only for its bearing on the role of the subjective factor in cognition.

The supporters of the hypothesis go back to Franz Boas and his views to add weight to their own opinions. But claiming such a tradition does not seem much to the point. True, Boas emphasized the importance of linguistic research for ethnology (today a normal procedure).[3] But at the same time—and this is important—he explicitly rejected those theories which gave language a role in creating culture and favored theories which emphasized the function of culture in shaping language.[4]

Edward Sapir, a pupil of Franz Boas, thought differently. The fact remains, however, that Sapir did not engage in any speculations or in the philosophy of language. He was an eminent and versatile linguist who rendered great services in the study of the languages of American Indians, and his reflections on the culture-forming role of language are an attempt to generalize the results of specialized research and penetrating observations. This must be borne in mind when we undertake a critical appraisal of the ideas of Sapir and his continuator Benjamin Lee Whorf. Sapir was Whorf's teacher and provided the general formulations which Whorf later tried to test, using his own studies of the Hopi Indian language.

Sapir's idea can be formulated as follows: the language in which a given human community speaks and thinks organizes the experience, and thereby shapes 'the world' and the 'social reality' of this community. In other words, a specific *Weltanschauung* is inherent in every language.

This immediately suggests an identity of Sapir's idea with the opinions of Humboldt and his present-day continuators. There is certainly some coincidence here, but the assertion of identity would be erroneous and based on quite superficial analogies.

Sapir was not only a linguist but an ethnologist as well, and as such he had to deal with the concrete social reality of the peoples he was studying. That is why he understood the influence of the social and economic aspects of the life of a given community upon its culture and language.[5] That is why the metaphysical tradition of 'the spirit of the nation', without which Humboldtism, especially in its present-day form, cannot be understood, was quite alien to him. That is why he had nothing in common with the conventionalist speculations of philosophers and logicians on the so-called 'choice' of language. And that, finally, is why we can find almost materialist ideas, treating language as a reflection of the environment, in his works.[6] (Such ideas are also to be found in Franz Boas and, contrary to current opinion, in B. L. Whorf though he was not consistent on this point.) Sapir's opinion was more balanced and moderate than the Humboldtists'! He simply stated that language, socially conditioned as it is, *influences* the way a community grasps reality. I think this idea is not only rational but also valuable and novel. True, in Sapir's works it occurs side by side with inaccurate radical formulations, but it is certainly inherent in his opinions and lies at the heart of the matter. It should not be lost in criticism.

Sapir avoided easy generalizations. While formulating his thesis concerning the influence of the various languages upon the *Weltanschauung,* he came out against the popular opinions of Lévy-Bruhl on the pre-logical and concrete nature of "primitive" thinking, as Boas did before him. Like many other ethnologists, Sapir did not accept the concept of 'primitive' thinking. He did not believe the thinking of primitive peoples to be pre-logical in nature or incapable of developing higher forms of abstraction. If such forms do not occur in the thinking of the primitive peoples, it is simply because they are not needed in the practical life of these peoples. When such a need appears, abstract categories, originating from the appropriate transformations of existing language, appear too.[7]

To sum up, Sapir was concerned with something essential for the problem of the active role of language in the process of cognition, namely, with the *heuristic* function of language, with its organizing influence upon our perception of reality, that is, with its influence upon our experience. At the same time, he strongly emphasized the influence of environment, through the intermediary of social experience, upon the formation of language. Thus his opinions reveal the dialectical problem of interaction between cognition and language, no one-sided idealist thesis on the influence of language in shaping the world. Let us quote some of Sapir's statements in order to become better acquainted with his way of thinking.

In his important article "Language," written for *Encyclopaedia of the Social Sciences,* Sapir analyzed the problem of how and why people who have not seen more than one elephant in their lives can speak freely of herds or generations of elephants and communicate with one another on that subject. According to Sapir, this is due to language.

> Language has the power to analyze experience into theoretically dissociable elements and to create that world of the potential integrating with the actual which enables human beings to transcend the immediately given in their individual experiences and to join in a larger common understanding. This common understanding constitutes culture, which cannot be adequately defined by a description of those more colorful patterns of behavior in society which lie open to observation. Language is heuristic, not merely in the simple sense which this example suggests, but in the much more far-reaching sense that its forms predetermine for us certain modes of observation and interpretation. This means of course that as our scientific experience grows we must learn to fight the implications of language. . . . Language

is at one and the same time helping and retarding us in our exploration of experience, and the details of these processes of help and hindrance are deposited in the subtler meanings of different cultures.[8]

This idea is pushed further by Sapir in his "Conceptual Categories in Primitive Languages," where he claims that language is a system which not only pertains to experience (acquired largely in a manner independent of that system) but defines experience in some way. Meanings are not so much discovered in experience as imposed upon experience, through the influence of linguistic forms on our orientation in the world. This leads to the conclusion (which is the nucleus of other, more general hypotheses) that the mutual correspondence between the various linguistic systems cannot be strict.[9]

Sapir's main idea, which became the inspiration and the starting point for Whorf, is contained in his work *The Status of Linguistics as a Science*. There reference is made explicitly to language as a 'guide to social reality', and the 'real world' is called a largely unconscious projection of linguistic habits upon the surrounding reality. In that work the thesis of the creative character of language in the process of thinking is formulated in its most radical form, and therefore serves the purpose of criticism best. But let Sapir speak for himself.

Language is a guide to "social reality." Though language is not ordinarily thought of as of essential interest to the students of social science it powerfully conditions all our thinking about social problems and processes. Human beings do not live in the objective world alone, nor alone in the world of social activity as ordinarily understood, but are very much at the mercy of the particular language which has become the medium of expression in their society. It is quite an illusion to imagine that one adjusts to reality essentially without the use of language and that language is merely an incidental means of solving specific problems of communication or reflection. The fact of the matter is that the "real world" is to a large extent unconsciously built up on the language habits of the group. No two languages are ever sufficiently similar to be considered as representing the same social reality. The worlds in which different societies live are distinct worlds, not merely the same world with different labels attached.

The understanding of a simple poem, for instance, involves not merely an understanding of the single words in their average significance, but a full comprehension of the whole life of the community as it is mirrored in the words, or as it is suggested by their overtones. Even comparatively simple acts of perception are very much more at the mercy of the social patterns called words than we might suppose. If one draws some dozen lines, for instance, of different shapes, one perceives them as divisible into such categories as "straight," "crooked," "curved," "zigzag" because of the classificatory suggestiveness of the linguistic terms themselves. We see and hear and otherwise experience very largely as we do because the language habits of our community predispose certain choices of interpretation.[10]

The fragments from Sapir's works quoted above may certainly be subject to different, or even mutually exclusive, philosophical interpretations. Everything depends on how we read them, that is, which elements we consider principal and stress and in which context we take them (and of course this is not the first time in the history of philosophy in which different philosophers have interpreted the same text differently). But the reasonable critic will always try to isolate and comprehend any new problems discovered by research workers or any contribution they make toward understanding problems already known. That is why the destructive criticism of the only Soviet work devoted to the opinions of Edward Sapir known to me (M. M. Gukhman, "E. Sapir i etnografičeskaya lingvistika," *Voprosy yazykoznaniya*, no. 1, pp. 122-127, 1954), cannot be considered successful Marxist criticism.

There is no doubt that Sapir's radical formulations concerning the role of language in creating human reality, formulations that border on idealism, cannot be supported by a materialistically minded philosopher or by any anthropologist or sociologist who understands the social conditioning of language. But Sapir's other opinions do not agree with those formulations. Thus Sapir's statements may not be analyzed and criticized in isolation from his system as a whole. For if we take the whole of his system into consideration, we see clearly that Sapir is not an idealist. On the contrary, he notes and appreciates the social conditioning of the origin, development, and function of language. He notes and appreciates the objective nature of reality which language reflects (in some sense of the word 'reflects'). In the light of his whole system, Sapir's suggestions acquire a quite different significance.

We have an objective world before our eyes—the world of physical objects and the world of social phenomena. We have people living in that world, who perceive things, who think, and who, thanks to their cognitive functions, act. People and their products must always be interpreted socially. Anthropologists especially emphasize the unity of the individual and the community because this is more evident in the case of the primitive peoples than in the case of the civilized peoples. Language is a reflection of natural and social reality; and it is also a social product. But is it *only* a reflection and a product? It is a social product of immense educational importance for the individual. It is a specific collection of social stereotypes. But does it not also *shape* the behavior of individuals, especially their cognitive behavior? Do not different language systems, which are specific reflections of the different milieus that have produced them (those milieus being always in some profound sense social), affect the different ways in which the people who use those systems and think in them see the world?

This is not a trivial problem, if only because it helps us approach the issue of the subjective factor in the process of cognition in a new and more profound manner. For should it turn out that in fact the environment, including the social milieu with its intricate interplay of class forces, affects human cognition *through the intermediary* of language (and here the decision belongs to empirical data, and not to philosophical whims), we would have to tackle the problem of the objective nature of cognition again. And the problems of the sociology of knowledge would acquire particular importance.

Contrary to what is suggested by some, this idea does not necessarily imply idealism and can quite successfully become an element of a materialist philosophy. Nothing prevents us from accepting the existence of subjective elements in the reflection of the world by human cognition in addition to the objective and material nature of the world. To assert that language simply *creates* an image of reality (an assertion in which the problem of the objective existence of reality is disregarded and its reflection by human cognition is denied) and to assert that subjective elements, including the cognitive influence of a socially shaped language, participate in the reflection of reality are two different things. The latter assertion may prove false (which has to be demonstrated), but it may not be rejected *a priori.*

Of course, a benevolent interpretation of Sapir's views is offered here, an interpretation which tries to bring out the rational elements of his theses and disregards his possible slips, inconsistencies, and even falsehoods. In view of the purposes of this work, this is quite proper. For it is not my concern to appraise Sapir's views *in toto,* but to deal with those ideas which became part of the Sapir-Whorf hypothesis. That is why we can afford the luxury of concentrating our attention on the constructive aspect of Sapir's opinions without absolving him of his philosophical sins and without fending off criticism of his errors.

After what has been said, we can view the two principal ideas inherent in the Sapir-Whorf hypothesis more objectively:

1. Language is a social product. The language system in which we are educated, and in which we think, shapes the way we perceive the world around us.
2. In view of the differences between the various language systems, people thinking in different languages perceive the world in different ways. These differences of language are reflections of the different environments that produce them.

There is a striking similarity between these theses and the neo-Humboldtist theses on the *Weltanschauung* implicit in every language. And yet they are different if only because Sapir's theses are empirically verifiable generalizations resulting from specialized research. The credit goes to Whorf for undertaking such empirical verification.

Benjamin Lee Whorf was an original personality, something rarely to be found among present-day scholars. Although a very gifted and creative ethnographer and linguist, he was an amateur scholar and preferred earning his living as an insurance agent, a rather extraordinary occupation for a linguist. Yet, as his own reminiscences tell us, he was first stimulated to study linguistics by his work as an insurance agent. He began working out his ideas himself and did not begin to cooperate with Sapir until he was thirty-four. Four years before his death at the early age of forty-four, he started to lecture at Yale University.

Whorf owed two things to an occupation which forced him to travel much in that part of the United States inhabited by various tribes of American Indians: first, his knowledge of American Indian languages, in particular Hopi, in which he later specialized; and second, his ideas concerning the links between language and thinking, which he deduced from his observations and analyses of the causes of fires.

Whorf reports[11] that he was induced by his practical experience, prior to his collaboration with Sapir, to reflect on the effect of the meanings of words adopted by a given social group upon human behavior. Upon analyzing hundreds of reports on the causes of fires, he came to the conclusion that the factors involved included not only technology but also the influence of meanings of words upon the behavior of the persons concerned. One example was a set of instructions on the safe storage of gasoline. The workers usually thought that safety measures did not have to be observed when empty gasoline drums were stored, because the drums were 'empty'. Someone would toss a cigarette stub and cause a dangerous explosion of the vapor contained in those 'empty' drums, which were more dangerous than drums filled with gasoline. The apparent ambiguity of the term 'empty drum' suggested a definite situation and affected human behavior. Observation of such cases suggested to Whorf the ideas which he later used in his research.[12]

Contacts with the cultures and languages of Indian tribes, reflections on these, and his research attitude made Whorf react enthusiastically to Sapir's suggestions and ideas when he came to study systematically under the latter's guidance. Whorf was more stimulated than guided directly. Nevertheless he developed his hypothesis under the influence of Sapir and his general ideas. Whorf resolved to verify those ideas using specific material, and his knowledge of the culture and language of the Hopi Indians made him very well qualified for that purpose. This gave rise to valuable studies, which only won renown after their author's death. He died early, and we have every reason to believe that what he left only marked the beginning of what would have been an interesting career as a scholar. But even what he wrote succeeded in making Sapir's ideas more concrete and much more radical, until he ended by discovering the principle of 'linguistic relativity', the main conception of the Sapir-Whorf hypothesis. Whorf's radical formulation is as follows:

We dissect nature along lines laid down by our native languages. The categories and types that we isolate from the world of phenomena we do not find there because they stare every observer in the face; on the contrary, the world is presented in a kaleidoscopic flux of impressions which has to be organized by our minds—and this means largely by the linguistic systems in our minds. We cut nature up, organize it into concepts, and ascribe significances as we do, largely because we are parties to an agreement to organize it in this way—an agreement that holds throughout our speech community and is codified in the patterns of our language. The agreement is, of course, an implicit and unstated one, *but its terms are absolutely obligatory*; we cannot talk at all except by subscribing to the organization and classification of data which the agreement decrees.

This fact is very significant for modern science, for it means that no individual is free to describe nature with absolute impartiality but is constrained to certain modes of interpretation even while he thinks himself most free. The person most nearly free in such respects would be a linguist familiar with very many widely different linguistic systems. As yet no linguist is in any such position. We are thus introduced to a new principle of relativity, which holds that all observers are not led by the same physical evidence to the same picture of the universe, unless their linguistic backgrounds are similar, or can in some way be calibrated.[13]

Whorf's assertion that the Hopi language and the Hopi *Weltanschauung* are not just different from the languages and *Weltanschauungen* of European peoples (the SAE languages—Standard Average European) but are their very opposites is a theoretical consequence of this principle of linguistic relativity.

We shall now investigate this principle in greater detail, because it is this (and not Sapir's formulations) which accounts for the specific philosophical and scientific climate of the Sapir-Whorf hypothesis.

We find here echoes of Sapir's ideas, but there is no doubt that Whorf moved far away from them. Continuators usually radicalize the ideas of theory makers; they eliminate vagueness and ambiguity and put an end to the original hesitations and the prudent caution of their masters.

Yet they often have to pay a high price. For the brilliance of many ideas consists precisely in their being vague and inconsistent. Perhaps Sapir and Whorf are an instance.

Sapir did not doubt the existence of an objective world, reflected by language, in the least. But Whorf thought that the world was only a kaleidoscopic flux of impressions that require organization by our minds or, to put it more precisely, by our linguistic system.

Sapir stated cautiously that "human beings do not live in the objective world alone," that language is not "merely an incidental means of solving specific problems of communication or reflection," and that "the real world is, to a large extent, unconsciously built up on the language habits of the group." But he never said that we comprehend the world in a definite way because "we are parties to an agreement to organize [nature] in this way," an agreement "codified in the patterns of our language." That conventionalist element in Whorf's opinion was alien to Sapir.

When Sapir soke of the dialectical links of language with environment, he meant the vocabulary only.[14] Like Franz Boas, he denied the existence of any direct connection between the environment and the grammar of a language (phonetics, morphology, syntax, etc.). Whorf, on the contrary, rejected all restrictions and identified a language system with grammar.[15] This was a radicalization of Sapir's theses which had far-reaching consequences.

On the other hand, the principle of linguistic relativity was implicit in Sapir's theses too, for he stated that different societies live in different worlds, and not in the same world—and these worlds may be labeled differently. Whorf interpreted this somewhat differently and stressed different things. He spoke, for instance, of the impossibility of an impartial description of reality by a scientist. Like Mannheim, he tried to evade the embarrassing consequences of extreme relativism by assuming that a linguist, thanks to his knowledge of widely different languages, could, in Mannheim's terminology, "recalculate perspectives" and thus reconstruct the objective state of things. But these are relatively unimportant details. The essential element, which is the principle of linguistic relativity and what it implies, comes from Sapir. Whorf took it over and made it into the cornerstone of his conception.[16]

Whorf's formulation lacks Sapir's moderation; it lacks that ambiguity which gives us the chance to appraise his views "benevolently."

What Whorf presents can indeed be classified as philosophical idealism or, still worse, as an extreme relativism which denies the possibility of the existence of objective truth.[17] Thus the Sapir-Whorf hypothesis is not, as its name would indicate, something homogeneous, since its authors hold different views on essential issues. But this is not the heart of the matter. Whorf is not interesting for the originality of his theory, which is known to have been derived from Sapir's views, but because of its particular form. Let us see what he has to say about linguistic relativity and what new facts and arguments he can adduce to defend his standpoint. Philosophical objections must always give way to empirical data if the data are unquestionable and the arguments are sufficiently weighty.

Thinking, Whorf says, always means thinking in some language. Every language is a comprehensive system of stereotypes which unconsciously control the forms of thinking.[18] Which stereotypes appear when we compare SAE with the Hopi language?

According to Whorf, we perceive the world in a given way depending on how our language divides the stress of events into parts. SAE languages tend to analyze reality as a set of *things* and focus their attention mainly on human products, such as tables and chairs and so forth—objects artificially isolated from the rest of the world. The Hopi language implies a different analysis, it analyzes the world as a set of *events*.[19] And how do the different languages cope with the real events in nature? Here is an example of Whorf's reasoning.

We might isolate something in nature by saying "it is spring." Apache uses the verb *ga* to formulate the statement "be white (including clear, uncolored, and so on)." With a prefix *no-* the meaning of downward motion enters: "whiteness moves downward." Then *to*, meaning both "water" and "spring," is prefixed. The result corresponds to our "dripping spring," but synthetically it is "as water, or springs, whiteness moves downward." How utterly unlike our way of thinking! The same verb, *ga*, with a prefix that means "a place manifests the condition" becomes *gohlga*: "the place is white, clear, a clearing, a plain." These examples show that some languages have means of expression—chemical combination, as I called it—in which the separate terms are not so separate as in English but flow together into plastic synthetic creations. Hence such languages, which do not paint the separate-object picture of the universe to the same degree as English and its sister tongues, point toward possible new types of logic and possible new cosmical pictures.[20]

Thus there exists a structure of sentences which differs from the subject-object structure sanctified by Aristotle. Our way of seeing the world in terms of 'things' resulted in the opposition of subject and predicate, actor and action, things and relations, objects and properties. But the verb is always combined with things and can never occur alone. The ideology based on the reification of the world is imposed upon us by our language, although it is beginning to conflict with contemporary field theory in physics, with mathematics, etc. The American Indian languages differ from the SAE languages, and taking examples from the Nootka language, Whorf concludes:

> When we come to Nootka, the sentence without subject or predicate is the only type. The term "predication" is used, but it means "sentence." Nootka has no parts of speech; the simplest utterance is a sentence, treating of some event or event-complex. Long sentences are sentences of sentences (complex sentences), not just sentences of words.[21]

There are also other, though less striking, differences which account for the fact that Indian languages, by dividing reality into different sorts or parts, condition a different way of perceiving the world. For instance, the Navaho Indians classify all inanimate bodies in two categories; "round objects" and "long objects," which obviously makes the whole linguistic classification system different from those of the SAE languages.[22]

But certainly the most important categories (since it is on them that the Sapir-Whorf hypothesis practically rests) are the categories of time and space in Hopi. Formulated briefly, Whorf's conclusion is this: the Hopi Indians know no such category of time as is encountered in SAE, while the category of space is similar in the two cases.

In his paper on the model of the universe of the Hopi language, Whorf described the category of time in that language.

> I find it gratuitous to assume that a Hopi who knows only the Hopi language and the cultural ideas of his own society has the

same notions, often supposed to be intuitions, of time and space that we have, and that are generally assumed to be universal. In particular, he has no general notion or intuition of *time* as a smooth flowing continuum in which everything in the universe proceeds at an equal rate, out of a future, through a present, into a past; or, in which, to reverse the picture, the observer is being carried in the stream of duration continuously away from a past and into a future. ... Hence the Hopi language contains no reference to "time," either explicit or implicit.

At the same time, the Hopi language is capable of accounting for and describing correctly, in a pragmatic or operational sense, all observable phenomena of the universe. ... Just as it is possible to have any number of geometries other than the Euclidean which give an equally perfect account of space configurations, so it is possible to have descriptions of the universe, all equally valid, that do not contain our familiar contrasts of time and space.[23]

According to Whorf, the Hopi Indians replace the metaphysics of three-dimensional space and one-dimensional time by the metaphysics of that which is objective and that which is subjective.[24] Time introduces subjectivity. The future tense is replaced by that which is subjective. The verbs do not occur linearly in the three aspects and one dimension of time, but on the basis of the operational gradation "earlier–later."[25]

Thus Whorf does not assert that the Hopi do not distinguish tenses, which would really be unbelievable, but claims that they do so in a way different from that of SAE languages, and that there is a difference between our category of "tense" and the Hopi category of "duration." This is Whorf's strongest argument in favor of the principle of linguistic relativity.

Whorf's argumentation pertains to two different problems: the relation between one language (comprehended as a vocabulary plus a grammatical structure) and another and the relation between a given language and individual behavior. Hence his hypothesis may be verified in these two fields. In the first case the issue is the translatability of one language into another if, by hypothesis, they imply different categories of reality and different *Weltanschauungen.* In the second case the issue is the effect of language upon individual behavior if the *Weltanschauung* inherent in the language affects the way in which the people who speak that language and think in it perceive the world.

This is a general outline of Whorf's thesis, which uses the Hopi language to illustrate Sapir's general hypothesis. The fragmentary nature and the narrow scope of Whorf's work make it impossible to answer his questions with an unqualified yes or no. But he formulated a controversial hypothesis as well, which interests the philosopher.

Let us see what others have done to verify the Sapir-Whorf hypothesis. Although people have more often discussed the hypothesis than effectively investigated its assumptions, there is considerable literature on the subject which directly or indirectly provides arguments in the controversy.

First, we have to consider a galaxy of ethnolinguists who have continued the study of the languages and cultures of American Indians and added to our knowledge of the subject, although it was not their intention to verify the hypothesis formulated by Sapir and Whorf. They have in fact posed a new culturological problem: how do we explain the fact that peoples speaking the same language often have different cultures and, conversely, the fact that peoples living on the same territory and showing cultural affinity speak different languages?

The Navaho Indians, neighbors of the Hopi, were investigated by Clyde Kluckhohn and Harry Hoijer.

Kluckhohn is in favor of the Sapir-Whorf hypothesis. I should even say that he formulates its ideas much better than Whorf and offers formulations that come closer to Sapir's ideas.[26] Kluckhohn's investigations of the Navaho language have demonstrated its concreteness. A Navaho never refers to any action in an abstract way, but always describes the concrete accompanying circumstances. For instance, in the Navaho language there is no word for our phrase "to ride," because the form of the verb requires qualification as to whether one goes on horseback or rides a cart, trots or gallops, etc. By combination with the appropriate form of a given verb, physical objects are classified into long, round, etc. Analysis of the extension of the various nouns reveals that in Navaho one term often covers different classes of objects (in agreement with the classification adopted in English), but that distinctions are often made that are unknown in European languages.

Such investigations, which are only indirectly connected with the Sapir-Whorf hypothesis, certainly contribute to our knowledge of the problems involved.

Similar investigations have been made by Hoijer, mainly concerning the Navaho Indians. A supporter and firm defender (at least at one time) of the Sapir-Whorf hypothesis, he has collected many data that may prove useful in the controversy over it. The perception of colors and the forms of kinship reflected in American Indian languages and in European languages are examples of the problems he is interested in. Hoijer's statements are marked by peculiar caution: in his opinion, language differences do not determine the perception of reality, but only lend direction to the perceptions of those who speak given languages.[27]

Dorothy Lee, also a firm adherent of the Sapir-Whorf hypothesis, analyzed the Wintu language and the language of the Trobriand Islanders in her works. While she emphasizes that the image of the world depends on the culture, and in particular the language in which the culture develops, she adds that this does not make it impossible for the people in question to cross the boundaries of the culture. It is a question of setting some general guide lines and limits within which the individual can function in his own way. This is certainly a moderate interpretation of the Sapir-Whorf hypothesis.

Her investigations of the Wintu language have led her to the following conclusions: *reality* as such exists objectively, but the isolation of individual *things,* to which we give definite terms, is a result of the interaction between the cognizing person and that reality. What we talk about is neither purely subjective nor purely objective. In European languages the important elements are the parts which make up the whole, while in the Wintu language the whole plays the dominant role, and a part is only a fragment of the whole. This distinction also holds for the category "I," which is reflected in the whole system of language and culture. These differences in the ways of classifying reality in the various languages must be borne in mind if we want to understand peoples who think and speak differently from us.

> ... for true communication, we cannot assume as a matter of course that our classifications are the same for people of all cultures; that translation is merely the substitution of one sound-complex for another. Once we are aware that the basis of

classification is not a universal one, we can find out whether our different words do name the same things, and if they do not, one can qualify our word.[28]

We must also take into account the investigations of ethnolinguists into kinship systems. Together with the study of numerical systems this is the sphere of problems best represented in the literature of ethnolinguistics (in American literature the works of Floyd Lounsbury may be mentioned) although it has not yet been properly utilized in the field of language and cognition we are considering in this book.

I could cite many examples which would testify to connections between contemporary ethnolinguistics and the problems implied by the Sapir-Whorf hypothesis. But these connections have only resulted from study of a similar subject matter, not from any deliberate attempt to verify that hypothesis. I only know two major scholarly undertakings over the past twenty years deliberately intended to discuss and/or verify the Sapir-Whorf hypothesis. One of these was the seminar organized by Hoijer which gave us the valuable book *Language in Culture* (1954); evidently a seminar could not achieve anything more than a confrontation of opinions on the data collected previously. The other was the genuine study of the assumptions of the hypothesis carried out as the Southwestern Project. But that study was part of psycholinguistic research, and so takes us into another field of research.

Psycholinguistics is organically connected with the Sapir-Whorf hypothesis, and psycholinguists have carried out a number of studies to verify the foundations of the hypothesis.

John B. Carroll defined psycholinguistics as the science that investigates the ways in which information is coded in a given language system by those who speak that language and decoded by the hearers.[29] Psycholinguistics makes a preliminary distinction between two categories: 'language' as a communication system (language in the sense of de Saussure's *langue,* and not *parole*) and 'cognition' as the state of language users. Psycholinguistic research establishes tangible relationships between the use of a given language and definite *behavior* of human beings. The problems must be formulated so that they can be tested experimentally, and the criteria of testability are strictly defined.[30]

According to Roger Brown,[31] Eric Lenneberg,[32] Carroll,[33] and others, the founders of psycholinguistics, this new trend in research, analyzed its problems in close connection with the Sapir-Whorf hypothesis of linguistic relativity and sought new ways of verifying it. Research was shifted to such problems as the effect of language upon the ability to distinguish colors, learning processes in children, memorization processes, and even speech pathology. The studies have been carried out within a single speech community, and not on a comparative basis.

Many psycholinguists who take up problems investigated by Sapir and Whorf begin by demonstrating the vagueness of the assumptions underlying the hypothesis. Brown and Lenneberg did just this in their study of language and cognition, which was important in the evolution of psycholinguistics. Carroll, in a paper on certain psychological consequences of the structure of language, made fine distinctions between the various possible interpretations of the Sapir-Whorf hypothesis. This was also done by many other researchers.

In addition to such endeavours to make the vague assumptions of the Sapir-Whorf hypothesis more precise, the main task of psycholinguistics has been the formulation of a strictly defined experimental basis for the verification of those assumptions. This has given rise to many research projects, projects which have been interesting and valuable though narrow in scope.[34]

All this indicates the motivation of the Southwestern Project mentioned above. It tried to apply the assumptions and methods of psycholinguistics to the comparative study of various language groups in an attempt to verify the Sapir-Whorf hypothesis. The southwestern part of the United States was particularly suited for that purpose because of the linguistic differentiation of its inhabitants, both Indians and whites. The study, directed by John B. Carroll, was carried out during the summer of 1956 (the summer of 1955 being devoted to preparatory work). It covered five culture and language groups: the Navaho, Zuni, Hopi, and Hopi-Tewa groups, and the American Spaniards of New Mexico. Only partial results were made public. As one may conclude from the report submitted by Carroll to the American Psychological Association in September, 1959 (I refer to a mimeographed text of that report), even the organizers of the project realize that the results were not entirely significant, and this probably accounts for the fact that they were never published in full. The data seem to indicate that a number of factors doomed the project to failure in advance: a short period of research (only *one* summer); a small number of researchers (four senior and twelve auxiliary workers); a wrong choice of the groups to be investigated (there are no representatives of a purely monolinguistic culture among American Indians, and the verification of the Sapir-Whorf hypothesis requires a comparative study of cultures and languages isolated from one another); and finally, the narrow scope of psycholinguistic problems.

Two problems come to the fore:

1. Do the phonemic differences between languages result in the appropriate reactions in the speakers? For example, the Zuni language makes distinctions among the lengths of vowels; does this mean that the Zuni Indians can measure temporal duration better than speakers of English, in which the length of vowels is not phonemic in nature?
2. Does the categorial system of a language affect practical human behavior?

The report claims the experiment "more or less" confirmed the predictions of the Sapir-Whorf hypothesis, but the results are considered to be insignificant. This could not have been otherwise under the conditions described. This point is worth making and must be emphasized, for one failure should not discourage further research on a broader scale and under more favorable conditions. From my personal contacts I have gotten the impression that the failure of the Southwestern Project has disappointed even the supporters of the hypothesis. And yet they should have realized that a bad starting point would doom the project to failure. I think that the failure of the project and the lack of constructive results by popularizers of the hypothesis have brought about a turn toward the study of linguistic universals at the expense of linguistic differentials. This brings us to a criticism of the Sapir-Whorf hypothesis, which is necessary for drawing some conclusions concerning the issue under consideration.

The Sapir-Whorf hypothesis has been criticized from many quarters, and in most cases justly. Carroll, Brown, Lenneberg, and others have correctly emphasized that the hypothesis in its original version may not be accepted since its assumptions are too ambiguous and vague, its generalizations too hasty, and its empirical foundations too weak. And yet it includes an idea that even the most severe critics have failed to refute, an idea that deserves both examination and an empirical confirmation. In science a hasty negation is as bad as an insufficiently grounded affirmation.

The valuable idea alluded to is the statement that the language system in which we think affects the way we perceive reality and consequently affects our behavior (the term 'behavior' here to be understood broadly as covering all human activity, including scientific activity). The Sapir-Whorf hypothesis does not claim that the whole *Weltanschauung* is shaped or that languages may be mutually untranslatable or that skewed *Weltanschauungen* emerge. On the other hand, such possibilities are not excluded. The formulation of such wider generalizations is made totally dependent on the empirical data. The moderate formulation that the language system not only is an instrument of communication in human cognition but also codetermines cognition is adopted as a working hypothesis, one that is based, first, on the observation of linguistic data and, secondly, on a specific interpretation of the unity of language and thinking and of the relation of language-thinking to objective reality.

The Sapir-Whorf hypothesis is often accused of idealism and circular logic. If language is treated as an arbitrary convention, idealism results; and if differences between *Weltanschauungen* are explained by differences among the structures of the language systems involved and the latter differences in turn are explained by differences among cultures, we have a perfect vicious circle. This objection is met by the statement that language, interpreted as a unity of language and thinking, is generated by society; it is a social product and reflects the given physical and social environment shaped by history. We are interested in how that social product, language, affects the perception of the world when it takes the form of a definite system. These are assumptions which depend on one's philosophical standpoint, but they at any rate eliminate idealism and the vicious circle. What is left is an undisputable problem which cannot be eliminated *a priori* by any materialist: the problem of the active role of language in the process of cognition and in human behavior. This formulation includes both materialism and dialectics. The problem itself can be settled (in the sense of verification or falsification) only on the strength of empirical data.

Is this concept of language as a social product to be taken as the Sapir-Whorf hypothesis? Certainly not. But the idea, for all the essential modifications, can be traced to that hypothesis, or has at least been inspired by its authors. There is no doubt that in such a general form it might be traced back to Herder's and Humboldt's philosophy of language, but there is an important difference here, especially for a materialist. The Sapir-Whorf hypothesis, with all the objections that may be raised against it, has been formulated as a generalization of empirical data. Whoever wants scientifically to approach the problem of the active role of language in the process of cognition must make use of that hypothesis (which does not mean accepting it *in toto*).

Today, after all the experiences and defeats in this field of inquiry, we must formulate a positive program for research, a program which, by taking into account all the failures and errors, will give us the optimal chance of finding the correct solutions. But before proceeding to this task, we have to refute those objections to the Sapir-Whorf hypothesis which might apply to our own plans. For though we do not intend to try to verify that hypothesis in its original version, we have accepted some rational ideas which it contains.

Let us begin with an argument which is more psychological than logical in nature. Some research workers prefer to study the phenomena observable in all languages rather than to study the differences among the functions of the various languages in culture. I call this argument psychological, for there is no incompatibility between these two types of research or between the corresponding standpoints, and only scientific fashion favors one approach or the other. Nothing prevents us from stating that there are phenomena and laws common to all languages and that every language (or group of languages) is marked by phenomena and properties specifically its own. There is nothing logically inconsistent here, the only question is whether certain phenomena and properties occur or not.

The problem of linguistic universals is currently fashionable, but the conference held at Dobbs Ferry, New York, in April, 1961, to discuss it demonstrated that we still have to define what is meant by linguistic universals and how these can be investigated. The work has only begun. But, nothing prevents us from again investigating both problems simultaneously. On the contrary, to do so may increase the attractiveness of research, since broader scope will increase the probability of obtaining conclusive results.

The criticism of the Sapir-Whorf hypothesis has touched all its component parts, from its philosophical assumptions to its theoretical and practical implications. We have to agree with the criticism made by authors, like Max Black and V. Zvegintsev, Charles Landesman and G. Brutian, Lewis S. Feuer and John B. Carroll or Eric Lenneberg. Despite their differing, even opposing, theoretical standpoints, they are all united in finding the original version of the Sapir-Whorf hypothesis untenable. Let us recall the objections. Its primary categories are ambiguous and badly defined. Its formulations are vague. The assumption that the language orders and organizes 'raw' cognition, which is 'a kaleidoscopic flux of impressions', and the assertion that language (interpreted autonomously, not as a reflection of reality) includes a *Weltanschauung* are metaphysical. And the principle of linguistic relativity in its radical form leads to an absurd claim that the various languages cannot be translated into another.

But for all this the important problem formulated above does remain. How can it be settled?

First of all, we must have suitable comparative material. We should select some ten different languages for investigation. They must satisfy the following conditions:

1. They must be historically isolated from one another, to exclude any possibility of mutual influence (e.g., the Eskimo language and the Ewe language of African Negroes).
2. They must be languages belonging to different linguistic types and spoken by societies at different levels of civilization (languages of primitive peoples and languages of the various civilized peoples).
3. They must be languages of societies whose history, including the history of culture, is known or at least can be studied in some way.[35]

The investigations would have to be carried out on many levels. Research teams would have to undertake many-sided studies of the language and culture of each nation involved. In order to obtain a comprehensive monograph of the language and culture of a given community, each research team would have to include linguists, historians, social anthropologists, and social psychologists.

The next stage would initiate comparative work proper, in which philosophers would also have to be engaged. But results can only be compared if the data are comparable. Thus the scientists and philosophers would have to work out an appropriate questionnaire and methodological principles to serve as guidelines for all the research teams working on the various languages before they began research studies. This would also define the foundation and nature of comparative studies.

In view of what has been said above there is no need to justify the significance of such an undertaking for the various humanistic disciplines and for an eventual integration of them. But it is obvious that it would be a difficult research project which would require years of work and immense effort, and which would require genuine international cooperation—something like an International Geophysical Year in the social sciences and the humanities. Is all this feasible? Of course, and such an undertaking has already been proposed. Let us hope that extrascientific considerations will not prevent it from being carried out.

Only such studies will answer important questions of philosophical significance; they cannot be answered by mere philosophizing. In all probability there are phenomena common to all languages and also phenomena specific to some of them or to language groups. But perhaps it is otherwise; perhaps one type exists and the other does not! Each of these answers has its own philosophical implications, but the concrete solution depends above all on empirical data.

Thus we have to wait for the facts and abstain from final decisions and conclusions (incidentally, even 'abstaining from decisions' also is philosophically significant). But philosophy is not doomed to a passive wait-and-see attitude. It has its active task as well: it must analyze the categories to be used in research. Though to do this is only to clear the way for research proper, this preliminary step is very important.

Let us try to 'clear the way' in Part 3 of this book.

Part 3

Analysis of the Problem

Chapter 4

Language and Thinking

In order to analyze the active role of language in cognition, we shall now consider a problem often called the problem of the relationship of thinking to language. By thinking I mean human thinking; in the context of this problem it makes no difference whether some other concept of thinking could be formulated to cover thinking processes both in man and in some higher animals. The essence of the problem is rather whether human thinking consists of two processes, 'pure' thinking and 'secondary' verbalization of thoughts, or of a single process of thinking in a language. The problem is not encumbered by the fact that the content of thoughts produced by thinking in different languages or in languages based on different material vehicles of meaning (verbal language versus a language of gestures) may be the same. It is also not contradicted by the fact that there are certain extralinguistic components of secondary importance in human thinking which are not typical of human thinking in general.

We shall begin by considering the concepts 'language' and 'thinking'. Linguistics makes a common distinction between 'speech' and 'language'. 'Speech' means the concrete process of human communication by means of phonic signs; 'language' means a system of rules of meaning and grammar abstracted from the real process of speaking. In accordance with this distinction, universally adopted after de Saussure, speech is an actualization of language, while language is an abstract potential aspect of the general phenomenon of speech.

Language is a system in which specific meanings are associated with their specific material vehicles, such as sound complexes. A being which emits certain sounds not meant as vehicles of meaning (even if the sounds have meaning in some language) does not use language and hence does not speak (e.g., a parrot trained to emit sounds that are words in some language does not speak). On the other hand, for several reasons it makes sense to treat the actualization of the same system of rules of meaning and rules of grammar in different material vehicles as the use of the same language (e.g., speaking, writing a phonetic notation, associating definite symbols with at least some words of the phonic language and using those symbols in human communication).

The physiology of the higher nervous functions occasionally tries to ascertain to what extent our thinking is 'speaking to oneself', i.e., to what extent it is a physiological process performed by our organs of articulation. We are not interested here in this aspect of the connection between thinking and speech, between thinking and language. I take it to be the case that 'inner speech', i.e., language as a process within the organism, usually exists within the brain. Such a process certainly takes place when a person 'talks to himself' or 'polishes his thoughts' before he writes down every fragment of his text.

In view of what has been said above on the essence of the use of language, *the use of language* (in every form and for everyone, for the user himself or for his fellow men) *implies thinking*. It does so since it implies comprehension of the meaning associated with the material vehicles in a given language. Hence the statement that one cannot use language (in inner speech or in intersubjective communication) without thinking is analytic, given the definition of the use of language, or, even more briefly, given the definition of language. This, however, does not make analytic the converse statement, namely, that all thinking, every act of (human) thinking, implies the use of a definite language, shaped and acquired by an individual in the course of human communication. This statement could be made analytic by defining 'thinking' appropriately. I shall, however, consider it a synthetic statement, the focal *hypothesis* in the considerations that follow, a hypothesis warranted, I think, by the achievements of the empirical disciplines concerned with human thinking and behavior. This hypothesis is also present in the statement that *one cannot think* (in a human way) and behave in a manner conditioned by such thinking *if one has not been taught to use some language in the human community in the proper period of one's life. Thinking always is thinking in some language,* and not something which can be divided into two stages: prelinguistic thinking and a subsequent, secondary formulation of thoughts in the words of some language, a condensation of thoughts in a language pattern (although, obviously, thoughts which are thought in one language may later be translated into another language).

I treat this statement as an hypothesis because of its synthetic character, and because it is not universally accepted. It is, on the contrary, an object of controversy. But I consider it very strongly supported by scientific data.

Theoretically, there are two different ways of solving the problem of the relationship between thinking and language. One consists in the 'pure' conceptual analysis that is performed by phenomenologists. But no philosophy that attempts to be scientific (by excluding assertions that contradict the theses of specialized disciplines) could abide the speculative character of such analysis. I shall therefore only note the existence of those speculative trends which assume the noble guise of scientific philosophy.

The second way consists in analysis of the data provided by the specialized disciplines. This makes philosophy, not an exalted 'queen of sciences', but more secure and less exposed to speculation. In my opinion only this second path is worthy of philosophy as a science.

Specialized disciplines offer two kinds of investigations interesting for philosophers concerned with the relationship between thinking and language. There are investigations of the processes which take place in the child when the child learns to speak, especially of the ways in which acquiring the means of participating in linguistic communication is connected with the formation of human linguistic behavior. And there are investigations of the behavior and psychology of aphasic persons who have lost their ability to participate in linguistic communication.

In the former case, we have access to the data of developmental psychology (child psychology) that describe the development of children who are mute as a result of deafness.

In the latter case, we have access to the data of disciplines that treat speech impairments caused by brain damage which resulted in loss of the ability of language-thinking.

I shall first present an analysis of the data provided by these specialized disciplines dealing with man and his cognitive functions and then return to a tentative justification of the general hypothesis formulated above.

Theoretically, developmental psychology ought to provide the most important data for our problem, the problem of the relationship between thinking and language. Unfortunately, it does not. This is not because it is unable to do so, but because it has not yet dealt with the problem explicitly, at any rate, has not conceived it on a sufficiently broad scale. This may seem strange, since this problem ranks among the most important in developmental psychology, yet analysis of the relevant available literature reveals that such is the case. Usually, either the problem is lost in a mass of detailed but quite fragmentary investigations, or a solution of the problem is assumed *without* painstaking investigations. This has undoubtedly been the case because developmental psychology has been concerned mainly with the *continuity* of the developmental process from its simplest to its most complicated forms, even in investigations of more general theoretical problems. The issue of continuity is certainly important, but this does not justify ignorance or neglect of the problem we are considering here.

Literature of the first type is so widely represented that it requires no illustration. We need only glance at almost any work presenting detailed investigations of the development of vocabulary in children of a given age, or the grammatical types dominant in children's speech, or the evolution of syntax (and such works are legion) to see that the investigations lack a broad theoretical conception. It is not my intention to minimize the importance of such contributions. I only want to assess them properly.

The work of Piaget in the 1920s, which assumed the unity of thinking and speech in the child and studied the child's thinking *through the intermediary* of his speech, is representative of the second kind of literature. For instance, the thesis concerning egocentrism in the child's thinking is based exclusively on the egocentrism of his speech, i.e., on the assertion that the child speaks about himself and is not concerned with his listener's standpoint in conversation. An interesting and penetrating criticism of such an approach can be found in L. S. Vygotsky's study of Piaget's works.[1]

Below, we shall see what psychological literature can contribute when we consider the Soviet school of developmental psychology based on Vygotsky's work. This school occupies an extraordinary position in the study of the connection between speech and thinking. It is the only psychological school in the world which has deeply attended to the significance of this connection and has done something significant about it. We can explain its extraordinary position by taking into account the influence of philosophical assumptions upon Vygotsky's approach to psychological problems. Starting from the assumptions of Marxist epistemology, one cannot fail to see the significance of the connection between speech and thinking in the developmental process of the child.

This does not mean that no other valid considerations of our problem can be found in the psychological literature. Yet their modest scope confirms the thesis that most psychologists underestimate or simply fail to notice the problem. As already noted, Piaget, in the methods of his works from the 1920s, *assumes* the unity of speech and language. This facilitates further study of the child's psychology on the basis of his speech. Likewise, Stern bases his theory of stages in the development of thinking and speech on personalistic assumptions, but *does not examine* the issue of the links between speech and thinking in the child's development. In other authors we find statements and ideas concerning this issue, some of them quite interesting but all of them without empirical evidence to support the author's standpoints. For instance, Delacroix speaks of the process of the intellectualization of the child (which is a qualitatively new stage in development) which accompanies the appearance of speech.[2] Kainz emphasizes the role of words in the formation of concepts by the child[3] and shows interest in the speech and economy of that process. But it is only in the Soviet psychological literature (and to a certain extent also the Polish literature, particularly that of the Cracow school) that our problem emerges fully as a genuine object of research.

The most important study in this field is Vygotsky's *Myšleniye i reč* (*Thinking and Speech*), which is completely dedicated to the problem under consideration.

Vygotsky interprets 'thinking' broadly, as "orientation in the world." Hence he examines the developmental factors of thinking and of speech separately, both in their phylogenetic and ontogenetic aspects. Given such an interpretation of thinking, it is obvious that the development of thinking precedes the development of speech in man's phylogenesis and ontogenesis. Vygotsky also assumes that in the early stages of phylogenesis and ontogenesis the developmental factors and paths of thinking and of speech are interdependent. Yet he does not doubt that at a certain moment the two lines of development meet to become one, that man's thinking becomes verbal.

> But what is most important in our knowledge of the development of thinking and speech in the child is the fact that at a certain moment, in an early period (about the age of two), the lines of the development of thinking and speech, until then independent, meet and begin to coincide, and give rise to an entirely new form of behavior, characteristic of man.[4]

Vygotsky also has no doubt that this is the turning point in the development of the child's psychology. He agrees with Stern that the child makes the greatest discovery in his life when he realizes that "things have names" (that the community in which the child grows up calls things by these names). Vygotsky did not stop at general hypotheses, but studied the problem by examining experimentally the ways in which concepts are formed. He and his collaborators investigated the use of words in directing attention and in the processes of analysis, abstraction, and synthesis.[5] These investigations totally undermined the idealist approach of the Würzburg school.

In examining our problem in the light of experimental research on the origin and evolution of conceptual thinking, Vygotsky grasps the real issue, the unity of thinking and speech. His research hypothesis is that such a unity exists from early childhood and accounts for the specific nature of human thinking. He believes that the thinking of a child who knows how to speak is always linguistic, always verbal, and that speech is always intellectual. That is why Vygotsky consistently identifies the concept and the meaning of a word.[6] He analyzes the problem of that identity in every detail: he makes a distinction between the physical and semantic aspects of speech and examines the evolution of the connections between them,[7] and he studies the development of concepts from 'pseudoconcepts' (general words used by the child but understood to denote concrete things) to proper concepts in close connection with the evolution of the functions of speech.[8] Vygotsky uses dynamic analysis. He not only wants to prove that thinking in an adult human being is linguistic thinking, but to investigate the dynamics of the process as well.[9] This enables him to offer an explanation of syncretism in the child's speech, and of the evolution toward analytic thinking, which differs from Piaget's explanation. This also helps him explain the function and nature of thinking aloud. He suggests that the child has a tendency toward hypostases because of his relatively strong linking of words with objects. I am only outlining the issues investigated by Vygotsky without endeavoring to present them in an exhaustive manner. I only want to emphasize that he realized the significance of the problem we are concerned with here and investigated it experimentally.

Vygotsky's school, by continuing his ideas, has succeeded in expanding his research into an imposing system not found elsewhere.[10] A. R. Luria's works, especially his studies of the role of words in the formation of new cognitive associations in man,[11] are of particular interest because he has tried to draw some theoretical generalizations. The large-scale research conducted by this Soviet school of thought covers all the issues connected with our problem.

In the Polish literature on the subject, research conducted by the Cracow school deserves particular attention. In addition to its numerous smaller contributions which describe the various manifestations of the child's speech in great detail, the Cracow school has formulated important theoretical generalizations. For example, there is Stefan Szuman's theory that the child constructs his world of objects by coming to know them together with their names. In this way Szuman explains the generalizing function of words, which eliminates the need for images.[12] This theory is similar to earlier research by the Soviet psychologists Lublinskaya and Rosensardt and by American psycholinguists (Eric Lenneberg and others) which emphasizes the effect of speech upon the perception of objects.

But we must bear in mind that even such partial results are exceptional. Developmental psychology has not solved or even properly formulated the problem which interests us. Hence the dissatisfaction of the philosopher who turns to that discipline for an answer to his questions. This state of affairs also affects developmental psychology itself adversely. As long as it fails to formulate central theoretical problems, its specialized research, undertaken without adequate theoretical and methodological preparation, will only yield minimal results. It may only result in the accumulation of facts without any clear notion of whether they will be useful in later research or of whether they are being collected and systematized in the right way.

The situation is no better in the analysis of the psychology of mute children and children brought up in the 'wilderness'. It may seem disrespectful to speak of people thus handicapped, but the fact remains that analysis of the development of these children would yield excellent experimental data. Unfortunately, what we are told about the relation between thinking and speech in such people (with a few laudable exceptions) consists of low-standard popularizations and speculations. This refers in particular to children brought up in the wilderness. The numerous studies concerned with deaf-mutes usually have had purely practical objectives in view; this partly defeated their purpose, because excessive limitation of the cognitive basis also restricted the possibilities of obtaining practical results. In this respect too the Soviet school is exceptional, but even there, workers have been hesitant to deal with the problem.[13]

What fantastic theoretical possibilities are opened up by the study of what are called 'wild' children, such as the wild boy of Aveyron, Caspar Hauser, or the two 'wolf' girls in India, Amala and Camala. But those cases were not (and at the time could not be) studied in a scientific manner. And yet these were unique cases. The natural development of speech and the effect of the lack of speech upon perception of reality, orientation in the world, and thinking are some of the problems which studies of the development of such children could clarify.

The things to investigate would be persistent *alali* produced by the lack of an environment of speech (as in the case of the two girls in India in the early twentieth century) and, above all, the nature of changes in orientation to the world caused by the emergence of the function of speech in a person who did not learn to speak at the usual age. Let us consider, in the latter regard, Caspar Hauser's case. He initially perceived the world as a collection of colored patches and only came to perceive it as a world of things when he learned the names of those things.[14] These facts are known from a report made by his teacher. I am not as concerned with the trustworthiness of that narrative as with the importance of the problems, which could have been examined in this connection.

Psychological studies of prelinguistic and postlinguistic stages of children born deaf and mute, and *a fortiori* those born deaf and blind, might also be valuable, if such studies concentrated on the relation between thinking and speech. The works available on such cases do not meet that condition. Even the classic cases of Helen Keller and Laura Bridgman were not studied in the proper way. The memoirs of Helen Keller, especially her account of the impact of her discovery that things have names upon the the further development of her psychic life,[15] are extremely interesting. Jerusalem, who investigated Laura Bridgman's case from her own reminiscences and the notes of her teachers, states that she only began to think abstractly when she learned to speak (speech in her case being signs perceived by touch).[16] Louis Arnould uses the example of Marie Hurtin, born deaf and blind, to emphasize the importance of the comprehension of the sign-object relation.[17]

Thus very little has been accomplished in a field which might provide a wealth of information on the mechanisms of the relationship of thinking and speech. We may find sporadic remarks on the significance of language signs for the development of abstract thinking in the works of various authors, but these are speculations and not scientific proofs.

Here too the Soviet school is a laudable exception. This can best be seen from the information on Soviet research studies in this area provided by Avgusta Yarmolenko in *Očerki psikhologii slepoglukhone-mykh* (*Notes on the Psychology of Blind Deaf-Mutes*).[18] These studies are, unfortunately, only first steps, but even they justify certain general conclusions that are extremely interesting from our point of view.

On the strength of the studies carried out so far, Soviet researchers claim first of all that if a child who is disabled and cannot speak is not *taught* a system of signs—i.e., *transmitted* a system of signs—he is doomed to lasting mental disability. This applies to individuals who are normal and even potentially capable of attaining a high intellectual level despite their physical disability.[19] It would be difficult to find a stronger and more explicit argument confirming the unity of thinking and speech and refuting metaphysical speculations about 'pure' thinking. The logical conclusion is that there is no thinking without a system of signs (although not necessarily phonic).

The Soviet research workers also have no doubts that in transmitting to a deaf and blind child a system of signs that is a transposition of a phonic language into a tactile language, we make his intellectual development possible. This is additional proof of the thesis that there can be no 'pure' thinking, thinking without speech, and that thinking is a *social* product, though always an individual act.[20]

This is also proved by the fact that a deaf and blind child starts on the path to human thinking, the path from sensory data to generalized ideas, once he has assimilated the first words translated into a tactile language.[21]

The research carried out by the Cracow school is also broad in theoretical perspective, and I should particularly mention a new research project of that school, which under favorable conditions may yield promising results.[22] I refer to its research on deaf and mute children who are in special schools and have already learned a language (including its written form). This research has been aimed at finding out whether these children comprehend abstract words, conjunctions, and prepositions denoting certain relations. Nine methods have been used for that purpose; one has been to ask the children to draw the situation described in a simple sentence that includes the preposition in question. The research carried out is still too fragmentary and too sparse to permit valid generalizations, but the results obtained thus far indicate clearly that while deaf-mutes comprehend the meanings of words that evoke concrete images (of things, persons, and actions), they do not comprehend the meanings of words that denote relations, even spatial relations. Continuation of these studies may add valuable information to our knowledge of the linkage between speech and thinking.

But even the partial and fragmentary results of research in the field of developmental psychology that we have permit certain generalizations.

First of all, they refute the hypothesis, which is still in circulation, that language is a natural product of a developed organism and can develop without being taught. This is refuted by the facts that children born deaf with no inborn defects of the organs of speech are mute too and that children who grow up in isolation from society (live closed up or among animals) develop a lasting speechless condition.[23] The faculty of speaking is 'innate' in man, but this only means that the structure of his brain and other organs, which are necessary conditions of the development of speech and thinking, is inherited and enables every normal child to *learn* to speak. Language and speech and thinking are social products which are transmitted to the human being through upbringing (in ontogenesis). Authors who otherwise differ widely in their opinions, such as Kainz[24] and Luria,[25] agree about this. This is important, since it sheds additional light upon the effects of the occurrence of speech in the development of the child. We can reject purely biological or personalistic theories which stress the development of the organism as such or the autonomous entity of the personality. We can then consider the role of the social factor in the child's upbringing and activities.[26]

Secondly, the results obtained (especially from the study of deaf-mutes) reinforce the conviction that there is an organic unity of thinking and speech. Lack of language and speech dooms a child to the mental level of an imbecile, and limited development of language and speech limits the developmental possibilities of thinking. The development of conceptual thinking in the child is doubtless associated with the development of the function of speaking, although the mechanism of that association is far from understood.

There is, as we can see, a well of knowledge to be tapped, but no efficient mechanism to extract the proper information. It is time we went about constructing the proper machinery for future research. And there are problems which can be and, in my opinion ought to be, investigated experimentally for that purpose.

Research should be focused upon the role of the verbal sign in the process of abstraction and in the organization of perception and indeed of the conceptualization of reality. In addition to a series of further studies on the development of the various functions, from the most primitive to the most complex forms of behavior of living organisms, and from incipient to fully developed forms of analysis, abstraction, synthesis, etc. (on which developmental psychology has focused its attention until now), a series of studies should be organized to explain the significance of the qualitative jump that occurs in the behavior of the human organism following the appearance of speech and verbal thinking.

Thus comparative research would have to be undertaken in the field of animal and human psychology, with special attention to the problem of animal 'language'. So far this problem has only been dealt with marginally, and much depends on how we define the concepts of language and speech. The controversy over what to call the communication system of animals is sterile. Comparative experimental research on the contribution of phonic speech (or its translations into other sign systems) to abstract thinking must also be undertaken. A continuation of Vygotsky's experimental observation of the ways children form concepts and of the role played in that process by the development of speech in the child might also be revealing.

A special study of children handicapped in hearing and speech should also be made.

First of all, the development of thinking should be investigated experimentally in a comparative way; this should be done on the strength of observations of normal children and deaf-mute (or deaf and blind) children who grow up under similar conditions. Mentally deficient children would be excluded. Up to the moment when the deaf-mute begins to learn to communicate by a system of gestures or a system of sounds, he and the normal child receive almost the same developmental stimuli. One of them receives *one type of stimulus less*; he does not hear. Hence we can study the function of that stimulus in the child's development. I would design the study in the following way. The literature of the subject reports cases in which a human child and a young chimpanzee were brought up in the same milieu to observe their development.[27] Analogous upbringing of two children, one normal and the other deaf-mute (or deaf and blind), would seem to be even simpler. The study should include two or three pairs of children, one of each pair normal and the other born deaf and mute, from six months up to three or four years, that is, up to the age when the deaf-mute begins to learn to speak systematically. The study would register data on the development of the children and focus on the turning point in this development which coincides with the appearance of speech in the normal child and with the appearance of its substitute in the disabled child.

No doubt, the study would encounter a number of difficulties; for instance, one would have to establish deafness early. It would also call for a very detailed program of research. It could not be a simple repetition of the studies made by Stern, the Bühlers, and others, who in a very detailed manner, day by day and hour by hour, *described* the behavior of the child, the sounds he emitted, his manifestations of speech, etc. The point would be to prepare a selective program, based on the studies and descriptions mentioned above and intended explicitly to establish the ways of studying the emergence and development of conceptual thinking. Above all, it would be essential to compare the change in the development of the child's orientation and his thinking in the strict sense which follows the emergence and the development of speech. Simultaneous observation of several pairs of children would help to eliminate the influence of casual or random factors. For optimal efficiency the experiment would require international cooperation. Its repetition in different national milieus would help eliminate random factors.

Such a study would provide a great step forward in our knowledge of how thinking evolves from simple reactions of the organism to stimuli, our knowledge of the mechanism of the evolution of the child's faculty of abstraction, analysis, and synthesis, and our knowledge of the emergence and development of concepts.

The study would include experiments on the development of conceptual thinking in deaf-mutes learning to speak. I refer to experiments of the type carried out by the Cracow school. They can contribute much to our knowledge of the function of speech in the development of thinking, as well as confirm once again the thesis that the study of pathological phenomena is often the best way of comprehending what is normal.

When we turn to the literature concerned with processes which take place when a normal person loses his faculty of speech as a result of injury or disease, we are struck by the similarities and differences with respect to the data provided by child psychology.

The difference consists primarily in the quantity and quality of data in these two fields. Scientists have been studying the phenomena covered by the general term 'aphasia' for over a hundred years. We are practically flooded by literature on the subject and by a wealth of facts examined with precision. Nevertheless the differences in the classification and interpretation of those facts, the discrepancies and even contradictions between the various schools which refer to those facts, prove that we are still in an early stage of the study of the various forms of aphasia. The scientists who have examined the patients cannot agree on many essential issues. Is there only one aphasia, or are there many different aphasias? Can aphasia be localized in a given part of the brain or does it affect the brain as a whole? Is aphasia a result of an impairment of mental processes, or vice versa? The list could be continued. The philosopher is sad to record such a chaos of opinions, yet feels some satisfaction that such a confusion is not endemic to philosophical disciplines.

At this point, we conclude that neither research in developmental psychology nor research on aphasia provide the philosopher with a well-documented answer to his questions about the interrelationship between speech and thinking. Perhaps the necessary precision has not yet been acquired in these fields. At any rate, the students of aphasia are unable to dispel the philosopher's doubts, and what is more they even, much to his astonishment, turn to him for assistance in solving many problems. For instance, Kurt Goldstein vigorously and boldly asserts that no clear demarcation line can be drawn between the specialized disciplines and philosophy in their treatment of this problem.

The main difficulty is that science is unable to state whether the loss of the ability to speak and to understand speech is the cause or the effect of the impairment of intellectual functions. This reduces, if it does not eliminate, the possibility of answering questions so intriguing to philosophers on the basis of research on aphasia. Are thinking and speech one, or are they distinct but complementary functions? Does language play an active role in thinking? In his fundamental *Psychologie der Sprache,* Friedrich Kainz traces the study of aphasia from Pierre Marie to Kurt Goldstein and concludes sadly that the problem of which depends on which, thinking on speech or speech on thinking, cannot be resolved.[28]

Although the study of aphasia in its present form cannot provide clear answers and solutions, we cannot reject the possibility of the philosopher learning important things from students of aphasia from the start. On the contrary, it is dismaying that philosophers, with the exception of Cassirer, have not drawn more on that source of information in their study of the relationship between language (speech) and thinking. Those who claim that we can learn most about that relationship when the natural unity of its elements is broken or damaged through disease or injury to the brain are very probably right.

On the other hand, students of aphasia, like students of child psychology, pay little attention to the issues that most interest the philosopher. But this is not so surprising. Their research is concerned mainly with medicine and the physiology of the brain. It deals with the relationship between pathological symptoms and injuries to the brain and with the etiology, syndromes, and therapy of such injuries. In most cases the studies are clinical, and general considerations of speech and thinking are exceptional; indeed, the studies do not even systematically pave the way for such considerations. Kurt Goldstein and his school are an exception to the rule. Goldstein not only raises general problems of interest to philosophers, but states that the student of aphasia will not be able to solve the problems with which he is confronted in practice without an appropriate philosophical standpoint.[29] It is no wonder, then, that Goldstein's research provides the most data for philosophical analysis.

It is not our business to decide whether the localizational or the organicist (holist) theory of aphasia is correct or to take sides in the controversy over the typology of the various forms of aphasia (almost every school uses a different classification and terminology, which makes these already complicated matters even more complicated). But both these problems are connected with issues in which the philosopher is directly interested. That is why he must recognize the significance of the differences of opinion involved.

Kurt Goldstein consciously adopts the antilocalizational approach, following Jackson, Marie, and Head. It is not a single part of the brain but the brain as a whole which becomes diseased in the case of aphasia, and this disease does not cause partial changes in this or that function, but changes in the entire personality, that is changes in attitudes and behavior. Goldstein distinguishes two attitudes, 'concrete' and 'abstracting'. These attitudes distinguish two different ways of using language, the concrete way and the abstracting way.

The concrete attitude or behavior consists in a situational approach to reality: things, phenomena, and words of a language are grasped in the concrete context of a given situation, and can only be known within the framework of that situation. The abstracting attitude or behavior on the contrary, dissociates things and phenomena from concrete situations and recognizes them from general characteristics. This also applies to language. Words acquire meaning, in the strict sense of the term, only within the framework of the abstracting approach.

The distinction between these two attitudes is connected by Goldstein with a definite conception of language. He is not alone in this; similar ideas are to be found in Head and in the Soviet school, in Vygotsky and Luria. What Goldstein calls the abstracting attitude, Head calls 'symbolic behavior'. Symbolic behavior is destroyed or impaired in the case of aphasia. Vygotsky's research went in the same direction,[30] and Luria holds the same opinion.[31]

Applying the concept of two attitudes or two types of behavior to the problems of language implies that language has an abstracting function, and is involved in concrete situations as well. Goldstein and his school present a number of interesting arguments in favor of such an interpretation.

In the case of nominal aphasia (the loss of the ability to *name* objects following the loss of the ability to comprehend names) the patient can still use a given object in the proper way, explain what purpose it serves thus avoiding naming it, and even use the word in question in a context, although he is unable to comprehend or to pronounce that word as a general name. (The patient who does not comprehend the general name 'umbrella' freely utters the sentence "I have two umbrellas at home".) Only the ability to use words abstractly is lost.[32]

The loss of the ability to name things is ascribable to the loss of the abstracting attitude and behavior. Every word generalizes, and the patient has lost the ability to generalize. But a word which loses its general meaning remains accessible to the patient in a concrete situational context as part of concrete behavior. And this only because the patient had learned the word and had associated it with a given situation before he became ill.

Observation of patients who have lost the ability to comprehend and reproduce the various conjunctions, such as 'though', 'or', 'yet', also proves this. The patient can only speak and write them in the company of other words. Similar conclusions can be drawn from the study of the loss of the ability to comprehend metaphors.

According to Goldstein, amnesic aphasia results from a change in the whole personality, and not only from a loss of verbal images (Luria's standpoint is similar). Transition from abstract language to concrete language occurs because the patient loses the comprehension of *meanings* of words. At this point we reach that aspect of Goldstein's analysis which is philosophically the most interesting.

The meaning of a word, Goldstein says, does not consist in an ordinary association of a set of sounds with a given object, but in the ability to denote general elements of the world of objects. Denotation organizes that world of objects by abstraction.[33] To reformulate Goldstein's idea: the patient loses the ability of *conceptual* thinking: though he may retain given words in a concrete individual situational context, he does not retain them as general names, as elements of conceptual thinking.

From this fact, Goldstein draws far-reaching conclusions. This explains why Ernst Cassirer, when discussing the pathology of speech in his fundamental work on the philosophy of symbolic forms,[34] makes use of Goldstein's research. If the words which perform the function of generalizing denotation are called symbols, then in amnesic aphasia (and it is precisely amnesic aphasia, in Goldstein's terminology, and semantic aphasia, in Luria's classification and terminology, which are interesting from the point of view of the philosophy of language) words lose their symbolic function. The patient loses his ability to order his perceptions of the world.[35]

The loss of the abstracting function of language is for Goldstein the loss of language in the proper sense of the term. And thus we return to the starting point of our investigation of aphasia. Does an aphasiac think? Can one think after having lost the faculty of speech?

Of course, we are not interested in cases of motor aphasia, where the patient understands what is said to him and retains his inner language, but cannot speak. From our point of view the cases of those aphasiacs who read philosophical books, or play cards or chess, do not involve any major problems of interpretation. We may not speak of an interdependence between the function of speech and thinking *in general,* but must always do so concretely with reference to a given type of mental paralysis and aphasia. But what about 'amnesic' or 'semantic' aphasia? (The extensions and intentions of these two terms do not strictly coincide but refer to the same kind of phenomena.)

Goldstein does not pose this question directly, but raises the issue indirectly. I am not concerned with what he says about the relationship between aphasia and intelligence. What he says has been summed up by Kainz in his thesis that mutual influence may vary, and besides, science cannot settle that relationship in a univocal manner for the time being.

But I am concerned with Goldstein's reflections on the 'language' of animals, primitive peoples, and aphasiacs.

Do animals have any language? If 'language' is to be understood in the qualified sense of 'abstract language' (or, as we would say, 'conceptual language') Goldstein's reply is firmly in the negative. Animals do not have the abstracting attitude specific to man, i.e., symbolic or categorial behavior (to use Head's nomenclature and Goldstein's early terminology).[36]

Similar reasoning leads Goldstein to answer the question of whether aphasiacs have a language in the negative.

In all these cases Goldstein's argument is based on the assumption that 'language' in the strict sense of the term means 'conceptual language' or 'abstract language'. Nor is Goldstein alone in this respect. In one of his latest works on the subject, Konorski supports the same view. This is astounding, since Konorski favors the physiological approach and is firmly opposed to Goldstein's making the problem a philosophical one. Konorski writes:

> Although ... primitive forms of 'communication' between individuals of the same species are fairly common among those animals which live in herds, speech in the stricter sense of the term, of naming and describing, has phylogenetically only developed in man.[37]
>
> Human speech appears only when definite sets of sounds (and in the speech of deaf-mutes conventional signs made by fingers) come to *symbolize* definite objects, actions, or concepts in general, i.e., when there is one-to-one correspondence between definite standard sounds and their "designata."[38]

Why do these authors, who otherwise do not deny the fact of communication among animals, emphasize the specific nature of human speech and protest the obliteration of the distinction between human language and the language of animals? They do so because human language has special properties and hence there is an *objective* difference between it and other types of communication. Given the continuity of the evolution of ways of communication and the fact that human language belongs to the class of communication systems, is it not artificial to single out human language by a special term? Are we not trying to settle the controversy over the specific nature of human language by definition, by convention? No. This distinction is based on a class of properties specific to the human type of communication. The distinction is objective in nature.

If a special name for this one system is not justified, then a special name for all communication systems regardless of differences between them is even less justified.

I have engaged in these somewhat speculative polemics with an imaginary opponent for a good reason. I want to use analogous reasoning in more controversial issues with real opponents who might be willing to admit the first train of argument. Mine, then, is a tactical move.

Are thinking and conceptual thinking (and thus 'linguistic thinking') identical? This is an important issue if we hope to solve our initial problem. Our opponents are mainly philosophers who would not hesitate to distinguish between human language and other communication systems, but who insist on the viability of 'prelinguistic thinking' or 'nonlinguistic thinking', which they take to mean adaptive behavior in general.

Obviously, the term 'thinking' is a troublemaker because of its ambiguity. The range of problems to which it is supposed to refer is interpreted in various ways. Let us, therefore, adopt a functional definition, acceptable to physiologists: the process of thinking occurs wherever we solve problems. But we soon realize that we have not eliminated the ambiguity, but have only shifted it to another level. For what does "solving problems" mean? A man who is playing chess is certainly solving problems. But so is a chimpanzee that puts smaller sticks together to make one big stick to get the banana outside the cage. What about the rat that learns to find the path leading to food in the maze? What about the amoeba that retreats on encountering acid and seeks another path to food?

What is common to all those cases is the behavior of an organism which reacts to external stimuli by striving for a definite objective. *In this respect* a normal thinking human being resembles both an aphasiac who has lost comprehension of the general meanings of words and the chimpanzee, the rat, and the amoeba. This resemblance can be explained by the evolutional continuity of living organisms. Can we use the common term 'thinking' to cover all behavior of this kind? Of course we are at liberty to do so, but this would be misleading, just as the use of one and the same term 'language' for the various systems of communication (human, animal, etc.) is misleading.

All behavior of every organism is connected with an orientation in the world. But among the various types of orientation in the world we may distinguish one which, thanks to the function of abstraction and generalization specific to linguistic signs, is characteristic *only* of men, or more exactly, only of men who have not been deprived by disease of the ability to make use of language. Studies in the pathology of speech shed new light upon this problem. The distinction made in these studies between concrete and abstract attitudes (behavior) is very important. Only in cases of abstract-attitude behavior may we speak of language (with its symbolizing, naming, and descriptive function mentioned by Konorski) and of thinking in the proper sense of both terms.

Goldstein uses the following example to illustrate the difference between concrete and abstract attitude. When I enter a dark room and switch on the light, I am behaving concretely; but when I abstain from doing so because I do not want to wake up the person sleeping in that room, I am behaving abstractly. A similar example may be used to explain the difference between behavior resulting from a conditioned response developed in an organism and behavior based on thinking. We can teach an animal to switch on the light in a dark room, but if the animal knew how to *abstain* from doing so in order not to awaken someone, it would no longer be an animal, it would think.

Such behavior must be connected with linguistic thinking. Why? The answer to this question is provided by the study of the pathology of speech. When man is unable to use his language, he loses his abstracting attitude and the ability to think in the strict sense of the word 'think'.

Are we not making the identification of thinking with linguistic thinking by definition? Not at all, just as we did not distinguish language from other communication by definition. Thinking in the sense of linguistic thinking is an *objectively distinguishable* type of orientation in the world. We do not deny that in many respects linguistic thinking is extensionally included in other concepts (such as 'physiological process' and 'behavior') and enables us to take the continuity of evolution of the behavior of living organisms into account. We are merely saying that in one respect—an all-important respect in this case—that type of behavior or orientation in the world differs from the others. It would be absurd to deny the difference between linguistic thinking and the orientation of a total aphasiac, an infant, a chimpanzee, or an amoeba.

It is often argued that linguistic thinking is sometimes an obstacle; that *homo alalus*, some Tarzan of the apes, would be more able-bodied and in certain respects would fare better in the world than a man who thinks in a language. Perhaps. We know that people deprived of one sense are more sensitive in their other senses than normal individuals. The memoirs of the deaf and blind woman, O. I. Skorokhodova,[39] describing her extraordinarily sensitive touch, are very instructive in that respect. But does it follow from this that a deaf and blind person has a better orientation in the world than a normal person? This is, of course, only an analogy. In our case we are not dealing with compensation for the lack of one of the senses, but with the elimination of the effect of conceptual thinking upon the perception of reality and upon responses of the organism to stimuli. A human organism formed under such a condition might be more dexterous in some respects, just as a cat or a dog is more dexterous than a man in some respects. But would not the price of such 'success' be too high? Would such an orientation in the world really be better? But it is not important which orientation in the world is better. What is important is the fact that the orientation in the world that is connected with linguistic thinking is *different* and *specifically human*. This suffices to justify its distinction.

To sum up: Even the study of the pathology of speech has not yet yielded the expected empirical solutions of the problem we are concerned with; it has, nevertheless, become a source of many reflections and intellectual stimuli. And for that the philosopher must be grateful.

We can now return to the initial problem: Are thinking and the verbalization of thoughts *separate* processes or a homogeneous process of speaking-and-thinking?

It is obvious that we must support one of two conceptions: either a monistic or a dualistic one. In other words, we may conclude that speaking-and-thinking is a homogeneous process or that speaking and thinking are two separate processes. And it is easy to see which solution was accepted by Marx (although in the passage from *The German Ideology* cited below he refers not to thinking, but to consciousness).

> From the start the 'spirit' is afflicted with the curse of being 'bur-dened' with matter, which here makes its appearance in the form of agitated layers of air, sounds, in short, of language. Language is as old as consciousness, language *is* practical consciousness, that exists also for other men, and for that reason alone it really exists for me personally as well; language, like consciousness, only arises from the need, the necessity, of intercourse with other men.[40]

Marx speaks in the spirit of a specific monism, in the spirit of antidualism. He does so again in another part of the same work.

> For philosophers, one of the most difficult tasks is to descend from the world of thoughts to the actual world. *Language* is the immediate actuality of thought. Just as philosophers have given thought an independent existence, so they had to make language into an independent realm. ... The philosophers would only have to dissolve their language into the ordinary language, from which it is abstracted, to recognize it as the distorted language of the actual world, and to realize that neither thoughts nor language in themselves form a realm of their own, that they are only *manifestations* of actual life.[41]

Marx was not at all isolated in his antidualism; many eminent thinkers made similar statements before him. I say that not to reduce the importance of Marx's statements, but quite the contrary, to increase it. This is a very controversial problem, the solution of which is not univocally settled by the choice of the materialist or the idealist standpoint in philosophy. Dualism and monism (in the specific sense of these terms, as used here) have found support among both materialists and idealists. And the fact that the history of the problem reveals eminent defenders of theses analogous to those of Marx only increases the value of Marx's standpoint.

Both groups, even today, can boast great names, philosophers and linguists alike. The monists may include Herder, Schelling, Humboldt, Steinthal, Marty, and Mauthner, but the dualists have Schopenhauer, Bergson, K. Bühler, Pick, and Preyer in their ranks. It is worth noting that N. Y. Marr supported the dualistic standpoint in this issue.

The controversy concerns the question, "Can thought (in the sense of conceptual thinking) occur without language?" or conversely, "Can language occur without thought?" But the controversy may also take the form of the problem of the identity of, or difference between, the functions of language and thinking. It then assumes a functional character. This typology comes from G. Révész, in my opinion the author of the best work on the problem. I shall adopt it as the basis for a critical analysis of this problem.

The first controversial question, i.e., that of the possibility of the occurrence of thought without language, may be examined either genetically or psychologically.[42]

If we reject speculations on the origin of language and thinking in early man, the genetic point of view must be confined to the data provided by developmental psychology. As we know, developmental psychology has not yet succeeded in satisfying our curiosity in that respect. We may dispute whether an infant thinks, but we cannot deny that it has a definite orientation in the external world, for it always reacts adaptively to stimuli coming from that world at least to a certain extent. Arguments against identifying thinking with orientation in the world are intended to demonstrate that the specific nature of conceptual thinking (which requires at least the realization of that which one is doing) are thereby eliminated. Such arguments are bolstered by Révész's argument, which is as follows: If we assume that the orientation of an infant in the world is equivalent to thinking, then, in all consistency, we must assume that animals think too, and thus we eliminate the specific nature of human thinking. For if we are satisfied with bringing out only what is *common* to all orientation in the world (a procedure which is legitimate and useful in a certain type of research), we lose what is *specific* to the various component parts of the phenomenon. This is the price we have to pay for the broad inexact use of the term 'thinking'.

A genetic analysis of the relation between language and thinking leaves various points unsettled, however, if only because of the insufficient data provided by developmental psychology. But psychological analysis of the acts of thinking of adult human beings puts the problem in a different light. In my opinion, psychological analysis forces one to reject any dualism of language and thinking unless one adopts an intuitionistic metaphysics, which either contradicts empirical data or simply misunderstands certain things.

In the literature on the subject I have encountered no defender of the claim that speech, i.e., actualization of language, is possible without thought. Since language is the unity of the material vehicle, i.e., sign system, and the semantic aspect of the signs involved (without which the signs cease to be a language), speech cannot exist without thought. Cases of automation, e.g., where a person repeats words learned previously but does not associate meanings with them or where a person repeats words in an unknown language without understanding them, do not refute this claim in the least, since these cases involve the production of articulate sounds but not speech (just as sounds repeated by a parrot reproducing words of human speech are not speech).

Thus the real problem is reached only when we ask, "Is extralinguistic non-verbal thought possible?"

Representatives of various shades of philosophical intuitionism believe that extralinguistic thinking not only is possible but is the very source of 'true cognition'. But the arguments they adduce to support their claim may be rejected without detailed analysis, since they are products of pure speculation based on quite arbitrary assumptions. Intuitionism opposes pure metaphysics and irrationalism to facts known from everyday experience and to the arguments of such empirical disciplines as the physiology and the pathology of brain functions. It can and must be stated that there *are* people who take such a standpoint (which is a social phenomenon that deserves attention), but there is no way of engaging in a discussion with intuitionists, for their theses cannot be analyzed in scientific terms. We can only point out that they violate the elementary principles of scientific analysis.

There are other theories, however, which are less ambitious in philosophical intent but more capable of verification or falsification. These deserve special attention because they contain certain observations which may be misunderstood and which actually have been used as empirical proofs of a dualistic interpretation.

Thus it is claimed, usually with reference to introspection, that not all thought processes are linguistic, or verbal, in nature. An analysis of the facts which the advocates of this thesis cite reveals a few misinterpretations, some of which I shall now describe.

I. People misinterpret the thesis, 'Thought cannot occur without language', to mean that thought and language are *identical* and that the process of thinking is an *exclusively* linguistic process complying with the requirements of grammar. The monistic conception of language and thinking is thus explicit, but thereby wrongly narrowed. Anybody who notices gaps and a lack of grammatical order in his thinking or who refers to the unconscious character of certain thought processes (the well-known facts of solving problems in sleep at a time when one apparently is not thinking about them) or who speaks of the supposedly extraverbal association of images in thinking must dispute such a notion.

The misunderstanding vanishes when we correct the interpretation of language-thought monism as *identification* of language and thinking. Monism is antidualism. It opposes the thesis that language and thinking are not only distinct but also mutually independent phenomena. Monism states that they are interdependent and form an organic whole. But 'to form a whole' does not mean 'to be identical and mutually interchangeable with another element of that whole'. There is no thought process without linguistic process, but this does not mean that the thought process *only* includes linguistic operations and that language and thinking are identical.

If we accept the assumptions of evolutionism, we must accept the thesis that man has evolved from the animal world physically and psychically, and this specifically includes human thinking. We may give different answers to the question of what thinking is: an orientation in the world, a subjective mirroring of objective reality, problem solving, etc. Each such formulation includes a grain of truth, but each is one-sided, and hence too narrow. None brings out the specific nature of *human* thinking. For the behavior of animals, in particular of higher mammals, shows some orientation in the world, some subjective mirroring of objective reality, some problem solving, etc. In the behavior of animals we observe within a small compass elements which form the foundation of human thinking. Engels wrote that when an ape cracks a nut in order to take the kernel out of the shell, its behavior includes a nucleus of analytic thinking. The specific nature of human thinking (in each interpretation of the term 'thinking' given above) consists in its conceptual character, which is inseparably linked with language as a system of signs. Nevertheless human thinking, a higher stage of orientation in the world, is not dissociated from earlier stages. The system of inputs to the human brain via the senses is analogous to the systems of inputs animals possess. Animals do not think, like men, but to a certain extent they do use means of orientation in the world analogous to those used by men, namely sensory images of the world. By associating those images with one another and by establishing more or less durable links between them, the animal orients itself in the world, adjusts its reactions to the external world, and behaves adaptively, in many cases in a better and more effective way than man does. The mechanism of orientation in the world—association of sensory images on the basis of experience—does not vanish in man, but becomes transformed. Human thinking, the human form of orientation in the world, is the unity of thought and language, since conceptual thinking cannot be achieved without language signs (which need not necessarily be phonic). But human thinking also includes image making, the specific mechanism of mirroring the world and shaping behavior, which can be traced back to the prelinguistic stage of animal orientation in the world. Of course, in human cognition it is combined with language and hence organized and structured in a different way, but it is something which goes beyond a *purely linguistic* process.

This is not strange to us if we comprehend the origin and evolution of the human cognitive faculty. But we need only narrow the interpretation of the initial thesis concerning language-thought monism and take into consideration the state of things described above to envisage the possibility of questioning the monistic thesis. This is so especially since observation shows that the linguistic aspect does not always appear in its full-fledged grammatical form during thinking. We can observe various jumps due to the shortcut nature of those thought processes, etc. But this is easily explained, given the example described above.

Hence the dualistic argument of those who see certain thought processes taking place unconsciously during sleep or when we 'suddenly' come upon the solution to a problem is fallacious. Such 'facts' do not deny the existence of an organic link between thought processes and linguistic processes. Unfortunately we still have no definite knowledge of how these 'unconscious thought processes' take place or of what role is played in them by mechanisms acquired as a result of linguistic thinking.

II. Another kind of misinterpretation of the role of language in the process of thinking is misunderstanding due to the erroneous conviction that one can think by a pure association of images and that language becomes a part of thinking only after the fact. Words and sentences are supposed to be the 'outer garment' of this extralinguistic process of thinking; they are indispensable in the communication of the results, but they are neither indispensable for the process itself nor for the use of its results by the thinker.

A symposium on problems of language and thinking was held in the early 1950s upon the suggestion of Révész. (Texts of the papers read were published in *Acta Psychologica*, vol. 10, no. 1-2, 1954.) During the symposium the mathematician B. L. van der Waerden supported the radical thesis that thinking was possible without language. His statement is so characteristic that we may take it as exemplary.

Van der Waerden claimed that in geometrical thinking language intervenes only *ex post facto*, when we *give a name* to some geometrical entity. I would like to quote in full the passage in which he did this, since it clearly reveals errors in reasoning often found (though in a less glaring form) in the statements of those who favor the language-thought dualism. (Compare the statements of various scientists quoted by Kainz in the same volume of *Acta Psychologica*.)

The issue at stake is that of Pascal's *limaçon*. After quoting Pascal's definition of this curve, van der Waerden says:

"In the mind of every mathematician who knows the concept of limaçon that concept is associated with three ideas.

1. The motoric idea, namely the notion of how the curve is produced by drawing a line, transferring segments, etc.
2. The visual idea, how the curve looks.

3. The linguistic idea, the name of the curve.

It is the first idea which is essential; when it is lost, the concept of the curve is lost, even if one knows how it looks. *... All this has nothing to do with language: one can draw a curve for one's own use and investigate its properties without the intention of communicating the results of such an investigation to anyone. Drawing a curve is a specific action, not a gesture.*

The second, visual, idea is not as indispensable: from the way the curve is produced one can always deduce its form.

The third idea, the name of the curve, is quite inessential. Pascal, who discovered the curve, first produced it motorically; secondly saw that it resembled a snail and only then, called it 'limaçon'. He had a clear concept of that curve before he invented a name for it." [43]

The faultiness of this reasoning is obvious, and that is why it is polemically so valuable for didactic purposes. We must polemicize with such a conception because the man who formulated it is an eminent specialist in his field—though it does not follow that his opinions must be taken as infallible reports about facts. Statements made by even the most eminent scientists about the ways in which mental activity take place may only be treated psychologically, as evidence of what they think about that problem, and not as a proof that such is the case. Unfortunately, sometimes good psychologists, such as Kainz, quote certain introspective protocol statements as *proof* that things are as these protocols state.

There are three essential issues in van der Waerden's statement that require analysis:

A. *Language is not needed to carry out geometrical operations; it is needed only to communicate the results.*

Van der Waerden states in express terms that Pascal's original idea of the curve was purely motoric: Pascal first produced the curve and then noticed its similarity to the snail. He had a quite clear concept of the curve before language intervened.

Two issues are of special interest here: the nature of a given creative activity and the nature of perception connected with that activity.

Van der Waerden's notion of creative activity is highly controversial (although he is a mathematician describing the creative work of another mathematician!). In order to force his assertion that language can be dispensed with in thought processes he describes creative activity in the following manner: Pascal was just sitting and drawing (it is inessential whether on paper or only in his imagination), and during this time he dare not have experienced any thought in a verbal form; he may only have experienced associations of images. Only when he drew the line and associated its shape with a snail did he associate it with the name 'limaçon.'

We have to defend the mathematicians, in this case Pascal: their intellectual work, reduced by van der Waerden to motoric ideas, is greatly degraded thereby. Such a description of the mathematician's thought processes cannot be taken seriously.

First of all, it disregards the fact that such a process usually begins *by raising a problem*. Like any scientist, the mathematician begins with a problem connected with his other works; he thus undertakes a research *task* which cannot be thought of other than in linguistic terms. It is inessential whether the language is current language or the specialized language of mathematical symbols; in most cases it is a specific mixture of both these languages.

Second, the process of solving the problem does not consist in thoughtlessly drawing lines and associating images, since the scientist has to confront his operations and their results with the task he has set himself, which is impossible without linguistic thinking.

Third, the mathematician not only draws lines and associates images but also reasons; indeed, he reasons in a much more precise form than other people do. And reasoning requires logic and logical formulas, which are always linguistic in nature, no matter *what kind* of language is being used. Van der Waerden claims that logic also is thinking in terms of images and associations, and not in terms of languages, but such a claim certainly cannot be defended.

B. *Sensory perception connected with geometrical operations is quite independent of language.* This idea, contained *implicitly* in the statement quoted above, is an axiom for its author, but it is precisely here that he reveals his ignorance of the issues.

Both introspection, highly unreliable because of its subjective nature, and objective studies of the pathology of language and of developmental psychology, prove that the structure of sensory perception and the sensory articulation of the world around us (e.g., the singling out of some objects and their properties) depend upon the conceptual schemata which are obtained in the process of acquiring knowledge of the world and which condition that knowledge. Without mental and linguistic abstraction Pascal would have been unable to imagine a straight line, a point, a circle, or a curve. Such abstract entities do not exist in reality. The fact that we can imagine the various geometrical entities without explicitly naming them does not in the least prove—as every psychologist knows—that we do not name them in some other, less manifest manner. Nor does it prove that our images would be possible without the appropriate articulation and structuralization introduced by conceptual thinking into our sensory perception of reality. Reproductive and productive perceptions and images, which in the opinion of van der Waerden are totally dissociated from linguistic thinking, are in fact closely connected with that thinking. Otherwise such perceptions—images *as such*—would be impossible. The naive conviction that they are possible, a conviction based on superficial introspection, has resulted in many an error in that field of analysis.

C. *One can have quite clear concepts without linguistic thinking, in particular, without names.*

In the light of van der Waerden's considerations this view seems consistent. But this does not mean it is correct. Such a thesis cannot be accepted by a student of the psychology of language, by a philosopher who bases his opinions on scientific data, nor even by an intuitionist. The first two cannot accept it because facts testifying to non-verbal formation of *concepts* are unknown; the third cannot accept it because in consistently defending the thesis of the intuitive nature of 'true cognition', he does not accept concepts (in their traditional interpretation) as elements of cognition.

In any case, scientific disciplines which treat of thought processes reject both the theorem that language need intervene in thinking *ex post facto* and only for the purpose of conferring names on ready products of extralinguistic thinking and also the theorem that concepts can be formed without language. Van der Waerden's theses that thinking is innate and speech acquired,[44] and that deaf-mutes think whether they have been taught to speak or not, are also false. The latter thesis maintains that, like normal people, deaf-mutes have an innate ability to think, their gesture language being an adjunct which expresses thought that existed independent of that language.[45]

III. Another misinterpretation of the role of language in the process of thinking involves analysis of what is sometimes called the 'asemantic' nature of artistic creation. A composer, some people claim, thinks in sounds, a nonrepresentational painter in colors. The holders of this view assert that this creative activity is thinking, although it has nothing to do with language.

Such reasoning makes two errors. One stems from the ambiguity of the term 'thinking', the other from a superficial interpretation of the relationship between the given types of mental activity and linguistic thinking.

We know that listeners are supposed to experience music 'purely in terms of sounds' and not to translate it into images. Music is to evoke emotional states directly. This theory deprecates program music. The requirement is clear, though to what extent it can be put into effect is another matter. At any rate, if the listener is to experience music 'purely in the terms of sounds', then apparently the same holds for the composer, who ought to convey his emotional states through sounds, without the intermediary of intervening images, and all the more of thoughts couched in words. Again, the requirement is clear; let us suppose it could be put into effect.

The question now arises: Whether the composer or the painter who 'purely' and 'directly' translates emotional states into sounds or a system of colors thinks. If we reply in the affirmative, as the supporters of the theory of nonlinguistic thinking in music and painting do, we must expand the meaning of the verb 'to think'. Arguments about asemantic artistic creation cannot support the existence of *conceptual* nonverbal thinking if we are to keep the terms unambiguous. Does experiencing such emotions as longing, homesickness, despair, and joy amount to thinking? Such emotions are usually accompanied by thoughts, if only in the form of reflections on one's own emotional state, but the experiencing of such emotions may not be termed thinking. Why, then, should a 'pure' translation of such emotions into, or their expression by, sounds or colors be thinking? We may use that term, but only if we grant its ambiguity and realize that the properties specific to the process of conceptual thinking do not coincide with the properties of other processes given the same name.

The issue becomes more complicated, however, when we consider the relationship between the 'pure' process of composing or painting and linguistic processes. I wish to discuss two elements of that relationship.

First, even if we assume a complete dissociation of composing and painting from *verbal* language, we cannot ignore the fact that these two forms of artistic activity use a *specific* language which is a product of intellect. Hence the activity is burdened with the 'sin' of being connected with language.

The system of mathematical symbols is certainly a specific language born of a verbal language and is ultimately translatable into the latter. Music also has its own language, rich and formalized (at least as far as notation is concerned), and its principles of harmony, counterpoint, composition, etc., can be expressed in verbal language. Only a layman could imagine a composer sitting down in an armchair, closing his eyes, and experiencing a tune. Composing, strictly speaking, never took place in this way, and this is even more the case now that music has become more reasoned and 'calculating' than it ever was. To a large extent the language of music becomes automatic once one knows how to handle it skillfully. But this does not alter the fact that a composer observes the rules of that language. The sequence of tenses may torture the student of Latin; the master of Latin uses it almost automatically and ceases to pay attention to rules, but he observes them all the time.

In musical composition the composer certainly 'thinks' in terms of a language, namely the language of music aside from any additional verbalization of his thoughts. Musical *composition*, in the proper sense of the word, has always been an *intellectual* activity, and today is more so than before. Music is composed in a definite language based on, and inseparably linked with, a verbal language.

Matters are more complicated when it comes to painting, since painting, in contradistinction to music, has no formalized language. Yet painting is connected with verbal language more than music. It is not true that a painter produces his works exclusively on the basis of 'pure' experiences of images or colors. The painter always has a fairly comprehensive *knowledge* of perspective, of the principles of combining colors, of composition, etc. The impressionists are perhaps the best example because we probably know more about their attitudes to art than those of any other group. They certainly experienced their works emotionally, but they expressed emotions consciously, deliberately, with the aid of wide theoretical knowledge. The same creative manner applies to a greater degree in contemporary abstractionism which, like contemporary music, is greatly intellectualized. It is a specific calculus manipulated consciously. (I do not refer to dabblers who use 'abstractionism' to veil their lack of talent, but to painters *sang pur*.)

The second element of the relationship between artistic and linguistic processes is this: Not only is the artist's language linked with verbal language in some way, but in *reflecting on what he is doing*, he must verbalize in some language. The artist not only produces his works but also *appraises* the effects of his activity and thereby corrects his work. Such an appraisal is preeminently intellectual and verbal, since it takes place in the sphere of certain accepted rules and conventions.

To sum up: The artist makes use (in most cases in a conscious manner) of some language connected with verbal language in his creative activity and reflects on his creative activity in a language. This reflection is not something external or posterior to the act of producing a work of art. It is organically connected with the very act of creating a work of art, affects it, and becomes part of it.

Thus musical and pictorial 'thinking' is not just extralinguistic and does not occur independent of thinking proper.

IV. A fourth kind of misinterpretation of the role of language in thinking is connected with the problem of the plurality and variability of languages. This kind of misinterpretation occurs in linguistics. Eric Buyssens' produalistic argumentation at the symposium organized by Révész is a good illustration.

A. The very fact that many different languages can express the same thought is used by Buyssens to support the thesis that thought is independent of language.

This implies two erroneous assumptions: that there is, in two places one 'identical' thought independent of language and that this ready-made thought is expressed in different languages. Thus the author *assumes* what he wants to prove, the dualism of language and thinking.

The fact is that the opposite thesis, that there is no ready, nonverbalized thought which is expressed (in the sense of an external manifestation of something which has an objective existence) in different languages is equally legitimate. According to this thesis cognitive and communicative processes are realized in different languages, which all refer to the same object and are mutually translatable. Thus the dualistic implications vanish, but the problem remains. The theses to be proved are not assumed in advance.

B. Buyssens asserts next that language variability, especially in the process of word formation, proves that thought exists prior to, and independent of, its verbalization. This is clearly erroneous. The change taking place in language need not be a *consequence* of changes in the way of thinking. A thought may be thought in different words at different levels of the development of language, but cannot first exist in a non-verbal form and as such stimulate modifications of the language, indispensable for its expression. Changes in language—in the sphere of phonetics and grammar—have nothing to do with the need to acquire new means of verbalizing new thoughts. The fact that changes in language are in part determined by changes in the knowledge of the world (the simplest examples are provided by the phenomena of word formation) does not warrant the assertion that changes in the way of thinking *precede* changes in language. Nor does it help refute the monistic thesis that language and thinking are two abstractly separated aspects of a uniform process, namely of the process of thinking in terms of concepts-and-language. The phenomena of word formation prove not that thought precedes language, but only that new phenomena taking place in reality require a new cognitive interpretation in terms of words-and-thought. This must have occurred when it became necessary to introduce such new terms as those quoted by Buyssens— 'agnostic', 'cyclone', 'radar', etc.

C. Teachers of foreign languages tell us that we have to abandon the habit of *translating* from our native language into foreign languages. According to Buyssens this proves that the words of a foreign language are *associated* directly with thought, since he *assumes* that ready-made thought exists independent of any language and can only later be 'expressed' by some linguistic apparatus. This is a quite erroneous and arbitrary assumption. We need only suggest that the person learning a foreign language should learn to *think* in that language, and Buyssen's intuition vanishes. I am not claiming to solve the problem, merely to demonstrate that Buyssens assumes *a priori* an idea he has set out to prove.

D. Finally the last argument of the dualists. Mathematicians use a special international symbolism. According to the dualists this proves that they think without using language.

The mistake here obviously consists in identifying all
language with national languages and in failing to comprehend the genetic and semantic connection between the
language of mathematical symbols and verbal everyday
language.[46]

In conclusion another idea is worth citing, an idea which
helps explain why people who resort to the method of
introspection (usually people not familiar with the achievements of the psychology of language) are under the illusion
that one can think without any language. I am referring to a
phenomenon, well known in the psychology of language,
called the 'transparency' of words to meaning. It demonstrates the fact, often emphasized by various authors, that
in verbal language meanings are associated directly with the
images of objects to which they refer, and not with the
images of words; the latter images, in view of the routine
use of verbal signs, vanish from the field of our vision. In
the process of thinking we fail to notice the verbal signs
which we are using, but we do not think nonverbally, and
this is the *main* difference. This helps us understand belief
in the existence of extralinguistic thinking. Even research
scholars (like Sechenov and Russell) formulated opinions
similar to the one refuted above. In this connection it is
well to recall A. Potebnia's statement that "the faculty of
human thinking without words is given us only thanks to
words." [47]

This laborious tracing of the dualistic argumentation reveals one
thing: there are no matter-of-fact arguments, arguments free from
errors and misunderstandings, that are sufficient to justify dualism. If
we do not assume intuitionist metaphysics, we cannot indicate any
observable occurrences of nonverbalized thought. On the contrary,
experience seems to support thought-language monism.

In this connection let us briefly consider Révész's opinions.

He agrees with the antidualistic part of the above formulation but
does not agree with the promonistic part. He interprets monism too
narrowly as a theory of the *identification* of thinking and language, a
theory which fails to notice the double aspect of conceptual thinking,
of *thinking in terms of a language*. Révész develops a kind of dualistic

monism. He accepts the monistic thesis of the existential unity of language and thinking but asserts the dualism of their functions. His *intentions* seem correct, but his conclusions lead us astray. An analysis of his argumentation will demonstrate this clearly.

The contrast Révész sees between the cognitive function of thinking and the communicative function of language is unfortunate, since, contrary to his declaration in favor of monism, it suggests that one may think 'for oneself' in an extralinguistic manner and that words are needed only for interpersonal communication. But the cognitive function of thinking cannot be performed *without* languages, and the communicative function of language cannot be performed *without* thinking. Hence Révész's idea of a dualism of functions contradicts his thesis of existential monism of the elements of that relation. This annihilating self-contradiction results from an *ad hoc* construction which may, in turn, be attributed to Révész's endeavor to avoid the consequences of the narrow interpretation of monism.

The same holds for the contrast of individual subjective thought with language, which is always social in nature (this contrast follows from the earlier one). It is true that a thought always is some individual person's thought, but is also a social phenomenon. Thinking is socially conditioned and is impossible without the thinking individual's participation in the human community, and the scientific or political or other thought of an individual affects his society. The same holds for language. It performs a social function as an instrument of communication but it also is an instrument of thinking by individuals.

It is equally erroneous to contrast the functions of thought and language on the grounds that thought uses mainly abstract images, while language uses symbolic signs; or on the grounds that phenomenological analysis of thinking and language reveals differences between the *acts* of thinking and the *acts* of speaking.

Révész wants to achieve the right goal. He wants to dissociate himself from a certain oversimplified interpretation of monism. But by using the wrong means for that purpose, he contradicts his own monistic thesis. The goal must be achieved without trying to combine existential monism with functional dualism.

I have indicated above the most proper and the most effective method of procedure and the manner of interpretation. I shall now try to expand that method.

When we adopt the monistic standpoint, we reject the claim that language and thinking can exist separately and independently of one another. Of course, we are talking about specifically *human* thinking, in other words about *conceptual* thinking. Thus we assert that in the process of cognition and communication, thinking and using a language are inseparable elements of one and the same whole. Integration is so perfect and interdependence is so precise that neither element can ever occur independently, in a 'pure' form. That is precisely why the functions of thinking and language may not be treated separately, let alone contrasted with one another.

Thinking and using a language must be interpreted as two aspects of one uniform process which includes man's acquisition of knowledge of the world, his reflection on this cognition (including his cognition of himself), and his communication of the results of cognition to other people. De Saussure compared the unity of sound and meaning in a word to two sides of a piece of paper. We may say the same thing of language use and thinking: you cannot remove one side without impairing the other. Thus the theory of the difference between the functions of language and thinking postulated by Révész in his specific interpretation of monism is replaced by the theory of different aspects of a uniform language-thought process. I must emphasize, though, that the latter theory, while asserting the unity of the two aspects of the process, does not identify them with one another.

The sources of the unity of the thought-and-language process are to be sought in its history. Human thinking has been shaped in the social process of labor. It is both its result and a factor of its further evolution. Human consciousness, as the specifically human faculty of abstract, generalizing, and conceptual cognition of reality, and language, as the means of human communication, have both developed in the course of cooperation between men. Our present knowledge of human evolution confirms the brilliant anthropogenetic and sociogenetic idea of Marx, formulated in *The German Ideology,* and Engels' opinions in his paper *The Role of Labour in the Transition from Ape to Man.*

The unity of thinking and language-use is the unity of elements of different origin which have been intertwined into an inseparable whole in the course of social evolution. Verbal language developed genetically, from animal cries which expressed emotions and served the purpose of emotionally contagious communication. Thinking is a continuation and development of the animal orientation in the world, which consists in the concrete, image-like mirroring of the surrounding world in the psychology of the animal. This animal orientation in the world contains in a nuclear form certain intellectual functions whose development by linguistic signs results in conceptual thinking.

These inseparable aspects of the uniform process of acquiring knowledge of the world differ both in origin and in content. Human thinking is linguistic, and that is why it is abstract and generalizing: every word generalizes. But thinking also makes use of some means of prelinguistic orientation in the world, namely, concrete sensory images and their associations. At the stage of linguistic thinking these cannot be separated from language, because the structure of sensory perception depends on the categories imposed upon cognition by language. Yet concrete sensory images differ from abstract words, from concepts. Connected with language and associated with its words, images of reality are nevertheless not linguistic in nature. At least for that reason thinking is not identical with language, but is richer than language. Hence the monistic rejection of the identity of language and thinking need not result in the acceptance of a dualism of their functions.

The differences between the two elements of the language-and-thought unity are manifested in the relative autonomy of the development of those elements. The phonic aspect of language is governed by its own laws of evolution, and it would be a vulgarization to look for an absolute interdependence between all phonetic and morphological (or even syntactical) changes, on the one hand, and changes in the mode of thinking, on the other. The difference between the two aspects of the language-and-thought process is also emphasized by the distinct characteristics of grammar and logic. But this is a subject for a separate study.

To sum up: there is a unity of language and thinking, but no identity; there is a monism of language-and-thought, but not a vulgarized theory of identification. These conclusions are of signal importance in the analysis of such problems as the relationship between language and reality: they modify the perspective of those problems and the manner of their interpretation. Hence the remarks made above concerning the relationship between language and thinking are certainly a good starting point for an analysis of the active role of language in mirroring reality—the problem to which we shall now turn.

Chapter 5

Language and Reality

Once we have analyzed the relationship between language and thinking, we are faced with a whole set of problems connected with the relationship between language and reality. When we speak of reality, we mean a class of objects which exists objectively, external to and independent of our own existence. The examination of these problems is the next step in our analysis of the active role of language in the cognitive process.

Speech, both audible and inaudible, is always speech *about something*. The subject matter may be natural reality, social reality, or psychic reality (the manifestations *of our individual* spiritual lives, exist for us objectively, i.e., outside us and independently of us, and thus form part of the reality which we investigate). The epistemological controversy is whether language, which *creates* our image of reality, or reality, which *is mirrored* (or reflected, or mapped) by language, is primitive. Two solutions are possible: either the linguistic process is an act of creating an image of reality, or it is an act of mirroring.

It has long been assumed that if the linguistic process is a cognitive reflection of reality, language plays no active role in the process and, vice versa, that if language does in fact play an active role, the linguistic process cannot be a cognitive reflection of reality. This is not the first time in the history of human thought that faulty formulation of problems has made solutions difficult or impossible.

Let me remove one source of possible misinterpretation at the outset. The subject of misinterpretation was treated extensively in the preceding chapter, but what was said there is worth restating, if only because misinterpretations are to be found in the literature of the subject we are concerned with. By language I mean a uniform product of signs and meanings actually functioning in human speech, not a system of sounds or other signs per se. Of course, there is a phonic aspect of language, dealt with by phonetics; but sounds alone are not language, and as long as they have no definite meanings, the controversy over whether they create an image of reality or merely mirror or map objective reality is meaningless.

What does the assertion that language creates human reality or the human world mean? Such an assertion is to be found in Cassirer's philosophy of symbolic forms, Carnap's principle of tolerance, and Ajdukiewicz's radical conventionalism; and of the wide range of trends which subscribe to the general formulation that language creates our image of the world (but differ, often quite radically in the interpretation of this formulation), I have purposely chosen only this one group. We shall not consider views which have a clearly idealistic ontology; and the view that language does not create an *image* of the world, but *the world itself* is a mystic fantasy, and will not be discussed here. Our interest will focus on those views which make epistemological statements concerning the *image* of the world.

Cassirer and, to a certain degree, Carnap were indifferent to matters of ontology, while Ajdukiewicz affirmed the objective existence of the world. But these verbal declarations were at odds with their technical refusal to leave room for anything but a subjective image of the world. These authors may be accused of inconsistency and *de facto* idealism in the sphere of ontology, but their views differ from the mysticism of subjective idealism. Hence an analysis of these views may prove useful for our purposes, especially since the arguments of these schools against the vulgarized copy theory of cognition include a hard core of rational ideas.

I shall also exclude such theories as the Sapir-Whorf hypothesis, since they combine the thesis of the creation by language of the image of the world with the inconsistent admission that language itself is a product of definite social conditions, a product formed under the influence of environment in the broad sense of the term (both natural environment and social milieu). Such conceptions are better analyzed within the copy theory.

What then, is the point of those who claim that language creates the reality given to man?

They mean above all that language contains a definite *Weltanschauung*, that it determines the way we perceive and grasp reality. Hence, in this sense of a perceptual perspective, language *creates* our image of reality and imposes this image upon us. It is, as it were, a mold which brings order into the original chaos of reality 'in itself'. By imposing upon the human mind, which always thinks in some language, a definite manner of combining elements of that chaos (in other words, of eliminating certain elements of that chaos), language decides *de facto* what is to be treated as thing, event, regularity, etc. Some trends make the conception apparatus creative (Carnap, Ajdukiewicz); others make the thought-shaping function of symbolic forms creative (Cassirer). In the first part of the present book we dealt with a number of ideas about this issue, from the rational to the mystic. These ideas underline the active role of language in the process of cognition—and that is their rational element. I shall return to this issue and try to interpret it in terms of the copy theory of cognition.

But the authors of those opinions combine the thesis of the *Weltanschauung*-shaping role of language with a second thesis, often tacitly assumed, that language is a product of an arbitrary convention (Carnap, Ajdukiewicz) or that language is a product of a symbolic function specific to human psychology (Cassirer).

This combination of two theses is characteristic of views which explicitly set out to refute the copy theory. By itself, the first thesis can be interpreted in a way consonant with a version of the copy theory.

The second thesis makes it possible to question the conception of language as the *maker* of our image of the world. It suffices to question the origin of the language which creates our image of the world, or determines our *Weltanschauung*, since to do so is to force the advocates of that idea to take scientifically untenable standpoints or to adopt an interpretation which enforces, indirectly, one version of the copy theory itself.

The first dilemma occurs when one claims that language is a product of an arbitrary convention. Neither a sociologist nor a psychologist of language nor a linguist will agree with the assumptions of Carnap's principle of tolerance or Ajdukiewicz's radical conventionalism (and these or similar concepts lay at the root of the logical positivist philosophy of language). Any theory which claims that the origins of language are to be found in arbitrary choice or convention must be considered fantastic. To a sociologist of science it might serve as a proof that claims to a strictly scientific character are often based on clearly antiscientific arguments (by 'antiscientific arguments' I mean theses which are in contradiction with positive knowledge achieved in a given field at a definite stage of its historical development). The fact that eminent and exact thinkers adopted basic theses which are obviously false (with reference to current empirical science) can probably be explained, psychologically, by their fascination with the methods of the deductive sciences. In these disciplines one usually adopts certain axioms and transformation rules regardless of their origin and concentrates one's attention on the calculus itself. Such reasoning, even if it is correct in the deductive sciences, fails completely when applied to products of social life like language. Carnap and Ajdukiewicz had special mathematical languages in mind and neglected to study the connections between these languages and natural languages. In doing so, they generalized theses valid with respect to specialized languages to cover all languages in general.[1]

The situation is no better when, like Cassirer, one claims that language is one of the forms in which the function of symbolizing occurs, a function characteristic of human thinking alone. In fact this does not answer the question posed, but avoids answering it altogether. We are not asking what it is that language is a form or realization of, but whether its present-day form is simply given (biologically? by a supernatural force?) or has developed under the influence of certain factors, and if the latter, what these factors may be. Our problem begins where the philosophy of symbolic forms stops.

The closer we approach the proper answer to this question, the more untenable the notion of language as the maker of the image of the world. For what else remains for us than to state that a language may *create*—in a definite sense of the word—our image of the world, but it is itself a product of social and historical processes. Lanugage-thinking is shaped in the phylogenetic evolution of mankind, and becomes a product and an element of the practical activity of man in transforming the world. In a word, the *maker* of the image of the world is himself a *product* of the world.

The consequences of such an approach become obvious when we come to the problem of the classification of real phenomena by language, to the problem of the articulation of the world by language. For the time being let us agree without reservation that language affects our mode of perceiving the world and that in this sense it creates our image of the world. Does our interpretation of the sense of the verb 'to create' mean that such a creation is arbitrary? Not in the least! Once we understand that language is a *social* product, genetically and functionally connected with man's *practical social activity*, we realize that the image of the world suggested or imposed by a given language is not arbitrary and cannot be changed in an arbitrary manner. The psychologist, the linguist, the historian, or the sociologist of culture will tell us explicitly that language is one of the most traditional and the most change-resistant elements of human culture. And this is easy to understand if we consider the social origin of language. Such scholars will tell us that Carnap's principle of tolerance, which refers to an arbitrary change of logic and of language, Ajdukiewicz's radical conventionalism, with its conception of a change in the perspective of the world following an arbitrary choice of a new conceptual apparatus, and Kolakowski's surrealistic ideas on the possibility of an arbitrary classification of real phenomena (the possibility of constructing such 'objects' as half a horse and a segment of a river)[2] are all fantastic ideas which have abounded in the history of the problem of language.

Hence it is one thing to assert that language creates the image of reality arbitrarily, depending on individual choice of language, and quite another to claim that it creates reality by imposing patterns and stereotypes shaped in the phylogenetic evolution of mankind upon the perception of the world manifested during the ontogenetic evolution of the individual. The second interpretation of the creative role of language may not be imposing, but it is rational in character and may be accepted by scientific disciplines concerned with the problems of culture. But such an interpretation is not compatible with the original theory of language as the maker of the image of the world and can be comprehended only in the light of the copy theory of cognition. It becomes part of the copy theory and imparts a specific, *dialectical* character to it. One need only step back a little, and the fantastic theory of language as the maker of the world image is immediately refuted. The logic of thinking points us in the direction of the copy theory of cognition.

What do people mean when they claim that language reflects (mirrors, copies, etc.) reality?

This is not merely a matter of the purely phonic aspect of language.

The phonic aspect is only important in the case of onomatopoetic effects, i.e., quite secondarily. What does it mean, then, when we say that language as a system of signs and meanings reflects (mirrors, copies) reality?

The copy theory is old, at least as old as the classical definition of truth, and hence burdened with the ambiguity resulting from different interpretations in different philosophical systems. We must bear in mind all these differences (often difficult to grasp) in the interpretations of the copy theory but emphasize its connection with the classical theory of truth. For when a person says that between human cognition and known reality there is a relation *analogous to* (no reasonable person will claim that it is *identical with*) the relation between a reflection in the mirror and the object being mirrored, or between the original and the copy, or between an object and its photograph, etc., then he expresses an opinion inseparably linked with the idea that a statement is true if in reality it is as stated. The classical definition of truth, which has dominated the theory of truth for a thousand years, is a specific formulation of the copy theory of cognition and it is simply impossible outside that theory. What else could Aristotle have had in mind but the copy theory when he wrote in the *Metaphysics* that a person is really pale not because we think so, but on the contrary, our statement about him is true because he is really pale. Once we comprehend the interconnection between these theories of truth and of cognition, we can understand the copy theory better and easily refute what I consider to be an incorrect interpretation of that theory, one which would claim that sense data and not thought reflects reality.

But let us return to the intuitions associated with the phrase 'copy theory'.

Helena Eilstein has correctly demonstrated that the term 'copy' (or 'mirroring', or 'reflection') may be interpreted in three ways in the theory of human thought.[3]

First, it is the name for the cause-and-effect relation holding between the stimuli originating from the material world and the psychic acts which they evoke. This relation is a copy in the *genetic* sense.

Secondly, the term denotes the relation between psychic acts and the properties of society which condition the former; society shapes the attitude of a given individual. This relation is a copy in the *sociological* sense.

Third, when we talk about a copy in the *epistemological* sense, we mean a specific cognitive relation between the contents of certain psychic acts and their correlates in the form of definite elements of the material world.

The distinction is interesting and valuable, although the classification is not exhaustive. The meanings distinguished for the term 'copy' demonstrate its ambiguity, but are interconnected and partly overlapping. Despite this reservation it is worthwhile bearing in mind that

> When we say that a theory 'copies' a given state of things faithfully or unfaithfully—'copies' in the epistemological sense— this means that it states the truth or untruth of that state of things. When we say that a theory 'copies' interests, opinions or attitudes of a social class, 'copies' in the sociological sense means that the rise, evolution and propagation of such a theory is conditioned by the existence of a class with such interests, aspirations, and attitudes, a class whose intellectual elite uses that theory as guidelines in the class struggle, as an instrument of propaganda, or as both.[4]

What is common to all these meanings of the term 'copy'?

First, they all imply the acceptance of the existence of some *objective* reality, i.e., reality existing outside any mind and independent of any mind, reality which is copied, mirrored, etc., by that mind. In each of its meanings the copy theory implies the acceptance of a *realistic*, though not necessarily materialist, standpoint. An objective idealist may also defend the 'copy' concept. This has actually occurred in the history of human thought. But the idea is not conceivable outside realism; if the mind is to copy something, in any meaning of the term, that something must exist *objectively*, i.e., independent of the mind.

Secondly, each of the meanings of the term 'copy' specified above accepts the relation of *genetic dependence* between an experience or its content and an objective reality which has evoked it, i.e., the acceptance of the causal nexus between the effect of reality upon the mind and that which the mind experiences.

Third, each of these meanings claims that a *mapping* relation holds between the content of a given experience and reality. The term 'mapping' is understood here more broadly than 'similarity' or 'correspondence', which are terms of the rival interpretations of 'copy'.

Fourth, the term 'copy' is connected with the distinction between an experience or its content, and reality. That is why the copy is always understood as something other than reality. It is something subjective compared to objective reality. This statement is very important for the analysis of the category of 'copy'.

As in the case of any fundamental philosophical category, here too certain implications result from a given solution of basic philosophical problems. Two philosophical positions are implied in the acceptance of the copy theory of cognition in any of the above interpretations. One is realism, which disputes subjective idealism, and the other is anti-agnosticism, which disputes the assertion that the world is unknowable.

Yet for all the common theses and common epistemological assumptions which connect the meanings and interpretations of the copy theory, differences are to be found between its various representatives. They are revealed in the interpretation of the term 'mapping'.

The controversy is whether the relation of copying is to be interpreted as similarity or as correspondence. Similarity entails a relation between what the mind experiences and reality where some qualities of the copy and what it copies are of the same kind, if not identical. Correspondence entails a parallelism of two orders, reality and what is experienced by a given mind. There is a one-one relation between these elements in that their structures as a whole are identical, but they are not similar because their qualities are neither of the same kind nor identical.

Zdzislaw Cackowski demonstrates in an important monograph[5] the significance for Marxist epistemology of this controversy. Nevertheless, I think that its role has been exaggerated. The controversy is significant when the copy theory is applied to sensory images, but not when it is applied to abstract ideas. It is at this point that the connections between the copy theory and the classical theory of truth becomes important. The latter also refers to *thoughts* about reality, and not to artificially isolated impressions or sensory images.

It can be disputed whether the sensory impression of redness shows 'similarity' or 'correspondence' with those properties of objective reality which evoke it, but thoughts may only be classified as true or false. Of course, a thought formulated as the statement "This tree is green," or a like statement is controversial, but such statements as "The category of honor is of great significance in the description of the

gentry community," "The indeterminacy principle establishes a correspondence between the precision of the measurement of the
momentum and the precision of the determination of the position of a
particle," and "The gamma rays are a kind of electromagnetic waves,"
are not. We may legitimately ask of such statements whether they are
true or false, i.e., whether they copy (mirror) reality in the human
mind, but the problem of similarity or correspondence makes no sense
here. The statement that the category of honor is of great significance
in the description of the gentry community is true, and can be proved
by research. Hence this statement copies in our mind a certain
objective state of things. We say that things are a certain way, and they
really are that way, and this can be verified according to certain criteria.
But the controversy over whether 'copying' is similarity or correspondence is simply senseless for this is not what we ask about, and we
cannot ask about it meaningfully in the given case.

But even statements about sensory images are not as simple as they
might seem at first glance. Here too a probing analysis is indispensable
for the proper interpretation of the copy theory of cognition.

First of all, we must bear in mind that 'pure' sensory impressions, or
'pure' sensory images or sensory cognition, are abstractions which are
useful in certain considerations but do not stop being abstractions. In
the real process of cognition we can neither separate sensory perception
from conceptual thinking nor separate conceptual thinking (associated
with language) from the sensory aspect of cognition. They have formed
an indivisible whole in the process of phylogenesis, a whole which can
be investigated from various points of view. A person who takes a
product of abstraction for reality errs, and if he tries to base his mental
constructions on it, he errs twice.

During analysis we may speak about the sensory aspect of the
process of cognition and consider it separately, but in doing so we must
bear in mind that we have artificially divided a whole for research
purposes. On the other hand, we should not use the expression 'the
sensory level of cognition', so common in Marxist epistemological
literature, because it suggests a temporal sequence in cognition: sensory
perception first, then abstract thinking, and finally practical experience.
Lenin was the indirect and unintentional culprit here. During his
readings in philosophy he made a note (not meant for publication) that
cognition proceeds from sensory perception through abstraction to

practical activity. But the guilty ones are really those who abuse Lenin's *Philosophical Notebooks*, in which preliminary notes made by the great thinker shed light upon the way he worked and upon some of his ideas. Such notes should not be treated as texts ready for publication; on the contrary, everything seems to indicate that the notes were made for private use, and in view of their brevity and interpolative character were only meaningful for the author himself in the context of his other ideas. That is why they should be quoted and interpreted with utmost caution. Even greater caution is required if one wants to use them as the foundation of a theory.

Hence it is not Lenin who is responsible for the theory of 'levels' of cognition (a theory we are concerned with here because it leads to a vulgarization of the copy theory of cognition); the responsibility devolves upon certain admirers of Lenin, who have unfortunately rendered a great disservice to Marxist epistemology. The theory of 'levels' of cognition would have us believe that in the process of cognition 'pure' sensory perceptions, or 'pure' sensory impressions isolated from one another, come *first* and are *followed* by 'pure' abstract reflection and conceptual thinking, to which practical experience is added finally. Such a conception of cognition must be rejected by the psychologist who studies the process of cognition empirically and by the Marxist epistemologist. In his *Theses on Feuerbach*, Marx claimed that the materialism of his own time was limited because it disregarded the subjective factor of practical experience in the cognitive process. Other things being equal, one cannot claim that the characteristic feature of Marxist epistemology is its constant and systematic elaboration of the role of practical activity in cognition (this is of course true) and at the same time claim that such activity only becomes significant in the last stage as a criterion of truth (this also is true but only if we do not reduce the cognitive function of practice to this alone). At any rate, in the normal process of human cognition there is no such thing as sensory perception independent of abstract thinking and its categories. On the contrary, we now have enough experimental data to state that perception is not only connected with language-thinking, but is dependent on language because it is directed by it. This statement is important because it enables us to oppose the degeneration of the copy theory into a form of naive realism. It was this naive realism which offended critically minded researchers.

Naive realism, as distinguished from critical realism, asserts that things are as they seem to be and that sensory qualities are inherent in the things themselves. We know that neither of these statements is tenable. Things *are not* as they seem to be. An analysis of common errors in perception reveals this fact, and science is constantly demonstrating the distance between our everyday image of the world and the microscopic and macroscopic images provided by additional instruments. Sensory qualities *are not* inherent in things themselves. Perception depends on the perceiving apparatus. It varies with the different kinds of perceiving apparatus and with changes in the properties of a given apparatus, e.g., following chemical treatment or mechanical injury.

Naive realism was a prescientific standpoint, and with the spread and advance of science it has become antiscientific. Unfortunately, it is the point of departure for certain interpretations of the copy theory of cognition. This is the case when the copy theory is illegitimately applied to an analysis of sensory perception taken as autonomous and isolated from the cognitive process as a whole. In interpreting the copy theory as supporting the idea that the qualities of sensory perception are *similar* to the qualities of objects (and hence are inherent in the objects themselves) and that objects are what they appear to be, we propagate naive realism and make our theory erroneous and embarrassingly shallow and primitive. In Marxists the error is astonishing, since it is based on theses that clearly contradict the epistemological assumptions of the Marxist doctrine that cognition is an endless process and that the results of cognition are not absolute truths (in a particular sense of the term).

What gave rise to this tendency which vulgarizes the copy theory and markedly contradicts the postulate that cognition is a process? Among other factors the use of such terms as 'copy', 'reflection', and 'mirroring', despite care, has contributed to misinterpretation.

Why do we use a misleading terminology? For historical reasons. The phrase 'copy theory' was the name of that intellectual trend shaped in the *struggle* with particular adversaries. In the struggle against subjective idealism, the term 'copy' emphasized the facts that what is given in the mind is evoked by something which exists independent of the mind and that thought (and not just the sensory image) is a copy of objective reality. In the struggle against agnosticism, the term emphasized the conviction that the world is knowable. In using the term 'copy' we sought to stress the material adequacy of what we state about reality, i.e., that reality is what we state it is and not what it seems to be. But this is not to state that there is some *physical similarity* between cognition and its object. Such an assertion makes no sense in reference to abstract statements about reality (though such statements can be interpreted by the copy theory of cognition as well).

Thus historical analysis justifies the use of our terminology, enables us to interpret the meanings of the various terms properly, and protects us against their abuse.

But there are other factors involved.

The idea suggests itself that this term 'copy' is only a metaphor! The copy theory does not apply to the sphere of visual perceptions exclusively, but covers all forms of cognition, our entire knowledge of the world, and, in its broadest interpretation, the sphere of our emotional, volitional, and aesthetic experiences, although in the latter case the problems of interpretation become greater. How, then, could such terms as 'copy', 'reflection', and 'mirroring', which suggest a mirror, an image, a photograph, be anything else but metaphors? If a formulation which is clearly metaphorical is interpreted literally, then the conclusions which are drawn from it are quite unwarranted.

The self-imposed comparison with the mirror makes the metaphorical interpretation of the terms 'reflection' and 'mirroring' indicative because the copy theory is meant to interpret more than just visual images. Thus a mirror has nothing to do with auditory images, let alone with abstract ideas. But here additional difficulties emerge, which I have discussed elsewhere.[6] They concern what is called the problem of the impartial observer, who would have to settle whether and to what extent there was a similarity between the reflection in the mirror and the object reflected, if the cognitive relation were *identical* with reflection in the mirror. But this possible objection can be waived, because the human mind is not a mirror and its function does not merely consist in *passive* reflection. Hence it follows that we are speaking about mirror reflection in a *metaphorical* sense. The terminology was dictated by the need to oppose subjectivism and agnosticism and by the attempt to bring out the fundamental difference between our theories and the ones presented by those trends. Nobody intended to adopt, together with the metaphor, the burden of the obsolete mechanistic traditions associated with that metaphor historically. And yet, even this comment only applies to rational interpretations of the problem and the endeavor to interpret the copy theory in accordance with Marxist philosophical assumptions. It does not alter the fact that some Marxists vulgarized the theory by taking the metaphor literally.

Marx's firm rejection of the mechanistic conception and his explicit requirement that a *subjective* factor be introduced into epistemology, a factor connected with human *practical activity*, makes our interpretation the only proper Marxist one. In the oft quoted but rarely understood *Theses on Feuerbach*, Marx is not talking about any external factor, but about a component element of human cognition, an element of the theory explaining such cognition.

In criticizing Feuerbach, Marx wrote:

> The chief defect of all previous materialism (including that of Feuerbach) is that things, reality, the sensible world, are conceived only in the form of *objects of observation*, but not as *human sense activity*, not as *practical activity*, not subjectively.[7]

And a little later in the same work:

> Feuerbach, not satisfied with *abstract thought*, wants *empirical observation*, but he does not conceive the sensible world as *practical*, human sense activity.[8]

We need only analyze Marx's criticism of "contemplative materialism" (*der kontemplative Materialismus*) in detail, in particular his postulate of inclusion of the subjective factor in the conception of the object, to see how remote Marxist epistemology (which consistently includes practical activity in the process of cognition) is from the vulgarized form of the copy theory which resulted from literal interpretation of the metaphor. That is why Lenin protested the interpretation of copying as 'dead mirroring' and emphasized that every generalization, even the simplest, includes a modicum of fantasy.[9]

On the other hand, when we analyze Marx's postulate further, we realize the error of all those who would see in him a subjectivist and a voluntarist, a supporter of an alternate articulation of the world either along the dividing line "the river–the horse" or along the dividing line "half a horse–half a river" (that would be that part of reality, distinguished by cognition, which functions as the object). Marx was a materialist, and it would be groundless and foolish to deny that; he was a materialist who understood the complicated nature of the process of cognition and the active participation in it of the subjective factor (that is why, among other things, Marxian materialism may be classified as dialectical).

The interpretation of the copy theory in the Marxian system is closely connected with the interpretation of the concept of the *human individual*. Objective reality is comprehended, reflected, mirrored, etc., by *a given man*, since cognition, for all its social conditioning, is always an individual act. Both in epistemology and in the philosophy of man, the logical (not genetic or chronological) starting point is the appropriate conception of the human individual. There is, therefore, nothing extraordinary in the fact that in the *Theses of Feuerbach* the problems of the subjective factor in cognition and of the conception of the human individual occur together and are closely interconnected. In the *Theses on Feuerbach* we find not only extremely valuable explanations of the role of practical activity and the subjective factor in the process of cognition, but important remarks on the construction of the concept of the human individual as well. In my opinion these remarks, often underestimated, are of fundamental significance for the development of historical materialism.

The human individual is a biological organism, a *separate* being, and a thinking organism which acts because it thinks. Hence an individual is always a *social product* and cannot be properly understood in isolation from society. Marx's formula that the human individual is the totality of social relations is in my opinion one of his most brilliant discoveries. It made it possible to develop the theory of historical materialism consistently and to oppose subjective voluntarism, religious personalism, and vulgarized sociologism in the analysis of the position of the human individual and of his practical activity. We shall see that this is also of great significance for epistemology.

In criticizing Feuerbach's opinion of religious alienation, Marx attacked Feuerbach's conception of the human individual.

> Feuerbach resolves the essence of religion into the essence of *man*. But the essence of man is not an abstraction inherent in each particular individual. The real nature of man is the ensemble of social relations.

Marx says that the adoption of such an attitude obliged Feuerbach "to postulate an abstract–*isolated*–human individual," which made him "conceive the nature of man only in terms of a 'genus', as an inner and mute universal quality which unites the many individuals in a purely natural (biological) way."

Marx's conclusion:

> Feuerbach therefore does not see that the 'religious senti- ment' is itself a social product, and that the abstract individual whom he analyzes belongs to a particular form of society.[10]

Only the combination of

1. the inclusion of the subjective factor in the conception of the object, and
2. the conception of the human individual as a social product, as the ensemble of social relations, lays the foundation for the proper interpretation of Marxian epistemology, for the Marxian interpretation of the copy theory of cognition.

Having such a foundation, we may return to specific problems of the copy theory and examine them in relation to the role of language in cognition. Marx spoke about the subjective interpretation of reality. In the language of epistemology we say that cognition is objective in nature (which means that cognition copies or mirrors objective reality), but that there is also a subjective factor in cognition. Cognition is copying, but copying with a subjective tinge. Unfortunately, when we approach the problem in such a general way, it is nothing but a cliché. It is not enough to say that the process of cognition is objective from one point of view and subjective from another. We must explain what the subjective element consists in. And it is here that the difficulty arises.

Usually emphasis is given to the facts that the image of reality must be related to the perceiving apparatus and that the quality of the image depends on the structure of that apparatus. This is certainly true and worth emphasizing, but rather trivial.

The problem begins to grow complicated only when, like Marx, we take into account the fact that man, in both phylogenesis and ontogenesis, comes to know the world through action and in *transforming* reality; thus cognition is not a passive 'mirror-like' copying, but an *active* way approaching objective reality. Cognition involves human practical activity in all its forms and is, in a sense, a *projection* of man. This means that man's approach to objective reality—from the articulation of that reality in sensory perception to the conception of regularities in its evolution—depends not only on what *reality* is like but also on what cognizing *man* is like. For *what* and *how* man perceives and cognizes depends on the kind of experience (accumulated in phylogenesis, the experience of the past generations, and in ontogenesis, individual experience) at his disposal. For that very reason the same reality can be, and is, perceived differently by different persons. This is, of course, the main channel through which the subjective factor, i.e., the factor which tinges cognition with the individual properties of the given cognizing *subject*, penetrates the process of cognition.

Now that a subjective element has been introduced into the process of cognition by including practical activity, we must try to formulate the general category called 'the subjective factor'. For that purpose let us examine the effect of language upon cognition, or, in other words, its effect on the copying of reality in the human mind.

When I spoke about the effect of human practical activity upon cognition, I made it clear that I meant practical activity accumulated in both the ontogenesis and the phylogenesis of man. It is not primarily one given individual human being's transformations of reality which become a part of his individual experience, but the products of all *social* practical activity, which are conveyed to the members of society in various ways. Foremost among these products is language, which quite effectively through education conveys society's experience to its present and future members. Thus we return to the problem of language as a product of social practical activity.

As we have seen, man always thinks in some language, and, in that sense, his thinking is always linguistic. His language consists of signs and meanings; it is language-thinking. Although thinking (in the sense of problem solving) includes elements of preverbal orientation in the world (sensory perception and the resulting mechanisms of concrete associations), at the stage of linguistic thinking those elements are clearly subordinate, as is demonstrated by the effect of words upon sensory perception. How a man thinks depends primarily on social phylogenetic experience conveyed to him by society in the process of linguistic upbringing. Thus Humboldt was right in saying that man thinks as he speaks. One might say that an individual looks at the world and grasps it conceptually "through social spectacles."

But this is only one aspect of the role of language in the process of the human mind's copying of reality. We have to realize that language, which affects the way the human mind copies reality, is in turn a *product* of copying, a product of social practical activity in the broadest sense of the term. Thus the second part of Humboldt's thesis—that man not only thinks as he speaks but also speaks as he thinks—proves true. It is only when we realize the significance of this complementary thesis that we obtain a full picture of the problem and the dialectics of its inner relationships.

When we speak of the effect of language upon the copying of reality in the human mind, we treat language as a *ready-made* system of signs. But that system, so essential for our cognition, is itself a *product* that is markedly social in nature. In order to emphasize the effect of language upon cognition, we often note the extraordinary number of terms which denote the aspects of reality of particular importance to speakers of particular languages (in the case of the Eskimos the large number of terms denoting the various kinds and states of snow, in the case of desert peoples the large number of terms for the various shades of brown and yellow colors, in the case of peoples living near the sea the large number of terms denoting the various kinds of fish, in the case of peoples living on the steppes the large number of terms denoting the various plants). But this example marvelously confirms the thesis that language is shaped by man's social practical activity. It is obvious why it is the Eskimos who have so many terms for snow and why it is the inhabitants of the desert who have so many terms for the various shades of yellow, and not vice versa. Men speak as life and practical activity prompt them to speak. This applies not only to the names of things but to names of actions, and possibly to the linguistic interpretation of spatial and temporal relations as well. According to certain hypotheses (for instance, Marr's) it is possible to demonstrate the effect of social practical activity upon the entire range of linguistic formations, their evolution, syntax, and morphology.

It is beyond doubt that the ready-made system of language determines our vision of the world in some way. If a given human community has thirty terms for snow rather than just one term, the difference is not only one of wealth of vocabulary: that community perceives snow as differentiated by those terms. It does not 'produce' the different kinds of snow in an arbitrary way. These exist in nature *objectively* (though the community may not pay attention to them when it concentrates on the properties common to all the kinds of snow, e.g., its whiteness and coldness). It is not in the least a matter of convention that the Eskimo does in fact include thirty terms for snow in its vocabulary. Life itself required them. Distinguishing between various kinds of snow has been a matter of life and death for the members of that community. Practical activity contributes to the evolution of a given language, and the social experience fixed in language dominates the minds of the members of the given human community. The Eskimos *see* thirty kinds of snow rather than snow 'in general', not because they want to do so or because they have agreed to do so by convention, but because they are unable to perceive reality in any other way.

An excellent illustration of this thesis is provided by Paul Zinski's analysis (contained in his interesting book *Grund und Grat*) of the differences in descriptions of the mountain landscape in literary German and in the Swiss dialect.

Phylogenesis powerfully influences ontogenesis. What language-thinking distinguishes in reality does exist objectively, but the image of the world may take something into account in a variety of ways, or not at all. In this moderate sense language does in fact create an image of reality.

These issues give rise to a question suggested by the Sapir-Whorf hypothesis: Given the differences in the occupations of various communities, might not some language systems exist which have *no points* in common, and would they not be mutually untranslatable? Given the information provided earlier, we must answer in the negative. For all the differences of environment, climate, level of cultural development, etc., human societies are linked by a common biological history, and their practical activity takes place in an objective reality which is similar even if not identical. That is why language records differences *and similarities* (the recently started search for linguistic universals will, then, probably prove successful). The various language systems are not closed, and hence are not mutually untranslatable. Of course, philosophers would be interested in whether a 'totally different' biological history of thinking beings (should such beings be found on other planets) would produce languages mutually untranslatable despite their reflection of reality (like thinking on the basis of an electromagnetic or x-ray mirroring of reality). The optimists now constructing languages for communication with intelligent beings living on other planets are of the opinion that all intelligent beings understand relations between numbers. This fascinating problem, which would contribute something new to our analysis of language, can be settled empirically, of course, only when man really establishes contacts with intelligent beings living on other planets.

The above analysis has provided the proper form of the copy theory of cognition. It is characterized by the constant interaction of the objective and subjective aspect, of human cognition. Human cognition is always cognition of something which stands in an objective cause-effect relation to the cognizing mind. It is in this sense that cognition is a copy (reflection, mirroring) of objective reality. But it is always a subjective copy. It takes place in a given individual whose characteristics (perceptive apparatus, knowledge accumulated, etc.) partly determine the character of the copying; it takes place in a given system of language-thinking whose properties, derived from social experience, also partly determine the character of the copying. Thus the copy, like the truth attained in the process of cognition, is both objective and subjective in nature. Only if we fully realize this can we comprehend the thesis of Marxist epistemology that cognition and truth are processes. But further, we can and should strive to examine the role of the subjective factor in the process of the copying of reality in human mind. This will enable us to reformulate problems of the sociology of knowledge and to view the problem of the active role of language in human cognition in a different way.

In conclusion let us return to the issues raised in the course of our preliminary reflections. Does language *create* an image of reality? Is the alternative that language *either* creates an image of reality *or* copies objective reality a genuine alternative? Language neither creates an image of reality in the literal sense of the word 'creates', nor is it a copy of reality in the literal sense of the term 'copy'. Its copy always includes a subjective element, and in that liberal sense language creates an image of reality. A copy of objective reality and a subjective creation of its image in the process of cognition do not exclude one another, but complement one another to form a single whole.

Chapter 6

Language, Cognition, and Culture

Our analysis is now drawing to an end, and the time has come to say something about the active role of language in man's mental activity. We cannot expect any definitive conclusions—the lack of appropriate empirical research makes such expectations illusory—but we may hope to broaden the interpretation of the problem.

The problem of the active role of language in man's mental activity may be approached, depending on our interpretation of that activity, either as the problem of the role of language in thinking or as the problem of the role of language in human cognition. Human cognition being only one special type of thinking, this means that we use a broader or a narrower context of analysis to reveal particular aspects of the main problem.

There is yet a third approach to this problem. We may treat language as a function of culture, where culture is understood both as a specific kind of behavior and as a specific product of behavior. This third approach overlaps the first and second, but has its own distinct range of problems and queries.

As the title of this chapter indicates, we shall now concentrate our attention on the problems of the active role of language in human cognition and in culture. But we shall have to deal with the problem of the active role of language in thinking as well, if only to recall the results of the foregoing analysis. The logic of the matter makes it mandatory to consider the problems in the following order: thinking, cognition, and finally culture.

As I said in analyzing the relationship between language and thinking, speaking is always thinking; it always means experiencing the meanings of words both in the form of concepts and in their accompanying images. Language as the abstract aspect of speaking is by definition a thought *in potentia*, because a linguistic sign has meaning by definition. Hence language is language-thinking. Thinking or, to be exact, *human* thinking (and not the prehuman orientation in the world characteristic of infants or abnormal individuals that is often called thinking) always takes place in some language, because without the signs of the phonic language (or some transcription of such signs) conceptual thinking is impossible. But it does not follow that human thinking can be reduced to concepts connected with linguistic signs. There is a certain imaginative element in human thinking which depends on language in many ways but is not identical with it. The connection between thinking and language is complex and permanent. But thought may not be *identified* with language (the statement that human thinking is impossible without language is not analytic).

This thesis of the active role of language in thinking may be interpreted in at least three ways:

1. One interpretation is that *without* language as a definite sign system (hence also a system of rules of meaning and rules of grammar without which we cannot speak about a system of *linguistic* signs), *conceptual* thinking would be impossible. This may be formulated otherwise: sign systems called language are carriers of conceptual thinking. Hence our thesis reduces to the statement that the existence of language is a *necessary condition* (physiology, psychology, linguistics explain what this entails) of conceptual thinking.

2. But the essential, proper sense of the thesis of the active role of language in thinking is different. It states that language is the social foundation of individual thinking. The ability to speak, the structure of the brain, and the organs of speech in a normal human individual are inborn. But speaking *as such* is not inborn and does not develop naturally without the social mediation of teaching. And since conceptual thinking is impossible without language, man learns to speak and think in the process of social education. He receives a ready product from society:

language-thinking, i.e., experience or society's knowledge about the world, fixed in linguistic categories and accumulated in phylogenesis. This crystallization of social experience is the starting point and foundation of all individual thinking, a foundation conveyed by society to the individual in a dictatorial manner independent of the individual's control and awareness (except in cases of particularly penetrating self-reflection). Individual thinking is creative and novel; otherwise the progress of knowledge and culture would be impossible. But though an individual is seldom able or inclined to admit this, he looks at the world through the eyes of past generations, and what little is novel in his behavior has deep roots in the past.

Language then is the social point of departure for individual thinking. It is the intermediary between the social and inherited, on the one hand, and the individual and creative, on the other, in individual thinking. And language not only conveys the experience and knowledge of past generations to individuals but communicates the new achievements of individual thinking as social products to *future* generations as well. Thus in the process of human thinking, language (language-thinking) becomes a creative factor in a particularly important sense of the word. It conveys the social message of phylogenetic experience actualized in the ontogenesis of the human individual. The content of this message is not arbitrary, since the experience of past generations contains *objective* knowledge of the world, without which man would be unable to act in a manner adjusted to his environment and could not survive as a species. By learning to speak and by learning to think, we acquire the achievements of past generations rather easily. We need not rediscover everything, and the necessity for such a rediscovery would make all intellectual and cultural progress impossible. But the message of past generations affects our actual vision of the world overwhelmingly and despotically from articulation in sensory perception to the emotional tingling of our cognitive thinking. To be cautious, let me repeat once again: This is not the *only* factor determining our thinking, but it is a factor of immense importance and influence.

Hence when we speak of the active role of language in the process of thinking in this second sense, we mean that language, conveyed to the human individual by society, forms the *necessary* foundation of that individual's thinking. This foundation links the individual with other members of the same language community and is the basis for the individual's own mental creative work.

We need only reject the mysticism of a 'spirit of the nation', a 'national vital force', associated with the explanations of that phenomenon to find supporting ideas which have existed in the humanities in Europe since Herder and Humboldt in various theoretical disguises. These include the rational elements of the theses that language acts as an intermediary between the human individual and the world of objects and that every language includes a definite *Weltanschauung*, a definite schema or stereotype of the way in which the world of things and events is perceived. Liberated from mysticism, such opinions are brilliant observations on the role of the subjective factor in human thinking.

3. The third interpretation of the thesis on the active role of language in thinking is only a modification, a special case, of the second interpretation, but in view of its significance it requires separate treatment. It is the assertion that language not only is the social point of departure and the foundation of individual thinking but also affects the 'level' of abstraction and generality of that thinking (this is of great importance for conceptual thinking).

It is a well-known fact that languages differ from one another not only in phonetics, morphology, syntax, and vocabulary but also in the degree of generality of vocabulary. To say which languages are highly developed and which primitive is not easy, since such an evaluation always requires some system of reference and varies with changes in this system. But there is no doubt that languages can be classified into types in accordance with the nature of the terms they include and that certain languages lack certain general terms and include a wealth of concrete terms in their stead. Syntax can work in the same direction, by making abstract reference to things and actions possible or impossible. The active influence of language upon thinking is explicitly revealed here, although that influence can fully be comprehended only when we realize that both language and thinking are, genetically, products of human practical activity.

We discover new aspects of the problem of the role of language in human activity when we shift our analysis from thinking in general to cognition. Cognition is a process of thinking (or its product) which results in a description of reality. The description includes information not only about individual facts but also about the various relationships between them, relationships in which we include regularities of coexistence and change.

The process of cognition is associated with practical activity in various ways. Cognition begins with a practical activity or, strictly speaking, with some practical needs and the resulting requirement for cognitive information. Quite often the links between cognition and practical activity are direct, but even in the most abstract and autonomous fields of scientific research we can at least demonstrate an indirect genetic linkage. It is obvious that in stating these things we resolve the problem of the origin and goal of cognition: cognition serves human practical activity directly or indirectly, even though some thinkers do not always realize it. Here, however, we are interested in another linkage between cognition and practical activity, the language linkage. It is the least obvious because it is the most pervasive.

Let us return to the fundamental idea that language fixes the accumulated experience and knowledge of past generations for us. Of course it does so as *language-thinking*, as a system of material vehicles of definite *meanings*, and hence as a system of rules of meanings and rules of grammar which associate definite meanings with definite sounds (or other material vehicles). Language is in that sense a kind of condensed practical activity, which affects our actual process of cognition in the most suggestive and easiest way.

First of all, language affects the way we *perceive* reality. We now have experimental data to support the thesis that our perception of reality is clearly affected by the language in which we think. This only means that language, which is a kind of copy of reality, is also a kind of maker of our image of reality. Our articulation of the world is not only a function of individual experience. It is a function of social experience as well, which is conveyed to the individual through upbringing, primarily through language. The problem is more complicated than is indicated by this formulation, since what we call individual experience is also embedded in schemata and stereotypes of social origin. But formulating the problem in this manner, we admit the effect of language upon sensory perception without falling into extremes of subjectivism or naive realism. Although an Eskimo sees dozens of kinds of snow, a European highlander sees a few kinds of snow, and a European lowlander sees just snow, none of them just creates a subjective image of the world in an arbitrary manner. Each of them articulates the objective world on the basis of different social activity and individual activity. But it is a fact that the Eskimo really does *perceive* the world, in this respect, in a different way. He sees it in a more concrete manner than an inhabitant of the tropical zone, and he does so under the influence of the language he has been taught, among other influences. His language *forces* him to perform a complicated articulation of the world by placing at his disposal a number of concrete names for various kinds of snow instead of a single general term. This formulation must be qualified to avoid subjectivism entirely, but the active role of language in the process of cognition is stated clearly and explicitly.

The same applies to a variation of the above thesis, which deals with the influence of sentence formulation (in particular the influence of syntax) upon the perception of reality. In the language of certain tribes of American Indians one cannot say that a person goes, kills game; such a statement must be defined by reference to the time, place, method of action, etc. Evidently, this is not only a matter of wording but also a matter of perceiving reality, connected with the way the Indians speak and think about reality. The Indian thinks in a certain language; the categories and grammatical rules of his language force him to view reality in a way that makes him take into account a number of concrete details usually unnoticed by members of the Indo-European language communities. This means that he not only *speaks* differently but also *perceives* differently. There is nothing mysterious or arbitrary in this fact. The language has been shaped by a definite social practical activity; it reflects certain facts and meets practical needs. Once shaped, it also affects human cognition and plays an active role in it. Is this refuted by the fact that every language can be translated into any other language, so that with the proper explanations such general categories as 'to go' can be conveyed even in the more concrete language of American Indians? As long as the categorial and grammatical system of a language is not changed, that language determines a given way of perceiving reality by the members of the language group in question.

But the most important element characterizing the active role of language in the process of cognition is the effect of the conceptual apparatus of a given language (by which we mean not only the vocabulary but also the set of grammatical rules) upon the way in which we ask questions about reality. This is the rational element of radical conventionalism, a fact I wish to emphasize, the more so since I have criticized that theory and similar ones many a time. In my opinion the radical conventionalists' error consisted in laying excessive stress on a single idea and ascribing to it absolute validity. But the idea itself was undoubtedly fertile and based on pertinent observation of the active role of language in the process of cognition.

As I have said before, one may argue about the sensibleness of applying the term "primitive" to the language of peoples usually called primitive, but there is no doubt that in a language which does not know general terms such as 'plant' and 'animal' and has no categories with which to construct a developed numerical system, neither algebra nor the theory of relativity can be discovered. Of course, the problem is much more complicated, but I want to emphasize the indisputable fact that if a question cannot be *thought* in a given language because the language lacks the proper terms, then that question simply cannot be *posed*. Thus language actively affects the possibility of studying reality and indirectly affects opportunities of acquiring knowledge about reality as well.

What about the defenders of various forms of linguistic relativism? Are they right? Not in the least, because linguistic relativism advances assertions more radical than those which can be defended in the light of the facts.

If by 'linguistic relativism' we mean the thesis that language plays an active role in cognition and that therefore we must, in certain circumstances, indicate the conceptual apparatus of the language within which cognition was achieved, then the thesis is self-evident and uncontroversial. But linguistic relativists do not propose such a moderate thesis on the role of language in cognition.

Linguistic relativism is usually the more radical thesis that different linguistic systems condition types of cognition so widely different from one another that they are not mutually translatable. This was the main idea of radical conventionalism, and the direction in which at least one interpretation of the Sapir-Whorf hypothesis tended. Linguistic relativism makes the entire structure of cognition depend upon language and reaches the conclusion that language is the *maker* of our image of the world (in contradiction to the copy theory of cognition); this is basically erroneous.

First, experience will not support the thesis that there are languages not mutually translatable. More specifically, experience refutes the thesis that languages can condition images of the world which differ so greatly that coordinated action by people speaking and thinking in one of those languages and people speaking and thinking in another would be impossible.

All languages are mutually translatable, although this may often be difficult (as in the examples quoted by Malinowski, where meaningful translation requires a thorough knowledge of the culture of a given community) and although the world of images and emotions associated with the language from which a translation has been made is often missing (especially in the case of language systems that are isolated from one another). We can successfully translate into European languages definite statements made in language of primitive peoples, and we also can translate abstract categories of European languages into the language of primitive peoples, provided we make the appropriate explanations and modifications.

The incorrectness of linguistic relativism becomes clearer when we carefully consider its implications (in their radical interpretation) for the sphere of human action and behavior. If two diametrically different (and hence mutually untranslatable) language systems should yield diametrically different images of the world, the people speaking those languages ought to behave quite differently under the same conditions. This is absurd, given the devastating biological consequences which would necessarily result from unadjusted behavior (and at least one of the complexes of behavior would be unadjusted). But in reality we do not observe such facts. Depending on their environment, men may formulate the same meanings in different ways; may experience them in the form of different images; may focus their attention on different things and phenomena, depending on the conditions imposed upon them by their struggle for existence; and may classify fragments of objective reality in different ways. But their image of reality is in general *the same*, and in the process of acquiring knowledge of reality all men, regardless of the language in which they think, prove capable of adjustment and of adaptive behavior. An Eskimo may associate height with an image of icebergs, an inhabitant of the Trobriand Islands may associate it with an image of palms, an inhabitant of Tibet with an image of Himalayan peaks, and an inhabitant of a great city who has never lived in the country with an image of skyscrapers. And their different ways of life may find some reflection in the languages those people use. But are their languages mutually untranslatable, and will not the speakers of those languages be able to communicate with one another and behave in an adjusted and coordinated manner?

The last example takes us to the second argument against linguistic relativism. For all the differences among the various systems of language and thought, connected with differences in origin and conditioning, they have something in common, something which accounts for the fact that languages are mutually translatable and which makes it possible for people coming from the most distant milieus and environments and living in the most different natural and social conditions to communicate with one another. What they have in common is the biological lot of the human species on our globe and the common reflection of our earthly reality in language-thinking. To be successful, the fashionable search for linguistic universals need only be conducted on an adequately large scale. Some universals must exist in all languages, regardless of the differences among them. Their existence is indicated by the possibility of communication among people brought up in different cultures. This is certainly a convincing argument against a radical interpretation of linguistic relativism.

Finally, let me point to one more argument against linguistic relativism, an argument connected with the dynamics of language. For all its conservatism, language is not invariable. On the contrary, it changes constantly, especially in semantics. Changes in social life require changes in language-thinking and enrich vocabulary. Contacts with alien cultures have similar consequences. The progress of civilization, which leads to increasing contacts between cultures, gradually obliterates differences between the conceptual apparatuses of the various languages, but hardly affects their phonetic and grammatical systems and emotional associations with the various images. We can draw two conclusions, both of which mitigate against linguistic relativism:

1. Since such changes may be brought about by contacts between widely differing cultures, the radical version of linguistic relativism with its thesis of the mutual untranslatability of widely different linguistic systems must be false.
2. The progress of civilization increasingly obliterates differences between the semantic aspects of the various languages.

Thus while the active role of language in human cognition deserves such examination, the *absolute* importance ascribed to this notion by linguistic relativists must be rejected.

The problem of the role of language in human activity may be considered on a third plane, as the set of definite cultural processes, their products, and forms of human behavior.

I shall not engage in complicated discussions about the definition of culture. I shall follow Sapir in adopting the broad imprecise statement that culture is what society thinks and does. Given such an approach, the relation between language and culture, interpreted as a relation between cause and effect, works both ways: we have an effect of culture upon language and, conversely, an effect of language upon culture.

The first aspect of the problem lies outside the scope of the present analysis. I do not deny it great significance—on the contrary. But it is a linguistic issue, which calls for linguistic expertise, especially in the field of comparative history. Such knowledge as a philosopher might glean from the literature of the subject does not authorize him to make broader generalizations, especially since the controversy over the fundamental question whether the development of culture affects the development of language has been conducted by linguists in a 'philosophical' manner and remains unresolved. Marr transformed language (interpreted by him as 'language-thinking') into ideology and based his theory of the development of language by stages on the assumption that a given linguistic formation is a reflection of the corresponding social formation ('social' being defined in terms of social classes). Sapir, on the contrary, thought that language in no way depends on the development of culture ('language' being interpreted as a phonetic and grammatical system, its semantic aspect being disregarded). It seems that the point of view adopted by Sapir and other thinkers holding similar opinions is narrowed by an improper definition of language. It does not follow, though, that we must accept Marr's radical conception; in my opinion, the approach which makes us seek an influence of a society and associated culture upon its language is more fertile than that which *a priori* excludes such a possibility. Sapir's argument that *what* people think (culture) does not affect *how* people think (language) is not convincing. But these matters are better left for the linguists. Unfortunately they have done little in this field. Both thinkers of Marr's school and pronounced idealists such as Karl Vossler (in his *Frankreichs Kultur im Spiegel seiner Sprachentwicklung*, Heidelber, 1913) have fallen victim to dangerous generalizations.

Let us turn to the other aspect of the problem, the effect of language upon the development of culture. Once culture is conceived to include the thoughts of people who are members of a given society, the products of their thoughts (especially such products as science, technology, and art) and their behavior, a definite program of research immediately emerges.

The first point of that program consists in the analysis of the effect of language upon thinking and cognition. We have already discussed this. Practically nothing needs to be added here.

The second point concerns the analysis of the effect of language upon such products of human thought as science, technology, and art. This is an immense culturological problem that can only be touched on here, since it requires a separate monographic study. In the light of the foregoing analysis of the linguistic nature of conceptual thinking it is obvious that language influences science and technology and also art (mainly literature, but music and painting as well). The theory of relativity cannot be formulated in the language of a primitive Australian tribe and hence cannot be thought in that language. But neither can contemporary music, or Bach's music, or contemporary painting be formulated in that language. Such music and painting may be imitations of primitive artistic production, but, perhaps just for that very reason, they remain products of highly developed conceptual thinking, which is impossible without an appropriately formed language. Authentically primitive artistic production and its reasoned imitation (of course, always stylized) are two different things. But this problem too remains open, since the experts have said little on this subject.

Point three—the study of the effect of language upon human behavior—has been carried out much better.

Social psychology, sociology, and other disciplines concerned with the social behavior of human beings have discussed the role of stereotypes in human attitudes and behavior. Social upbringing in a definite environment and in a definite social group conveys accumulated social knowledge to a human individual both in the form of language-thinking and in the form of approved systems of values and associated stereotypes of human behavior. Unfortunately, we still know too little about that socially vital subject. The study of taboos in primitive societies is certainly much more advanced than the analogous study of stereotypes of behavior in civilized societies, especially the role of language in such stereotypes.

In primitive societies language interferes with the sphere of behavior primarily as a part of the binding system of taboos or as part of the system of religion and magic. In civilized societies the magic function of language does not vanish, although it is sublimated in such a clear form. But I am more interested in the more sublimated form. Through language society conveys to the individual certain attitudes, valuations, and stereotypes; these are fixed by the society's language and powerfully influence the consciousness of the individual. Because of their everyday character and suggestiveness they are difficult to decipher and are in most cases accepted as natural.

Consider, for instance, a society in which for some reason or another religious, class, racial, national, and other prejudices and dislikes are rampant. A child brought up in that society takes over certain attitudes and stereotypes of behavior. In most cases they are connected by language with a name which covers the full semantic 'wealth' of the prejudice, dislike, hatred, or positive valuation. Words are not something external to human attitudes and behavior but become part of them (just as they are not external to definite contents associated with them). The analogy is between the experiencing of definite emotions and stereotypes, elicited by such words as 'heathen', 'Protestant', 'lower-class', 'bourgeois', 'Negro', and 'Jew', and the experiences which doubtless are connected with *taboos*. But this is only an analogy since the situation of so-called societies is, from various points of view, very complicated. Therefore the "tyranny of words" which was talked about by the so-called general semantics is in no way meaningless. Indeed this entire matter, which is derided by academic semantics and judged to be reactionary in the Marxist literature (which incidentally usually jumbles general semantics together with academic semantics in a pitiless fashion) nevertheless conveys an unusually important idea: language brings about the forms of human behavior. Now, general semantics carried this to an absurd length; the author of this view, Korzybski, even considered language to be the source of various sicknesses—but that should not prejudice us against realizing the distinct value of this significant and powerful discovery. The truthful aspect of his view explains why general semantics turned out to be so effective, to the surprise of the critics of its work, in therapeutic activities. For if the goal of these semantic interferences is primarily to make people conscious of the role of language in their accepted attitudes and stereotyped ways of acting, then such general semantic therapy can become effective; the goal is also to convince people that general and even universal concepts are closely bound up with stereotyped concepts and prejudgments. It is enough to overthrow the suggestion that we are dealing here with something "natural" in order to bring the attitudes and stereotyped ways of behavior into doubt. The goal of such therapy can be reached with the help of the so-called semantic differential of Korzybski, and its function is to make this truth plain in the most suggestive and simple way possible. In any case, his work opened up a broad field for future investigations: even while one may cling to general semantics in a naive and exaggerated way, one may also find genuine results within it.

This issue might be treated as part of a larger research problem. This is the broadly interpreted sociology of knowledge, which I have referred to previously and which we are now viewing from a different angle. The sociology of knowledge states that the world (especially the social world) is always cognized from some definite point of view, a point of view determined by the interests of the social group in question. This may be expanded to include the point of view determined by the role of language in cognition and in the development of culture. The angle of approach and the problem of social conditioning not only apply to cognition in general and scientific cognition in particular, they apply to human attitudes and stereotypes of behavior as well. In this field the active role of language, one of the important determining elements, is of special significance. Such a broad interpretation of the problems gives new meaning, I think, to the statement that language is not only an element but also a coauthor of culture. When we get rid of the ballast of mysticism which usually permeates considerations of such matters, language reveals new aspects and new possibilities of research. The discovery, made early in our century, that language is not only an instrument but also an *object* of research in epistemology acquires new meaning. This is usually so when we come to face a truly important discovery.

Bibliography[*]

LINGUISTICS: FROM HERDER TO THE THEORY OF THE 'LINGUISTIC FIELD'

1. Artanowski, S. N. *Critique of Semantic Idealism and Some Philosophical Problems of Language.* Leningrad dissertation, 1959 (in Russian).
2. Basilius, H. "Neo-Humboldtian Ethnolinguistics," *Word 8* (August, 1952), no. 2, pp. 95–105.
3. Benes, B. *Wilhelm von Humboldt, Jacob Grimm, August Schleicher.* P. G. Keller, Winterthur, 1958.
4. Brie, S. *Der Volksgeist bei Hegel und in der historischen Rechtsschule.* W. Rothschild, Berlin, 1909.
5. Bühler, K. *Sprachtheorie. Die Darstellungsfunktion der Sprache.* Gustav Fischer, Jena, 1934.
6. Finck, F. N. *Die Aufgabe und Gliederung der Sprachwissenschaft.* Rudolf Haupt, Halle a.S., 1905.
7. Finck, F. N. *Der deutsche Sprachbau als Ausdruck deutscher Weltanschauung.* N. G. Elwert, Marburg, 1899.
8. Funke, O. "Zur Frühgeschichte des Terminus 'Innere Sprachform'," in *Festschrift zum 80 Geburtstag von Ernst Otto.* Walter de Gruyter, Berlin, 1957, pp. 289–294.
9. Guchmann, M. M. "The Linguistic Theory of L. Weisgerber" in *Problems of the Theory of Language in Contemporary Foreign Linguistics.* Academy of Science U.S.S.R., Moscow, 1961, pp. 123–162 (in Russian).
10. Hartmann, P. *Wesen und Wirkung der Sprache im Spiegel der Theorie Leo Weisgerbers.* Carl Winter, Heidelberg, 1958.
11. Haym, R. *Herder.* Aufbau-Verlag, Berlin, 1954, vols. 1 and 2.
12. Haym, R. *Wilhelm von Humboldt. Lebensbild und Charakteristik.* Aufbau-Verlag, Berlin, 1954 (originally published by R. Gaertner, Berlin, 1856).
13. Hegel, G. W. F. *Encyclopedia of the Philosophical Sciences. Ed. note:* Available in English translations: part I, *The Logic of Hegel*, translated by William Wallace. Oxford University Press, London and Oxford, 2d ed., 1892; part II, *Hegel's Philosophy of Nature*, translated by A. V. Miller. Oxford University Press, London and New York, 1969; part III, *Philosophy of Mind*,

---

[*]*Ed. note:* Wherever possible, English translations have been substituted for the original works in foreign languages which were cited by the author. Russian and Polish titles are given in English translation, and full translations are listed where available.

translated by William Wallace. Oxford University Press, Oxford and London, 1894.

14. Hegel, G. W. F. *The Phenomenology of Mind*, translated by J. M. Baillie. George Allen and Unwin, London, and Macmillan, New York, 2d ed., 1931.

15. Hegel, G. W. F. *Philosophy of History*, with prefaces by Hegel, translated by J. Sibree, and with new introduction by C. J. Friedrich. Dover, New York, 1956.

16. Hegel, G. W. F. *Philosophy of Right*, translated by T. M. Knox. Oxford University Press, Oxford, 1942.

17. Heintel, E. "Gegenstandskonstitution und sprachliches Weltbild," in *Sprache, Schlüssel zur Welt*, H. Gipper (ed.), pp. 47-55. [See No. *48.*]

18. Herder, J. G. *Abänderungen und Zusätze der zweiten Ausgabe der ersten Sammlung der Fragmente über die neuere deutsche Literatur* (1768). Gustav Hempel, Berlin and Leipzig, 1869-1879.

19. Herder, J. G. *Fragmente über die neuere deutsche Literatur. Abänderungen und Zusätze der zweiten Ausgabe der Fragmente. Erste Sammlung 1768*, in *Herders Werke*, part 19. Gustav Hempel, Berlin, 1877. *Ed. note:* New edition of *No. 18.*

20. Herder, J. G. *Ideen zur Philosophie der Geschichte der Menschheit*. Deutsche Bibliothek in Berlin, (n.d.).

21. Herder, J. G. *Journal meiner Reise im Jahr 1769*, in *Herders sämtliche Werke*. Weidmannsche Buchhandlung, Berlin, 1878, vol. 4, pp. 343-461. *Ed. note:* see *Journal of My Travels in the Year 1769*, translated, introduction, notes by John Francis Harrison. University Microfilms, Ann Arbor, 1953 (Columbia University dissertation, 1952).

22. Herder, J. G. *Sprachphilosophische Schriften*. Felix Meiner, Hamburg, 1960.

23. Herder, J. G. *Über den Ursprung der Sprache*. Akademie-Verlag, Berlin, 1959.

24. Humboldt, W. v. *Über das Entstehen der grammatischen Formen und deren Einfluss auf die Ideenentwicklung*, in *Gesammelte Werke*. Reimer, Berlin, 1843, vol. 3, pp. 269-306.

25. Humboldt, W. v. *Über die Sprachen der Südseeinseln*, in *Gesammelte Schriften*. B. Bohr's Verlag, Berlin, 1907, vol. 6, part 1, pp. 37-51.

26. Humboldt, W. v. *Über das vergleichende Sprachstudium in Beziehung auf die verschiedenen Epochen der Sprachentwicklung*, in *Gesammelte Werke*, vol. 3, pp. 241-268. [See *No. 24.*]

27. Humboldt, W. v. *Über die Verschiedenheit des menschlichen Sprachbaues*, in *Gesammelte Schriften*, vol. 6, part 1, pp. 111-303. [See *No. 25.*]

28. Humboldt, W. v. *Von dem grammatischen Baue der Sprachen*, in *Gesammelte Schriften*, vol. 6, part 2, pp. 337-486. [See *No. 25.*]

29. Ipsen, G., "Der neue Sprachbegriff," *Z.f. Deutschkunde*, 1932, pp. 1-18.

30. Ipsen, G. *Sprachphilosophie der Gegenwart*. Junker u. Dünnhaupt, Berlin, 1930.

31. Ipsen, G. "Stand und Aufgaben der Sprachwissenschaft," *Festschrift für Streitberg.* Heidelberg, 1924.
32. Kandler, G., "Die Lücke im sprachlichen Weltbild," in *Sprache, Schlüssel zur Welt,* H. Gipper (ed.), pp. 256–270. [See *No. 48.*]
33. Kantorowicz, H. U., "*Volksgeist und historische Rechtsschule,*" *Historische Z.* 108 (1912), pp. 295–325.
34. Kelkel, L., "Monde et langage: Réflexions sur la philosophie du langage de Wilhelm von Humboldt," *Les Études Philosophiques (Le Langage),* 1958, no. 4, pp. 477–485.
35. Marty A. *Über Wert und Methode einer allgemeinen beschreibenden Bedeutungslehre.* A. Francke, Bern, 1950.
36. Marty A. *Untersuchungen zur Grundlegung der allgemeinen Grammatik und Sprachphilosophie.* M. Niemeyer, Halle a.S., 1908.
37. Müller, G., "Wortfeld und Sprachfeld," in *Otto Festschrift,* pp. 155–163. [See *No. 8.*]
38. Öhman, S. "Theories of the 'Linguistic Field'," *Word 9* (August, 1953), no. 2, pp. 123–134.
39. Öhman, S. *Wortinhalt und Weltbild.* Dissertation, Stockholm, 1951.
40. Porzig, W. *Das Wunder der Sprache.* A. Francke, Bern, 1957.
41. Ramischvili, G. W. *Some Problems of W. v. Humboldt's Linguistic Theory.* Tbilisi dissertation, Academy of Science, Georgian S.S.R., 1960 (in Russian).
42. Rothacker, E. "Ontologische Voraussetzungen des Begriffs Muttersprache," in *Sprache, Schlüssel zur Welt.* H. Gipper (ed.), pp. 39–46. [See *No. 48.*]
43. Saussure, R. de. *Cours de linguistique générale.* Payot, Lausanne, 1916 and Paris, 1942.
44. Savigny, F. C. v. *Vom Beruf unserer Zeit für Gesetzgebung und Rechtswissenschaft.* Mohr und Zimmer, Heidelberg, 1814, especially pp. 8–15.
45. Schankweiler, E. *Wilhelm von Humboldts historische Sprachkonzeption.* Berlin, 1959. *Ed note:* An unpublished dissertation.
46. Schmidt-Rohr, G. *Die Sprache als Bildnerin der Völker.* Eugen Diederichs, Jena, 1932.
47. Schpet, G. *The Inner Word Form.* State Academy of Arts, Moscow, 1927 (in Russian).
48. *Sprache, Schlüssel zur Welt. Festschrift für Leo Weisgerber,* H. Gipper (ed.). Pädagogischer Verlag Schwann, Düsseldorf, 1959.
49. Trier, J. "Deutsche Bedeutungsforschung," in *Germanische Philologie. Festschrift für Otto Behaghel.* Carl Winter, Heidelberg, 1934, pp. 173–200.
50. Trier, J. *Der deutsche Wortschatz im Sinnbezirk des Verstandes: Die Geschichte eines sprachlichen Feldes.* Carl Winter, Heidelberg, 1931.
51. Trier, J. "Das sprachliche Feld," *Neue Jahrbücher für Wissenschaft und Jugendbildung 10* (1934), pp. 428–449.
52. Trier, J., "Über die Erforschung des menschenkundlichen Wortschatzes," in *Actes du Quartrième Congrès International de Linguistes.* Einar Munksgaard, Copenhagen, 1936, pp. 92–98.

53. Ufimtseva, A. A. "Theories of the 'Semantic Field' and the Possibilities of Their Application to the Extension of Word-Construction in Language," in *Problems of the Theory of Language in Contemporary Foreign Linguistics*. Academy of Science, U.S.S.R., Moscow, 1961, pp. 30–63 (in Russian).

54. Ullman, S. *The Principles of Semantics: A Linguistic Approach to Meaning*. Basil Blackwell, Oxford, 1957.

55. Vossler, K. *Frankreichs Kultur im Spiegel seiner Sprachentwicklung*. Carl Winter, Heidelberg, 1913.

56. Vossler, K. *Gesammelte Aufsätze zur Sprachphilosophie*. Max Hueber, Munich, 1923.

57. Vossler, K. *Positivismus und Idealismus in der Sprachwissenschaft*. Carl Winter, Heidelberg, 1904.

58. Vossler, K. *The Spirit of Language in Civilization*, translated by Oscar Oeser. Kegan Paul, London, 1932.

59. Weisgerber, L. "Die Bedeutungslehre — ein Irrweg der Sprachwissenschaft?" *Germanisch-Romanische Monatsschrift 15* (1927), pp. 161–183.

60. Weisgerber, L. "Der Geruchssinn in unseren Sprachen," *Indogermanische Forschungen 46* (1928), pp. 121–150.

61. Weisgerber, L. *Die geschichtliche Kraft der deutschen Sprache*. Pädagogischer Verlag Schwann, Düsseldorf, 1959.

62. Weisgerber, L. *Das Gesetz der Sprache*. Quelle und Meyer, Heidelberg, 1951.

63. Weisgerber, L. *Die Muttersprache im Aufbau unserer Kultur*. Pädagogischer Verlag Schwann, Düsseldorf, 1957.

64. Weisgerber, L. "Das Problem der inneren Sprachform und seine Bedeutung für die deutsche Sprache," *Germanisch-Romanische Monatsschrift 14* (1926), pp. 241–256.

65. Weisgerber, L. "Sprache und Begriffsbildung," in *Actes du Quatrième Congrès International de Linguistes*. Einar Munksgaard, Copenhagen, 1936, pp. 33–39.

66. Weisgerber, L. *Die Sprache unter den Kräften des menschlichen Daseins*. Pädagogischer Verlag Schwann, Düsseldorf, 1954.

67. Weisgerber, L. "Die Sprachfelder in der geistigen Erschliessung der Welt," in *Festschrift für Jost Trier*, Westkulturverlag Anton Hain, Meisenheim a. Glan, 1954, pp. 34–39.

68. Weisgerber, L. "Die sprachlichen 'Zugriffe'," in *Festschrift zum 80. Geburtstag von Ernst Otto*, pp. 295–299. [See *No. 8.*]

69. Weisgerber, L. "Sprachwissenschaft und Philosophie zum Bedeutungs-problem," *Blätter für deutsche Philosophie 4*, Berlin (1930/1931), pp. 17–46.

70. Weisgerber, L. *Vom Weltbild der deutschen Sprache. 1. Halbband: Die inhaltbezogene Grammatik; 2. Halbband: Die sprachliche Erschliessung der Welt*. Pädagogischer Verlag Schwann, Düsseldorf, 1953/1954.

71. Weisgerber, L. "Die Wiedergeburt des vergleichenden Sprachstudiums," *Lexis 2* (1951), pp. 3–22.

72. Weisgerber, L. "Das Wort in der Welt als sprachliche Aufgabe der Menschheit," *Sprachforum. Zeitschrift für angewandte Sprachwissenschaft 1* (1955), no. 1, pp. 10–19.

73. Weisgerber, L. "Die Zusammenhänge zwischen Muttersprache, Denken und Handeln," *Zeitschrift für deutsche Bildung 6* (1930), pp. 57-72, 113-126.
74. Wundt, W. *Völkerpsychologie*, vols. 1 and 2: *Die Sprache.* W. Englemann, Leipzig, 1911/1912.
75. Yermolajewa, L. S., "The Neo-Humboldtian Tendency in Contemporary Bourgeois Linguistics," in *Problems of General and Technical Linguistics.* Moscow, 1960, pp. 47-84 (in Russian).
76. Zinsli, P. *Grund und Graf. Die Bergwelt im Spiegel der Schweizerdeutschen Alpenmundarten.* A. Francke, Bern, 1945.

THE PHILOSOPHY OF SYMBOLIC FORMS: NEO-KANTIANISM

77. Bakradse, K. S. *Outlines of the History of Recent and Contemporary Bourgeois Philosophy* (section on the neo-Kantian philosophers). State Publishing House, Tbilisi, 1961 (in Russian).
78. Buczynska, H. *Ernst Cassirer's Philosophy of Language*, Warsaw dissertation (in Polish).
79. Cassirer, E. *Der Begriff der symbolischen Form im Aufbau der Geisteswissenschaften*, in E. Cassirer, *Wesen und Wirkung des Symbolbegriffs.* Bruno Cassirer, Oxford, 1956, pp. 169-200.
80. Cassirer, E. *An Essay on Man.* Doubleday, New York, 1954. Chap. 8: "Language," especially pp. 169-174.
81. Cassirer, E. "The Influence of Language upon the Development of Scientific Thought," *Journal of Philosophy 39* (1942), no. 12, pp. 309-327.
82. Cassirer, E. "Le Langage et la construction du monde des objets," in *Psychologie du langage*, H. Delacroix (ed.). Librairie Felix Alcan, Paris, 1933, pp. 18-44.
83. Cassirer, E. "Le Langage et le monde des objets," *Journal de Psychologie Normale et Pathologique 30*, January 15 - April 15, 1933, no. 1/4, pp. 18-44.
84. Cassirer, E. *Language and Myth*, translated by S. K. Langer. Harper, New York and London, 1946; Dover, New York, 1953.
85. Cassirer, E. *The Philosophy of Symbolic Forms*, translated by R. Manheim, vol. 1 (1953), vol. 2 (1955), vol. 3 (1957). Yale University Press, New Haven.
86. Cassirer, E. *Zur Logik des Symbolbegriffs*, in E. Cassirer, *Wesen und Wirkung des Symbolbegriffs*, pp. 201-230 [See *No. 79.*]
87. Hartman, R. S. "Cassirer's Philosophy of Symbolic Forms," in *The Philosophy of Ernst Cassirer*, P. A. Schilpp (ed.). Tudor, New York, 1958, pp. 289-334.
88. Kant, *Prolegomena*, edited and translated by Paul Carus. Open Court, Chicago, 1933.
89. Kaufmann, F. "Cassirer, Neo-Kantianism and Phenomenology," in *The Philosophy of Ernst Cassirer*, pp. 799-854. [See *No. 87.*]
90. Langer, S. K. "On Cassirer's Theory of Language and Myth," in *The Philosophy of Ernst Cassirer*, pp. 379-400. [See *No. 87.*]
91. Langer, S. K. *Philosophy in a New Key: A Study in the Symbolism of Reason, Rite and Art.* Harvard University Press,

Cambridge, Mass., 1957.
92. Leander, F. "Further Problems Suggested by the Philosophy of Symbolic Forms," in *The Philosophy of Ernst Cassirer*, pp. 335–358. [See *No. 87.*]
93. Popov, S. I. *Kant and Kantianism.* Moscow University Press, Moscow 1961 (in Russian).
94. Urban, W. M. "Cassirer's Philosophy of Language," in *The Philosophy of Ernst Cassirer*, pp. 401–442. [See *No. 87.*]
95. Vaihinger, H. *The Philosophy of 'As-If'; A System of the Theoretical, Practical and Religious Fictions of Mankind*, 2d ed., translated by C. K. Ogden. Routledge and Kegan Paul, London, 1968.
96. Werkmeister, W. H. "Cassirer's Advance beyond Neo-Kantianism," in *The Philosophy of Ernst Cassirer*, pp. 757–798. [See *No. 87.*]

PHILOSOPHY OF CONVENTION: MODERATE CONVENTIONALISM

97. Boutroux, E. *Natural Law in Science and Philosophy*, translated by Fred Rothwell. Macmillan, New York, 1914.
98. Dingler, H. *Die Grundlagen der Physik.* Walter de Gruyter, Berlin-Leipzig, 1923.
99. Dingler, H. *Der Zusammenbruch der Wissenschaft und der Primat der Philosophie.* E. Reinhardt, Munich, 1926.
100. Duhem, P. *The Aim and Structure of Physical Theory*, translated by Philip P. Wiener from 2d ed. of 1914. Princeton University Press, Princeton, 1954.
101. Kolakowski, L. "Philosophy of Non-Intervention," *Philosophical Review (Mysl Filozoficzna)*, Warsaw, 1953, no. 2/8, pp. 335–373 (in Polish).
102. Le Roy, E. *Essai d'une philosophie première.* Presses Universitaires de France, Paris, 1956.
103. Le Roy, E. "Un Positivisme nouveau," *Revue de Métaphysique et de Morale*, 1901, pp. 138–153.
104. Le Roy, E. "Science et philosophie," abstract in *Revue de Métaphysique et de Morale*, Paris, July, 1899.
105. Le Roy, E. "Sur quelques objections adressées à la nouvelle philosophie," *Revue de Métaphysique et de Morale*, 1901, pp. 292–327 and 407–432.
106. Poincaré, H. *Science and Hypothesis*, translated by W. J. Greenstreet. Dover, New York, 1952.
107. Poincaré, H. *Science and Method*, translated by Francis Maitland. Dover, New York, 1958.
108. Poincaré, H. *The Value of Science*, translated with an introduction by G. B. Halsted. Dover, New York, 1958.

RADICAL CONVENTIONALISM; NEO-POSITIVISM

109. Ajdukiewicz, K. *Language and Cognition: Selected Writings 1920–1939.* PWN Publishers, Warsaw, 1969 (in Polish).

110. Ajdukiewicz K. "On Professor Schaff's Article about My Philosophical Views," *Philosophical Review (Mysl Filozoficzna) 1953*, no. 2/8, pp. 292-334 (in Polish).
111. Ajdukiewicz, K. "Sprache und Sinn," *Erkenntnis 4* (1934), pp. 100-138.
112. Ajdukiewicz, K. "Das Weltbild und die Begriffsapparatur," *Erkenntnis 4* (1934), pp. 259-287.
113. Ajdukiewicz, K. "Die wissenschaftliche Weltperspektive," *Erkenntnis 5* (1935), pp. 22-30. *Ed. note:* Available in English translation: "The Scientific World-Perspective," in *Readings in Philosophical Analysis*, H. Feigl and W. Sellars (eds.). Appleton-Century-Crofts, New York, 1949, pp. 182-188.
114. Anscombe, G. E. M. *An Introduction to Wittgenstein's Tractatus.* Hutchinson, London, 1959.
115. Bergmann, G. *The Metaphysics of Logical Positivism.* Loagmans, Green, New York, 1954.
116. Black, M. *Language and Philosophy.* Cornell University Press, Ithaca, 1949.
117. Carnap, R. *The Logical Structure of the World*, translated by Rolf George. University of California Press, Berkeley and Los Angeles, 1967.
118. Carnap, R. *The Logical Syntax of Language.* Routledge and Kegan Paul, London, 1937.
119. Carnap, R. "Psychologie in physikalischer Sprache," *Erkenntnis 3* (1932/1933), pp. 107-142. *Ed. note:* Available in English translation: "Psychology in Physical Language," translated by G. Schick, in *Logical Positivism*, A. J. Ayer (ed.), pp. 165-198. [See *No. 127.*]
120. Carnap, R. "Überwindung der Metaphysik durch logische Analyse der Sprache," *Erkenntnis 2* (1931), pp. 219-241. *Ed. note:* Available in English translation: "The Elimination of Metaphysics through Logical Analysis of Language," translated by A. Pap, in *Logical Positivism*, A. J. Ayer (ed.), pp. 60-81. [See *No. 127.*]
121. Carnap, R. *The Unity of Science*, translated by M. Black. Routledge and Kegan Paul, London, 1934.
122. Feibleman, J. K. *Inside the Great Mirror: A Critical Examination of the Philosophy of Russell, Wittgenstein and Their Followers.* Martinus Nijhoff, Hague, 1958.
123. Franck, Philipp. *Modern Science and Its Philosophy.* Harvard University Press, Cambridge, Mass., 1950.
124. Hempel, C. G. "On the Logical Positivists' Theory of Truth," *Analysis 2*, no. 4, 1935, pp. 49-59.
125. Hempel, C. G. "Le Problème de la vérité," *Theoria 3* (1937), pp. 206-246.
126. *Logic and Language: Studies Dedicated to Professor R. Carnap on the Occasion of His Seventieth Birthday.* D. Reidel, Dordrecht, 1962.
127. *Logical Positivism*, A. J. Ayer (ed.). George Allen and Unwin, London, and Free Press, Glencoe, Ill., 1959.

128. Mises, R. v. *Positivism: A Study in Human Understanding.* Harvard University Press, Cambridge, Mass., 1951.
129. Neubert, A. *Semantischer Positivismus in den USA.* M. Niemeyer, Halle a. S., 1962.
130. *The Philosophy of Bertrand Russell,* P. A. Schilpp (ed.). Tudor, New York, 1951.
131. Reichenbach, H. *The Rise of Scientific Philosophy.* University of California Press, Berkeley and Los Angeles, 1956.
132. Russell, B. *The Analysis of Mind.* George Allen and Unwin, London, 1921.
133. Russell, B. *Human Knowledge: Its Scope and Limits.* George Allen and Unwin, London, 1948.
134. Russell, B. *An Inquiry into Meaning and Truth.* George Allen and Unwin, London, 1951.
135. Russell, B. *Logic and Knowledge: Essays 1901–1950.* George Allen and Unwin, London, 1956.
136. Schaff, A. "Concerning the Philosophical Views of K. Ajdukiewicz," *Philosophical Review (Mysl Filozoficzna),* 1953, no. 3 (in Polish).
137. Schaff, A. *Introduction to Semantics,* translated by Olgierd Wojtasiewicz. Pergamon Press, New York and London, 1962. Original edition PWN Publishers, Warsaw, 1960 (in Polish).
138. Schaff, A. *The Philosophical Outlook of K. Ajdukiewicz.* KiW Publishers, Warsaw, 1952 (in Polish).
139. Schaff, A. "The Philosophical Views of K. Ajdukiewicz," *Philosophical Review (Mysl Filozoficzna),* 1952, no. 1 (in Polish).
140. Schaff, A. *Zu einigen Fragen der marxistischen Theorie der Wahrheit.* Dietz Verlag, Berlin, 1954. *Ed. note:* Translation of first Polish edition; a second edition was published, in Polish only, by KiW Publishers, Warsaw, 1959 (in Polish).
141. Schlick, M. "Die Wende der Philosophie," *Erkenntnis 1,* (1930/1931), pp. 4–11. ("The Turning Point in Philosophy," translated by D. Rynin, in *Logical Positivism,* A. J. Ayer (ed.), pp. 53–59.) [See *No. 127.*]
142. *Semantics and the Philosophy of Language,* L. Linsky (ed.). University of Illinois Press, Urbana, 1952.
143. Weinberg, J. R. *An Examination of Logical Positivism.* Routledge and Kegan Paul, London, 1936.
144. Wittgenstein, L. *Philosophical Investigations,* translated by G. E. M. Anscombe. Macmillan, New York, 1953.
145. Wittgenstein, L. *Tractatus Logico-Philosophicus,* translated by C. K. Ogden and F. P. Ramsey with introduction by Bertrand Russell. Kegan Paul, London, 1922.

THE LANGUAGES OF SO-CALLED PRIMITIVE PEOPLES

146. *Les Carnets de Lucien Lévy-Bruhl,* Maurice Leenhardt (ed.). Presses Universitaires de France, Paris, 1949.
147. Elkin, A. P. *The Australian Aborigines: How to Understand*

Them. Angus and Robertson, Sydney and London, 1954.

148. Firth, J. R. "Ethnographic Analysis and Language with Reference to Malinowski's Views," in *Man and Culture: An Evaluation of the Work of Malinowski,* R. Firth (ed.). Routledge and Kegan Paul, London, 1957, pp. 93–118.

149. Graebner, F. *Das Weltbild des Primitiven.* Ernst Reinhardt, Munich, 1924.

150. Howitt, A. W. *The Native Tribes of South-East Australia.* Macmillan, London, 1904.

151. Kainz, F. *Psychologie der Sprache,* vol. 1: *Grundlagen der allgemeinen Sprachpsychologie,* 1954; vol. 2: *Vergleichend-genetische Sprachpsychologie* (2d ed.), 1960; vol. 3: *Physiologische Psychologie der Sprachvorgänge,* 1954; vol. 4: *Spezielle Sprachpsychologie,* 1956. Ferdinand Enke, Stuttgart.

152. Lévi-Strauss, C. *The Savage Mind.* University of Chicago Press, Chicago, 1966.

153. Lévy-Bruhl, L. *Les Fonctions mentales dans les sociétés inférieures.* Librairie Felix Alcan, Paris, 1912. *Ed. note:* Available in English translation: *How Natives Think* translated by Lillian A. Clare. George Allen and Unwin, London, 1926.

154. Malinowski, B. *Argonauts of the Western Pacific.* George Routledge and Sons, London, 1922.

155. Malinowski, B. *Coral Gardens and Their Magic,* vol. 1: *The Description of Gardening;* vol. 2: *The Language of Magic and Gardening.* George Allen and Unwin, London, 1935.

156. Malinowski, B. "The Problem of Meaning in Primitive Languages." Supplement to: C. K. Ogden and I. A. Richards, *The Meaning of Meaning.* Routledge and Kegan Paul, London, 1953.

157. Steinen, K. von den. *Unter den Naturvölkern Zentral-Brasiliens.* D. Reimer, Berlin, 1894.

THE SAPIR-WHORF HYPOTHESIS

158. Achmanova, O. S. *On Psycholinguistics.* Moscow University Press, Moscow, 1957 (in Russian).

159. Achmanova, O. S. *Studies in General and Russian Lexicography.* Educational Publishing House, Moscow, 1957, pp. 36–57 (in Russian).

160. Alexandre, P. "Note sur quelques problèmes d'ethnolinguistique," *L'Homme, 1,* (January–April 1961), no. 1, pp. 102–106.

161. *Anthropology Today. An Encyclopedic Inventory,* A. L. Kroeber (ed.). The University of Chicago Press. Copyright 1953 by the University of Chicago. All rights reserved. Copyright 1953 under the International Copyright Union. Extracts quoted by permission.

162. *An Appraisal of Anthropology Today,* Sol Tax et al. (eds.). The University of Chicago Press, Chicago, 1953.

163. *Biennial Review of Anthropology 1959,* B. J. Siegal (ed.). Stanford University Press, Stanford, 1959.

164. Black, M. "Linguistic Relativity," *Philosophical Review, 68* (1959), pp. 228–238.

165. Boas, F. *Introduction,* in *Handbook of American Indian Languages,* part I, F. Boas (ed.), *Bureau of American Ethnology, Bulletin 40.* U.S. Government Printing House, Washington, 1911, pp. 5–83.

166. Boas, F. *Race, Language and Culture.* Macmillan, New York, 1949.

167. Brown, D. W. "Does Language Structure Influence Thought? Comments on the Psycho-Linguistics Experiment at Michigan," *ETC 17,* no. 3, 1960, pp. 339–345.

168. Brown, J. C. "Loglan," *Scientific American 202,* (June, 1960), no. 6, pp. 53–63.

169. Brown, R. W. *Words and Things.* Free Press, Glencoe, Ill., 1958, especially pp. 229–263.

170. Brown, R. W. and Lenneberg, E. H. "A Study in Language and Cognition," *The Journal of Abnormal and Social Psychology 49,* no. 3 (July, 1954), pp. 454–462.

171. Brutjan, G. "Toward a Philosophical Appraisal of Linguistic Relativity," *Historical-Philosophical Journal,* Academy of Science, Armenian S.S.R., 1961, no. 2/13, pp. 169–183 (in Russian).

172. Carroll, J. B. "Process and Content in Psycholinguistics," in *Current Trends in the Description and Analysis of Behavior,* Robert Glaser et al. (eds.). University of Pittsburgh Press, Pittsburgh, 1958.

173. Carroll, J. B. "Some Psychological Effects of Language Structure," in *Psychopathology of Communication,* vol. 12, P. H. Hoch and J. Zubin (eds.), Proceedings, American Psychopathological Association, 1956. Grune and Stratton, New York, 1958.

174. Carroll, J. B. *The Study of Language.* Harvard University Press, Cambridge, Mass., 1955.

175. Carroll, J. B. and Casagrande, J. B. "The Function of Language Classifications in Behavior," in *Readings in Social Psychology,* E. E. Maccoby et al. (eds.). Holt, New York, 1958, pp. 18–31.

176. Chang Tung-sun. "A Chinese Philosopher's Theory of Knowledge," *ETC 9,* no. 3, 1952, pp. 203–226.

177. Cohen, L. J. *The Diversity of Meaning.* Methuen, London, 1962, especially sec. 9 "Can a Language Be a Prison?"

178. *Culture in History,* S. Diamond (ed.). Columbia University Press, New York, 1960.

179. Degtereva, T. A. *The Development of Contemporary Linguistics 1,* Moscow, 1961 (in Russian).

180. Emenau, M. B. "Language and Social Forms. A Study of Toda Kinship Terms and Dual Descent," in *Language, Culture and Personality,* L. Spier et al. (eds.), pp. 158–179. [See *No. 210.*]

181. Fearing, F. "An Examination of the Conceptions of Benjamin Whorf in the Light of Theories of Perception and Cognition," in *Language in Culture,* H. Hoijer (ed.). University of Chicago Press, Chicago, 1954, pp. 47–81.

182. Feuer, L. S. "Sociological Aspects of the Relation between Language and Philosophy," *Philosophy of Science 20* (1953), pp. 85-100.
183. Fishman, J. A. "A Systematization of the Whorfian Hypothesis," *Behavioral Science 5* (1960), pp. 323-339.
184. Goldstein, K. "Concerning the Concept of 'Primitivity'," in *Culture in History*, S. Diamond (ed.), pp. 99-117. [See *No. 178.*]
185. Granet, M. "L'Expression de la pensée en chinois," *Journal de Psychologie* (1928), no. 8, pp. 617-656.
186. Guchman, M. M. E. "Sapir and Ethnographic Linguistics," *Problems of the Science of Language*, 1954, no. 1, pp. 122-127 (in Russian).
187. Hallowell, A. I. "Cultural Factors in the Structuralization of Perception," in *Social Psychology at the Crossroads*, J. H. Rohrer and M. Sherif (eds.). Harper, New York, 1957.
188. Haudricourt, A. G. and Granai, G. "Linguistique et sociologie," *Cahiers Internationaux de Sociologie 19* (1955), pp. 114-129.
189. Herzog, G. "Culture, Change and Language: Shifts in the Pima Vocabulary," *Language, Culture and Personality*, pp. 66-74. [See *No. 210.*]
190. Hocket, F. C. "Chinese versus English. An Exploration of the Whorfian Theses," *Language in Culture*, H. Hoijer (ed.), pp. 106-126. [See *No. 211.*]
191. Hoijer, H. "Anthropological Linguistics," in *Trends in European and American Linguistics 1930-1961.* Spectrum Publishers, Utrecht, 1961, pp. 164-195.
192. Hoijer, H. "Cultural Implications of Some Navaho Linguistic Categories," *Language 27* (1951), pp. 111-120.
193. Hoijer, H. "Linguistic and Cultural Change," *Language 24* (1948), pp. 335-345.
194. Hoijer, H. "Native Reaction as a Criterion in Linguistic Analysis," *Proceedings of the VIII International Congress of Linguists*, Eva Sivertsen (ed.). Oslo University Press, Oslo, 1958, pp. 573-583.
195. Hoijer, H. "The Relation of Language to Culture," *Anthropology Today*, pp. 554-573. [See *No. 161.*]
196. Hoijer, H. "The Sapir-Whorf Hypothesis," in *Language in Culture*, pp. 92-105. [See *No. 211.*]
197. Hoijer, H. "Semantic Patterns of the Navaho Language," in *Sprache, Schlüssel zur Welt*, H. Gipper (ed.). Pädagogischer Verlag Schwann, Düsseldorf, 1959, pp. 361-373. [See *No. 48.*]
198. Hollowell, A. J. "Ojibwa Ontology, Behavior and World View," in *Culture in History*, pp. 19-52. [See *No. 178.*]
199. Hymes, D. H. "Linguistic Aspects of Cross-Cultural Personality Study," in *Studying Personality Cross-Culturally*, pp. 313-360. [See *No. 257.*]
200. Hymes, D. H. "On Typology of Cognitive Styles in Language," *Anthropological Linguistics 3* (1961), pp. 22-54.

201. Istomina, M. W. "On the Reciprocal Relation between Perception and Meaning of Flowers by Children of Pre-School Age," *Reports of Academy of Pedagogical Sciences of R.S.F.S.R.*, no. 113 (1960) Moscow, pp. 76-102 (in Russian).

202. Jakobson, R. "Boas' View of Grammatical Meaning," *American Anthropologist 61* (1959), pp. 139-145. *(Memoir 89* of American Anthropological Association entitled *The Anthropology of Franz Boas.)*

203. Kluckhohn, C. "Navaho Categories," in *Culture in History*, pp. 65-98. [See *No. 178.*]

204. Kluckhohn, C. "Patterning as Exemplified in Navaho Culture," *Language, Culture and Personality*, pp. 109-130. [See *No. 210.*]

205. Kluckhohn, C. and Leighton, D. *The Navaho*. Harvard University Press, Cambridge, Mass., 1947.

206. Kroeber, A. L. *Anthropology*. Harcourt, Brace, New York, 1948.

207. Kroeber, A. L. "Some Relations of Linguistics and Ethnology," *Language 17* (1941), pp. 287-291.

208. Landar, H. J., Ervin, S. M. and Horowitz, A. E. "Navaho Color Categories," *Language 36* (1960), pp. 368-382.

209. Landesman, C. "Does Language Embody a Philosophical Point of View?" *Review of Metaphysics 14* (1961), pp. 617-636.

210. *Language, Culture and Personality. Essays in Memory of Edward Sapir*, L. Spier, A. I. Hallowell, and S. S. Newman (eds.). Sapir Memorial Publication Fund, Menasha, Wis., 1941.

211. *Language in Culture*, Harry Hoijer (ed.). University of Chicago Press, Chicago, 1954.

212. *The Language of Wisdom and Folly*, I. J. Lee (ed.). Harper, New York, 1949.

213. *Les Langues du monde*, A. Meillet and M. Cohen (eds.). C.N.R.S., Paris, 1952.

214. Lee, D. "Being and Value in a Primitive Culture," in D. Lee, *Freedom and Culture*, pp. 89-104. [See *No. 219.*]

215. Lee, D. "Categories of the Generic and the Particular in Wintu," *American Anthropologist 46* (1944), pp. 362-369.

216. Lee, D. "Codifications of Reality: Lineal and Nonlineal," in *Freedom and Culture*, pp. 105-120. [See *No. 219.*]

217. Lee, D. "The Conception of the Self among the Wintu Indians," in *Freedom and Culture*, pp. 131-140. [See *No. 219.*]

218. Lee, D. "Conceptual Implications of an Indian Language," *Philosophy of Science 5* (1938), pp. 89-102.

219. Lee, D. *Freedom and Culture*, Prentice-Hall, Englewood Cliffs, N. J., 1959. (Selected Papers.)

220. Lee, D. "Linguistic Reflection of Wintu Thought," in *Freedom and Culture*, pp. 121-130. [See *No. 219.*]

221. Lee, D. "Stylistic Use of the Negative in Wintu," *International Journal of American Linguistics 12* (1946), pp. 79-81.

222. Lee, D. "Symbolization and Value," in *Freedom and Culture*, pp. 78-88. [See *No. 219.*]

223. Lenneberg, E. H. "Cognition in Ethnolinguistics," *Language 29* (1953), pp. 463-471.

224. Lenneberg, E. H. "Color Naming, Color Recognition, Color Discrimination: A Re-appraisal," *Perceptual and Motor Skills 12* (1961), pp. 375-382.
225. Lenneberg, E. H. "Language, Evolution and Purposive Behavior," in *Culture in History,* pp. 869-893. [See *No. 178.*]
226. Lenneberg, E. H. "A Note on Cassirer's Philosophy of Language," *Philosophy and Phenomenological Research 15* (1955), pp. 512-522.
227. Lenneberg, E. H. "A Probabilistic Approach to Language Learning," *Behavioral Science 2* (1961), pp. 1-12.
228. Lenneberg, E. H. and Roberts, J. M. *The Language of Experience: A Study in Methodology.* Supplement to *International Journal of American Linguistics 22* (1956). (Indiana University Publications in Anthropology and Linguistics, Memoir 13.)
229. Lévi-Strauss, C. "Language and the Analysis of Social Laws," *American Anthropologist 53* (1951), pp. 155-163.
230. Ljubimowa, E. D. "On the Problem of Verbal and Emotional Generalization." *Reports of the Academy of Pedagogical Sciences of the R.S.F.S.R.,* no. 113 (1960), Moscow, pp. 62-71 (in Russian).
231. Lohman, J. "Einige Bemerkungen zu den Genus-Kategorien des Wintu," *Zeitschrift für vergleichende Sprachforschung 68* (1943), pp. 99-121.
232. Lounsbury, F. G. "Language," in *Biennial Review of Anthropology 1959,* pp. 185-209. [See *No. 163.*]
233. Lounsbury, F. G. "A Semantic Analysis of the Pawnee Kinship Usage," *Language 32* (1956), pp. 158-194.
234. Maclay, H. "An Experimental Study of Language and Non-Linguistic Behavior," *Southwestern Journal of Anthropology 14* (1958), pp. 220-229.
235. Maclay, H. and Ware, E. E. "Cross-Cultural Use of the Semantic Differential," *Behavioral Science 6* (1961), pp. 185-190.
236. Mead, M. "Native Languages as Field-Work Tools," *American Anthropologist 41* (1939), pp. 189-205.
237. Mounin, G. "A propos de *Language, Thought and Reality* de Benjamin Lee Whorf," *Bulletin de la Société de Linguistique 56* (1961), pp. 122-138.
238. Nakamura, H. (ed.). *The Ways of Thinking of Eastern Peoples.* Japanese National Commission for UNESCO, Printing Bureau, Ministry of Finance, Tokyo, 1960. *Ed. note:* Revised English translation, edited by Philip P. Wiener, East-West Center Press, Honolulu, 1964.
239. *Personality in Nature, Society and Culture,* Kluckhohn, C. and Murray, H. A. (eds.). Alfred A. Knopf, New York, 1949.
240. Pike, K. L. *Language in Relation to a Unified Theory of the Structure of Human Behavior.* Summer Institute of Linguistics, Glendale, Calif., 1954. *Ed note:* 2d rev. ed.: Mouton, The Hague, 1967.
241. *Psycholinguistics,* Sol Saporta (ed.). Holt, Rinehart and Winston, New York, 1961.

242. *Psycholinguistics, A Survey of Theory and Research Problems,* C. E. Osgood and T. A. Sebeok (eds.). (Indiana University Publications in Anthropology and Linguistics, Memoir 10), 1954.
243. Rapoport, A. "General Semantics: Its Place in Science," *ETC 16,* (1958), pp. 80-97.
244. Rapoport, A. and Horowitz, A. "The Sapir-Whorf-Korzybski Hypothesis: A Report and a Reply," *ETC 17* (1960), pp. 346-363.
245. *Relativism and the Study of Man,* H. Schoeck and J. W. Wiggins (eds.). Van Nostrand, New York, 1961.
246. Sapir, E. "Conceptual Categories in Primitive Languages," *Science 74* (1931), p. 578.
247. Sapir, E. "Grading: A Study in Semantics," in *Selected Writings of Edward Sapir in Language, Culture and Personality,* David G. Mandelbaum (ed.). University of California Press, Berkeley, 1951, pp. 122-149. Originally published by the University of California Press; quoted material reprinted by permission of the Regents of the University of California.
248. Sapir, E. "Language," in *Selected Writings,* pp. 7-32.
249. Sapir, E. "Language and Environment," in *Selected Writings,* pp. 89-103.
250. Sapir, E. "The Status of Linguistics as a Science," in *Selected Writings,* pp. 160-166.
251. Sapir, E. "Time Perspective in Aboriginal American Culture: A Study in Method," in *Selected Writings,* pp. 389-462.
252. Schemjakin, F. N. "On the Problem of Verbal & Emotional Generalization," *Reports of the Academy of Pedagogical Sciences of the R.S.F.S.R.,* pp. 72-75 (in Russian). [See *No. 230.*]
253. Schemjakin, F. N. "On the Problem of Verbal & Emotional Generalization," pp. 49-61 (in Russian). [See *No. 230.*]
254. Schemjakin, F. N. "On the Question of the Relation of Word to Material Appearance," pp. 5ff (in Russian). [See *No. 230.*]
255. Sommerfelt, A. "Language, Society and Culture," *Norsk Tidsskrift for Sprogvidenskap 17,* pp. 5-81.
256. Sommerfelt, A. *La Langue et la société.* H. Aschehoug, Oslo, and Harvard University Press, Cambridge, Mass., 1938.
257. *Studying Personality Cross-Culturally,* Bert Kaplan (ed.). Harper and Row, New York, 1961.
258. Swegincev, W. A. "Neo-Positivism and Recent Directions in Linguistics," *Problems of Philosophy,* no. 12 (1961), pp. 92-101 (in Russian).
259. Swegincev, W. A. "Presuppositions of the Sapir-Whorf Hypothesis in Theoretical Linguistics," in *Recent Linguistics,* part I, Swegincev (ed.). Publishing House for Foreign Literature, Moscow, 1960, pp. 111-134 (in Russian).
260. Thompson, L. *Culture in Crisis: A Study of the Hopi Indians.* Harper, New York, 1950.
261. Trager, G. L. "The Systematization of the Whorf Hypothesis," *Anthropological Linguistics 1* (1959), pp. 31-35.

262. "Translation between Language and Culture. A Symposium" (F. R. Kluckhorn, G. L. Trager, S. Diamond, M. Swadesh, Z. Salzmann, C. F. and F. M. Voegelin, N. A. McQuown, D. H. Hymes), *Anthropological Linguistics 2* (1960), pp. 1-84.

263. Voegelen, C. F. *Anthropological Linguistics in the Context of Other Fields of Linguistics*, in "A. William Cameron Townsend en el XXV Aniversario del I.L.V." [Instituto Linguistico de Verano (Summer Institute of Linguistics)], Mexico City, 1961.

264. Voegelen, C. F. "Linguistics without Meaning and Culture without Words," *Word 5* (1949), pp. 36-45.

265. Voegelin, C. F. and Voegelin, F. M. *Hopi Domains: A Lexical Approach to the Problem of Selection.* Supplement to *International Journal of American Linguistics 23* (1957).

266. Waterman, J. T. "Benjamin Lee Whorf and Linguistic Field-Theory," *Southwestern Journal of Anthropology 13* (1957), pp. 201-211.

267. Whorf, B. L. "An American Indian Model of the Universe," in B. L. Whorf, *Language, Thought and Reality*, pp. 57-64. [See *No. 270.*]

268. Whorf, B. L. "Language: Plan and Conception of Arrangement," in *Language, Thought and Reality*, pp. 125-134.

269. Whorf, B. L. "Language, Mind and Reality, in *Language, Thought and Reality*, pp. 246-270.

270. Whorf, B. L. *Language, Thought and Reality: Selected Writings*, edited with introduction by John B. Carroll. M.I.T. Press, Cambridge, Mass., 1957.

271. Whorf, B. L. "Languages and Logic," in *Language, Thought and Reality*, pp. 233-245.

272. Whorf, B. L. "A Linguistic Consideration of Thinking in Primitive Communities," in *Language, Thought and Reality*, pp. 65-86.

273. Whorf, B. L. "Linguistic Factors in the Terminology of Hopi Architecture," in *Language, Thought and Reality*, pp. 199-206.

274. Whorf, B. L. "Linguistics as an Exact Science," in *Language, Thought and Reality*, pp. 220-232.

275. Whorf, B. L. "The Relation of Habitual Thought and Behavior to Language," in *Language, Thought and Reality*, pp. 134-159.

276. Whorf, B. L. "Science and Linguistics," in *Language, Thought and Reality*, pp. 207-219.

BEGINNINGS AND DEVELOPMENT OF LANGUAGE–THE PSYCHOLOGY OF THE CHILD

277. Antonow, I. P. "The Development of Thinking and of Language in Children of Pre-School and School Age," *Soviet Pedagogy* (1953), no. 2, pp. 56-74 (in Russian).

278. Arnould, L. *Ames en prison.* Boivin, Paris, 1934.

279. Berko, J. and Brown, R. "Psycholinguistic Research Methods," in *Handbook of Research Methods in Child Development*, P. H.

Musen (ed.). John Wiley, New York and London, 1960, pp. 517-557.

280. Bühler, Charlotte. *Soziologische und psychologische Studien über das erste Lebensjahr.* Gustav Fischer, Jena, 1927.

281. Bühler, Karl. *The Mental Development of the Child.* Routledge and Kegan Paul, London, and Harcourt, Brace, New York, 1930.

282. Busemann, A. *Die Sprache der Jugend als Ausdruck der Entwicklungsrhythmik.* Gustav Fischer, Jena, 1925.

283. Carroll, J. B. "Language Development in Children," in *Psycholinguistics,* S. Saporta (ed.), pp. 331-345. [See *No. 241.*]

284. Daumer, G. F. *Mittheilungen über Kaspar Hauser.* Heinrich Haubenstricker, Nürnberg, 1832.

285. Delacroix, H. *Le Langage et la pensée.* Librairie Felix Alcan, Paris, 1924.

286. Elkonin, D. B. *The Development of Speaking in the Pre-School Age.* Academy of Pedagogical Sciences, Moscow, 1958 (in Russian).

287. Geppertowa, L. "The Basic Structure of Sign Language and the Understanding of Speech Sentences," *Educational Psychology (Psychologia Wychowawcza)* 6, Warsaw (1963) (in Polish).

288. Geppertowa, L. "Development in Children up to Five Years of Age of the Understanding and Usage of Concepts Which Express Definite Relation by the Conjunctive 'in order that (to)'," *Psychological Review (Przeglad Psychologiczny),* Warsaw (1959), no. 3, pp. 47-86 (in Polish).

289. Geppertowa, L. "Understanding by Deaf-Mute Schoolchildren of Relations Indicated by Certain Prepositions," *Educational Psychology (Psychologia Wychowawcza)* 6, Warsaw (1963), pp. 17-31 (in Polish).

290. Gesell, A. and Ilg, F. L. *Child Development,* vol. 1: *Infant and Child in the Culture of Today;* vol. 2: *The Child from Five to Ten.* Harper, New York, 1949.

291. Grégoire, A. "L'apprentissage de la parole pendant les deux premières années de l'enfance," *Journal de Psychologie* (1933), pp. 375-389.

292. Gwosdev, A. N. "Problems in the Study of Children's Speech." Academy of Pedagogical Sciences, R.S.F.S.R., Moscow, 1961 (in Russian).

293. Hayes, C. *The Ape in Our House.* Harper, New York, 1951.

294. Hurlock, E. B. *Child Development.* McGraw-Hill, New York, 1956.

295. Isaacs, S. *Intellectual Growth in Young Children.* Routledge, London, 1945.

296. Jakobson, R. "Kindersprache, Aphasie und allgemeine Lautgesetze," *Selected Writings,* vol. 1. Mouton, 'S-Gravenhage, 1962, pp. 328-401.

297. Jerusalem, W. *Laura Bridgman. Erziehung einer Taubstumm-Blinden.* Verlag von A. Pichler's Witwe, Vienna, 1890.

298. Jesperson, O. *Language. Its Nature, Development and Origin.* George Allen and Unwin, London, 1954, especially book 2: *The Child*, pp. 103–190.

299. Kainz, F. *Psychologie der Sprache 2.* Ferdinand Enke, Stuttgart, 1960.

300. Kawerina, E. K. *On the Development of Speech in Children in the First Two Years of Life.* Medical Publishers, Moscow, 1950 (in Russian).

301. Keller, Helen. *The Story of My Life.* Doubleday, New York, 1902 (1954).

302. Kellog, W. N. and Kellog, L. A. *The Ape and the Child.* Hafner, New York, 1933.

303. Kolcowa, M. M. "The Comparative Role of Different Analyses in the Development of the Generalizing Function of Words by Children," *Problems of Psychology* (1956), no. 4, pp. 129–134 (in Russian).

304. Kowalski, S. *The Development of Speech and Thought in the Child.* PWN Publishers, Warsaw, 1962 (in Polish).

305. Leontiev, A. N. *Problems in the Development of the Psyche.* Academy of Pedagogical Sciences, R.S.F.S.R., Moscow, 1959 (in Russian).

306. Leontiev, A. N. and Luria, A. R. "Die psychologischen Anschauungen L. S. Wygotskis," *Zeitschrift für Psychologie 162* (1958), pp. 165–205.

307. Leopold, W. F. "Patterning in Children's Language Learning," in *Psycholinguistics,* S. Saporta (ed.). pp. 350–358. [See *No. 241.*]

308. Luria, A. R. "The Development of Speech and the Formation of Psychological Processes," in *The Science of Psychology in the U.S.S.R.,* vol. 1, Academy of Pedagogical Sciences, R.S.F.S.R., Moscow, 1959, pp. 516–577 (in Russian).

309. Luria, A. R. "The Directive Function of Speech in Development and Dissolution," *Word 15* (1959), pp. 341–352.

310. Luria, A. R. "The Genesis of Voluntary Movements," in *Recent Soviet Psychology,* N. O'Connor (ed.). Pergamon, London, 1961, pp. 165–185.

311. Luria, A. R. "The Role of Speech in the Emergence of Psychological Processes in Children," *Educational Psychology (Psychologia Wychowawcza) 2,* Warsaw (1959), pp. 132–148 (in Polish).

312. Luria, A. R. *The Role of Speech in the Regulation of Normal and Abnormal Behavior.* Pergamon, London, 1961 and Liveright, New York, 1961.

313. Luria, A. R. "The Role of Words in the Emergence of the Time-Reaction in Human Beings," *Problems of Psychology* (1955), no. 1, pp. 73–86 (in Russian).

314. Luria, A. R. and Judowich, F. J. *Speech and the Development of Psychological Processes in Children,* Academy of Pedagogical Sciences, R.S.F.S.R., Moscow, 1956 (in Russian).

315. Meumann, E. *Die Entstehung der ersten Wortbedeutungen beim Kinde.* Wilhelm Engelmann, Leipzig, 1908.

316. Piaget, J. *The Construction of Reality in the Child*, translated by Margaret Cook. Basic Books, New York, 1959.
317. Piaget, J. *Judgment and Reasoning in the Child*, translated by Marjorie Warden. Routledge and Kegan Paul, London, 1959.
318. Piaget, J. *The Language and Thought of the Child*, translated by Marjorie and Ruth Garbain. Routledge and Kegan Paul, London and Humanities Press, New York, 1959.
319. Piaget, J. *Play, Dreams and Imitation in Childhood*, translated by C. Gattegne and F. M. Hodgson. Norton, New York, 1962.
320. Przetacznikowa, M. "Some Problems in the Development of Sentence Structure in the Case of Two Children up to Three Years of Age," *Psychological Review (Przeglad Psychologiczny)* Warsaw (1959), no. 3, pp. 23–46 (in Polish).
321. Rubinstein, S. L. *Principles of General Psychology*. Pedagogical Institute Press, Moscow, 1946 (in Russian). *Ed. note:* Available in German translation: *Grundlagen der allgemeinen Psychologie*, Volk und Wissen, Berlin, 1958.
322. Sankov, L. W. and Solovev, I. M. *Studies in the Psychology of Deaf-Mute Children*. Pedagogical Institute Publishing House, Moscow, 1940 (in Russian).
323. Skinner, F. B. *Verbal Behavior*. Appleton-Century-Crofts, New York, 1957.
324. Skorochodowa, O. L. (ed.). *How I Experience and Imagine the World around Me*. Academy of Pedagogical Sciences, Moscow, 1954 (in Russian).
325. Smoczynski, P. *Acquisition of the Foundation of a System of Speech in the Child*. Ossolineum Publishers, Lodz, 1955 (in Polish).
326. Sochin, F. A. "On the Emergence of Speech Generalizations in the Process of the Development of Speech," *Problems of Psychology* (1959), no. 5, pp. 112–123 (in Russian).
327. Sokoliansky, I. A. "Some Observations on Blind-Deaf-Mutes," in Skorochodowa (ed.). [See *No. 324.*]
328. Solovev, I. M. "Questions of Psychology in the Deaf-Mute Child," in *Science of Psychology in the U.S.S.R.*, vol. 2. Academy of Pedagogical Sciences, R.S.F.S.R., Moscow, 1960, pp. 512-541 (in Russian).
329. Stern, C. and Stern, W. *Die Kindersprache*. J. A. Barth, Leipzig, 1907.
330. Stern, W. *Psychologie der frühen Kindheit bis zum sechsten Lebensjahre*. Quelle und Meyer, Leipzig, 1930.
331. Szuman, S. "The Development of Proper and Personal Names in the Speech of Children, and Their Role in the Apprehension of Parental and Non-Parental Surrounding," in *Ten Years of the Pedagogical Institute of Cracow*. Cracow, 1957, pp. 81–118 (in Polish).
332. Szuman, S. "Development of the Content of Children's Vocabulary," *Pedagogical Studies (Studia Pedagogiczne) 2*, Warsaw (1955), pp. 5–74 (in Polish).

333. Szuman, S. "On Psychic Factors of Repression in the Development of the Child," *Philosophical Review (Przeglad Filozoficzny)* 30, Warsaw (1927), pp. 28-52 (in Polish).

334. Szuman, S. "On the Expressed and the Unexpressed Content of Linguistic Utterances of Children in the First Years of Life," *Psychological Review (Przeglad Psychologniczny)* Warsaw (1959), pp. 3-21 (in Polish).

335. Szuman, S. "On the Factor Which Forms the Psyche of the Pre-School Age Child," *Psychological Quarterly* (1959), pp. 145-158 (in Polish).

336. Szuman, S. "On the Understanding of Speech and the Control of Favorable Conditions and Adequate Methods of Teaching," *Pedagogical Quarterly (Kwartalnik Pedagogiczny)* Warsaw (1957), pp. 68-104 (in Polish).

337. Szuman, S. "The Origin of Objects," *Psychological Quarterly (Kwartalnik Psychologiczny)* 3, Warsaw (1932), pp. 363-394 (in Polish).

338. Szuman, S. *The Role of Activity in the Mental Development of Small Children.* Ossolineum Publishers, Wroclaw, 1955 (in Polish).

339. Szuman, S. and Dzierzanka, A. "The Development of Ability in the Child to Describe and Explain the Complexity of Events Set Forth in a Picture," *Scientific Journal, University of Cracow (Zeszyty Naukowe Uniw. Jagiellonskiego Krakow),* Cracow (1957), no. 11, pp. 9-58 (in Polish).

340. Tyborowska, K. W. "Action and Speech in the Thought of Pre-School Children," *Psychological Studies (Studia Psychologiczne) 1,* Warsaw (1956), pp. 110-126 (in Polish).

341. Vygotsky, L. S. *The Development of the Higher Mental Functions.* Academy of Pedagogical Sciences, Moscow, 1960 (in Russian). *Ed. note:* Abridged translation in *Psychological Research in the U.S.S.R.,* vol. 1, Progress Publishers, Moscow, 1966, pp. 11-46.

342. Vygotsky, L. S. *Selected Psychological Works.* Academy of Pedagogical Sciences, Moscow, 1956 (in Russian).

343. Vygotsky, L. S. *Thought and Language,* translated by E. Hanfmann and G. Vakar. M.I.T. Press, Cambridge, Mass., 1966. (Also Russian text in *Selected Psychological Works,* pp. 39-388.) [See *No. 342.*]

344. Wallon, H. *Les Origines de la pensée chez l'enfant.* Presses Universitaires de France, Paris, 1945.

345. Watts, A. F. *The Language and Mental Development of Children.* George G. Harrap, London, 1944.

346. Werner, H. and Kaplan, E. *The Acquisition of Word Meaning: A Developmental Study.* Monographs of the Society for Research in Child Development, vol. 15. Northwestern University Press, Evanston, 1952.

347. Yarmolenko, A. W. "Conceptions of Time in Blind-Deaf-Mutes," *Publications Leningrad Bechterew Institute for Brain Research 18* (1947), Leningrad, pp. 174-181 (in Russian).

348. Yarmolenko, A. W. "The Dialectical Materialist Conception of the Condition of Blind-Deaf-Mutes, and the Critique of Idealist Theories," *Proceedings of Second Symposium on Scientific Understanding of Defects*, Moscow, 1959, pp. 161-165 (in Russian).

349. Yarmolenko, A. W. *Studies in the Psychology of Blind-Deaf-Mutes.* Leningrad University Press, Leningrad, 1961 (in Russian).

PATHOLOGY OF SPEECH—APHASIA

350. Ananev, B. G. *Psychology of Emotional Learning.* Academy of Pedagogical Sciences, R.S.F.S.R., Moscow, 1960 (in Russian).

351. Cassirer, E. *The Philosophy of Symbolic Forms* vol. 3, especially part 2, chap. 6. Yale University Press, New Haven, 1957.

352. Delacroix, H. [See *No. 285.*]

353. Gelb, A. "Remarques générales sur l'utilisation des données pathologiques pour la psychologie et la philosophie du langage," in *Psychologie du langage.* Librairie Felix Alcan, Paris, 1933, pp. 430-496.

354. Goldstein, K. "L'Analyse de l'aphasie et l'étude de l'essence du langage," in *Psychologie du langage.* Librairie Felix Alcan, Paris, 1933, pp. 403-429.

355. Goldstein, K. "Bemerkungen zum Problem 'Sprechen und Denken' auf Grund hirnpathologischer Erfahrungen," *Acta Psychologica 10* (1954), pp. 175-196.

356. Goldstein, K. *Language and Language Disturbances.* Grune and Stratton, New York, 1948.

357. Goldstein, K. "The Nature of Language," in *Language: An Enquiry into Its Meaning and Function,* R. N. Anshen (ed.). Harper and Row, New York, 1957, pp. 18-40.

358. Goldstein, K. "Über Aphasie," *Schweizer Archiv für Neurologie und Psychiatrie 19* (1926), pp. 3-38.

359. Goodglass, H. and Hunt, J. "Grammatical Complexity and Aphasic Speech," in *Psycholinguistics,* S. Saporta (ed.), pp. 448-454. [See *No. 241.*]

360. Head, H. *Aphasia and Kindred Disorders of Speech,* vols. 1 and 2. Cambridge University Press, Cambridge, 1926.

361. Head, H. "Hughlings Jackson on Aphasia and Kindred Affections of Speech," *Brain 38* (1915), pp. 1-27.

362. Jackson, J. H. *Selected Writings,* vol. 2: *Affections of Speech.* Staples Press, London, 1958, pp. 121-212.

363. Jakobson, R. "Aphasia as a Linguistic Problem," in *Psycholinguistics,* S. Saporta (ed.), pp. 419-427. [See *No. 241.*]

364. Jakobson, R. "Two Aspects of Language and Two Types of Aphasic Disturbances," in R. Jakobson and M. Halle, *Fundamentals of Language.* Mouton, 'S-Gravenhage, 1956, pp. 55-82.

365. Jakobson, R. [See *No. 296.*]

366. Kainz, F. [See *No. 299.*]

367. Konorski, J. "Pathophysiological Analysis of Various Speech

Disturbances," *Reports, Section on Medical Sciences, Polish Academy of Sciences, 2,* Warsaw, 1961 (in Polish).

368. Lee, L. L. "Brain Damage and the Process of Abstracting. A Problem in Language Learning," *ETC 16* (1959), pp. 154-162.

369. Lee, L. L. "Some Semantic Goals for Aphasia Therapy," *ETC 18* (1961), pp. 261-274.

370. Luria, A. R. "Aphasia and the Analysis of Speech Processes," *Problems of Linguistic Science,* 1959, no. 2, pp. 65-72 (in Russian).

371. Luria, A. R. "Problems of Aphasia in the Light of Brain Pathology," *Soviet Neuropsychiatry 6* (1941), pp. 286-294 (in Russian).

372. Luria, A. R. "The Study of Brain Disturbances and the Restitution of Impaired Brain Functions," in *Psychological Science in the U.S.S.R.,* B. E. Ananev et al. (eds.), vol. 2, *Academy of Pedagogical Sciences, R.S.F.S.R.,* Moscow, 1960, pp. 428-458 (in Russian.) *Ed. note:* See the full translation of this major Soviet survey, available from JPRS (Joint Publications Research Service), U.S. Government, Washington, vol. 1 (1961), vol. 2, (1962).

373. Luria, A. R. *Traumatic Aphasia.* Mouton, The Hague, 1965 [original ed.: Moscow, 1947 (in Russian)].

374. Maruszewski, M. "Some Observations on Psychological Investigations into the Specific Qualities of Human Action," in *Problems of Psychology and the Theory of Knowledge,* C. Nowinski (ed.). PWN Publishers, Warsaw, 1958, pp. 101-194 (in Polish).

375. Ombredane, A. *L'Aphasie et l'élaboration de la pensée explicite.* Presses Universitaires de France, Paris, 1951.

376. *Problems of the Pathophysiology of the Higher Nervous Functions of Human Beings during Brain Disturbances,* J. Konorski, H. Kozniewska, L. Stepien, J. Subczynski (eds.). *Reports, Section on Medical Sciences, Polish Academy of Sciences, 2,* Warsaw, 1961 (in Polish).

377. Ruesch, J. *Disturbed Communication.* Norton, New York, 1957.

378. Russell, W. R. and Espir, M. L. E. *Traumatic Aphasia.* Oxford University Press, Oxford and New York, 1961.

379. Schuell, H. and Jenkins, J. J. "The Nature of Language Deficit in Aphasia," in *Psycholinguistics,* S. Saporta (ed.), pp. 427-448. [See *No. 241.*]

380. Sejgarnik, B. W. *Pathology of Thought.* Moscow University Press, Moscow, 1962 (in Russian).

381. Wilson, S. A. K. *Aphasia.* Kegan Paul, London, 1926.

LANGUAGE AND THOUGHT

382. Abramjan, L. A. *Signal and Conditioned Reflex.* Academy of Sciences Armenian S.S.R., Erevan (Armenia), 1961 (in Russian).

383. Albrecht, E. *Die Beziehungen von Erkenntnistheorie, Logik und Sprache.* M. Niemeyer, Halle a.S., 1956.

384. Beljaev, B. W. "On the Reciprocal Relations of Thought, Language

and Speech," *Problems of Psychology*, Moscow, 1958, no. 3, pp. 11–24 (in Russian).

385. Goldstein, K. [See *No. 355.*]

386. Gorski, D. P. *Problems of Abstraction in the Formation of Concepts.* Academy of Sciences, U.S.S.R., Moscow, 1961 (in Russian).

387. Gorski, D. P. "The Role of Language in Knowledge," in *Thought and Language*, D. P. Gorski (ed.). Economics and Politics Publishers, Moscow, 1957, pp. 73–116 (in Russian).

388. Marr, N. J. *Language and Thought (Selected Works*, vol. 3). Publishing House for Social and Economic Literature, Moscow, 1934, pp. 90–122 (in Russian).

389. Mestchaninov, I. I. *A New Theory of Language.* Sotsekgiz, Leningrad, 1936 (in Russian).

390. Natadze, R. G. "Studies on Thought and Speech Problems by Psychologists of the Georgian S.S.R.," in *Recent Soviet Psychology*, N. O'Connor (ed.). Pergamon, London, 1961, pp. 304–326.

391. Panfilov, W. S. "On the Question of the Reciprocal Relation of Language and Thought," in *Thought and Language*, D. P. Gorski (ed.). pp. 117–165 (in Russian). [See *No. 387.*]

392. Pavlov, I. P. *Lectures on Brain Functions.* Academy of Sciences U.S.S.R., Moscow, 1949 (in Russian).

393. Potebnia, A. *Thought and Language*, vol. 1. (Moscow?) 1922 (in Russian).

394. Protasenja, P. F. *The Origin of Knowledge and Particularities.* Belorussian University Press, Minsk, 1959 (in Russian).

395. Révész, G. *Thinking and Speaking, Acta Psychologica 10* (1954), pp. 3–50.

396. Révész, G. *The Origins and Prehistory of Language.* Longmans, Green, London, 1956.

397. Révész, G. "Thought and Language," *Archivum Linguisticum 2* (1950), pp. 122–131.

398. Rossi, E. *Die Entstehung der Sprache und des menschlichen Geistes.* Ernst Reinhardt, Munich-Basel, 1962.

399. Russell, B. *Human Knowledge: Its Scope and Limits.* George Allen and Unwin, London, 1948. [See *No. 133.*]

400. Stalin, J. W. *On Marxism in Linguistics*, 1950. *Ed. note:* For a full set of Stalin's articles and the papers of other participants through 1950, see *The Soviet Linguistic Controversy*, translated from the Soviet press by J. V. Murra, R. M. Hawkins, F. Holling. King's Crown Press of Columbia University Press, New York, 1950.

401. Swegincev, W. A. *Studies in General Linguistics.* Moscow University Press, Moscow, 1962 (in Russian).

402. "Thinking and Language: A Symposium" (Iris Murdoch, A. C. Lloyd, G. Ryle), in *Freedom, Language and Reality: Publications of the Aristotelian Society 25* (supplementary volume). London, 1951, pp. 25–82.

403. *Thinking and Speaking: A Symposium*, G. Révész (ed.), *Acta Psychologica 10* (1954) (G. Révész 3–50, J. Piaget 51–60, F.

Kainz 61–92, W. G. Eliasberg 93–110, J. Cohen 111–124, J. Joergensen 125–135, E. Buyssens 136–164, B. L. van der Waerden 165–174, K. Goldstein 175–196, H. W. Gruhle 197–205).
404. *Thinking and Speech, Reports of Academy of Pedagogical Sciences, R.S.F.S.R.*, no. 113, Moscow, 1960 (in Russian).
405. Vostrikov, A. W. "The Marxist-Leninist Classics on the Connection between Language and Thought," *Problems of Philosophy*, 1952, no. 3, pp. 47–64 (in Russian).
406. Waerden, B. L. van der. *Thinking and Speaking, Acta Psychologica 10* (1954). [See *No. 403*.]
407. Yarmolenko, A. W. "The Role of Language in the Perception of Space," in *Problems of the Perception and Representation of Space*. Academy of Pedagogical Sciences, R.S.F.S.R., Moscow, 1961, pp. 69–71 (in Russian).

LANGUAGE AND KNOWLEDGE OF REALITY

408. Andreyev, I. D. *Foundations of the Theory of Knowledge*. Academy of Science, U.S.S.R., Moscow, 1959 (in Russian).
409. Antonow, N. P. *Origin and Nature of Knowledge*. Ivanowski State Pedagogical Institute, Ivanovo, 1959 (in Russian).
410. Baudouin de Courtenay, J. "Einfluss der Sprache auf Weltanschauung und Stimmung," *Philological Proceedings (Prace Filologiczne) 14*, Warsaw (1929), pp. 185–255.
411. Black, M. "Language and Reality," in *Models and Metaphors*. Çornell University Press, Ithaca, 1962, pp. 1–16.
412. Čačkowski, Z. *The Cognitive Content of Sense Impressions*. KiW Publishers, Warsaw, 1962 (in Polish).
413. Carmichael, L., Hogan, H. P. and Walter, A. A. "An Experimental Study of the Effect of Language on the Reproduction of Visually Perceived Form," in *The Language of Wisdom and Folly*, I. J. Lee (ed.). Harper, New York, 1949, pp. 251–258. [See *No. 212.*]
414. Cassirer, E. *The Philosophy of Symbolic Forms*, vol. 1: *Language*. Yale University Press, New Haven, 1953.
415. De Laguna, G. A. "Perception and Language," in *The Language of Wisdom and Folly*, I. J. Lee (ed.). Harper, New York, pp. 247–250. [See *No. 212.*]
416. Eilstein, H. "An Essay on the Meanings of the Theory of Reflection," *Philosophical Review (Mysl Filozoficzna)* (1957), no. 1, pp. 78–107 (in Polish).
417. Engels, F. *Anti-Duhring*. International Publishers, New York (many editions).
418. Engels, F. *Dialectics of Nature*. International Publishers, New York (many editions).
419. Gellner, E. *Words and Things*. Victor Gollancz, London, 1959.
420. Goodstein, R. L. "Language and Experience," in *Philosophy of Science*, Arthur Danto and Sidney Morgenbesser (eds.). Meridian Books, New York, 1960, pp. 82–100.
421. *The Importance of Language*, M. Black (ed.). Prentice-Hall,

Englewood Cliffs, N.J., 1962.
422. Janoska, G. *Die sprachlichen Grundlagen der Philosophie.* Akademische Druck- u. Verlagsanstalt, Graz, 1962.
423. Joergensen, J. "Some Remarks Concerning Languages, Calculuses and Logic," in *Logic and Language.* Reidel, Dordrecht, 1962, pp. 28ff. [See *No. 126.*]
424. Klaus, G. and Segeth, W. "Semiotik und materialistische Abbildtheorie," *Deutsche Zeitschrift für Philosophie,* 1962, no. 10, pp. 1245-1260.
425. Kluckhohn, C. "The Concept of Culture," in *Culture and Behavior,* R. Kluckhohn (ed.). Free Press, Glencoe, 1962, pp. 19-73.
426. Kochanski, Z. "Knowledge as Subjective Reflection of Objective Reality," *Philosophical Review (Mysl Filozoficzna)* (1956), no. 5, pp. 48-66 and no. 6, pp. 68-79 (in Polish).
427. Kolakowski, L. "Karl Marx and the Classical Definition of Truth," in *Marxism and Beyond: On Historical Understanding and Individual Responsibility,* translated by Jane Zielonko Peel, Pall Mall Press, London, 1969, pp. 58-86; also published as *Toward a Marxist Humanism,* Grove, New York, 1968, pp. 38-66. (Original essay published 1959 in Polish).
428. Krajewski, W. "On Some Problems of the Leninist Theory of Reflection and the Classical Conception of Truth," *Philosophical Studies (Studia Filozoficzne)* (1960), no. 2, pp. 49-94 and no. 4, pp. 95-115 (in Polish).
429. Lenin, V. I. *Materialism and Empirio-Criticism.* International Publishers, New York (many editions).
430. Lenin, V. I. *Philosophical Notebooks. Collected Works,* vol. 38. Foreign Languages Publishing House, Moscow, 1961.
431. Lewin, G. A. *Problems of the Theory of Knowledge in Lenin's 'Materialism and Empirio-criticism'.* Bielorussian State University Press, Minsk, 1960 (in Russian).
432. Luria, A. R. *Higher Cortical Functions in Man,* translated by B. Haigh. Basic Books, New York, 1966.
433. Marx, K. *Selected Writings in Sociology and Social Philosophy,* T. B. Bottomore and M. Rubel (eds.). McGraw-Hill, New York, 1961.
434. Marx, K. and Engels, F. *The German Ideology* (many editions); references given to Progress Publishers edition, Moscow, 1964.
435. *On Translation,* R. A. Brower (ed.). Harvard University Press, Cambridge, Mass., 1959.
436. Orlow, W. W. *Dialectical Materialism and the Psychological Problem.* Perm Publishing House, Perm, 1960 (in Russian).
437. Pavlov, Todor. *The Theory of Reflection.* Publishing House for Foreign Literature, Moscow, 1949 (in Russian; originally in Bulgarian).
438. Protasenja, P. F. [See *No. 394.*]
439. *Psychologie du langage,* H. Delacroix (ed.). Librairie Felix Alcan, Paris, 1933.
440. Quine, W. V. van O. *Word and Object.* M.I.T. Press, Cambridge,

Mass., 1960.

441. Rubinstein, S. L. *Being and Consciousness.* Academy of Science, U.S.S.R., Moscow, 1957 (in Russian). *Ed. note:* Available in German translation. *Sein und Bewusstsein,* 4th ed., translated by Maria Uhlmann. Akademie-Verlag, Berlin, 1966.

442. Russell, B. *An Inquiry into Meaning and Truth.* George Allen and Unwin, London, 1951. [See *No. 134.*]

443. Sapir, E. "Culture, Genuine and Spurious," in *Language, Culture and Personality,* D. G. Mandelbaum (ed.). University of California Press, Berkeley, 1959, pp. 308-331. [See *No. 247.*]

444. Sapir, E. *Language: An Introduction to the Study of Speech.* Harcourt, Brace, New York, 1949.

445. Schaff, A. [See *No. 140.*]

446. Schorochowa, E. W. *The Problem of Knowledge in Philosophy and the Natural Sciences.* Publishing House for Social and Economic Literature, Moscow, 1961 (in Russian).

447. Sechehaye, A. "Les Mirages linguistiques," *Journal de Psychologie* (1930), no. 5-6, pp. 337-366.

448. Sechehaye, A. "La Pensée et la langue, ou: Comment concevoir le rapport organique de l'individuel et du social dans le langage," in *Psychologie du langage,* H. Delacroix (ed.), pp. 57-81. [See *No. 439.*]

449. Swegincew, W. A. [See *No. 401.*]

450. Tcherkessov, V. I. *Materialist Dialectic as Logic and Theory of Knowledge.* Moscow University Press, Moscow, 1962 (in Russian).

451. *Theory and Critique of Translation,* B. A. Larin (ed.). Leningrad University Press, Leningrad, 1962 (in Russian).

452. Wetter, G. A. *Dialectical Materialism,* translated by P. Heath. Praeger, New York, 1963.

453. Wittgenstein, L. *Philosophical Investigations.* Basil Blackwell, Oxford, 1953.

454. Wittgenstein, L. *Tractatus Logico-Philosophicus.* Kegan Paul, London, 1922.

Endnotes*

PART ONE

Chapter 1

1. J. G. Herder [*19*], p. 340.
2. *Ibid.*, p. 342.
3. *Ibid.*, p. 343.
4. *Ibid.*, p. 347. I cannot deny myself the pleasure of quoting a fine passage from the *Fragmente*, which is interesting not only from the point of view of the problem we are discussing but also because its ideas were ahead of their time.

   "Ist's wahr, dass wir ohne Gedanken nicht denken können und durch Worte denken lernen, so gibt die Sprache der ganzen menschlichen Erkenntnis Schranken und Umriss. . . . Es muss diese allgemeine Betrachtung der menschlichen Erkenntnis durch und mittelst der Sprache eine negative Philosophie geben . . . . Wie vieles man hier ausfegen kann, was wir sagen, ohne dass wir was dabei denken; falsch denken, weil wir es falsch sagten; sagen wollen, ohne dass wir es denken können." J. G. Herder [*22*], pp. 99-100. *Ed. note:* Reprint of part of [*19*].

   If I am not mistaken, then ideas from our entire metaphysical ontology, up to and including the natural wisdom of God, to which mere words have given entry and false citizenship, would slide away and it is primarily these—namely the words—about which there has been the most argument. About nothing is there more argument than what neither party understands, and unfortunately mankind likes nothing better than to want to explain what it cannot explain to itself.
5. *Ibid.*, pp. 348-349.
6. "Die Sprache geht gewiss mit innerer Nothwendigkeit aus dem Menschen hervor, es ist nichts zufällig und willkürlich in ihr; *ein Volk spricht, wie es denkt, denkt so, weil es so spricht, und dass es so denkt und spricht, ist wesentlich in seinen körperlichen und geistigen Anlagen gegründet, und wieder in diese übergegangen.* Doch nicht der abgezogene allgemeine Begriff des menschlichen Geistes und menschlichen Denkens ist der Grund der Sprachen, sondern die ganze vollständige und lebendige Volksindividualität, die nur an der wirklichen Erscheinung studiert werden kann." W. von Humboldt [*28*], p. 344 (italics added).
7. "In die Bildung und den Gebrauch der Sprache geht nothwendig die ganze Art der subjectiven Wahrnehmung der Gegenstände über. Denn das Wort entsteht ja aus dieser Wahrnehmung, und ist nicht ein Abdruck des Gegenstandes an sich, sondern des von diesem in der Seele erzeugten Bildes. Da aller objectiven Wahrnehmung

---

*Ed. note: Italicized numbers within brackets, following the names of authors, refer to items listed in the *Bibliography*.

unvermeidlich Subjectivitaet beigemischt ist, so kann man schon unabhängig von der Sprache jede menschliche Individualität als einen eignen Standpunkt der Weltansicht betrachten. Sie wird aber noch viel mehr dazu durch die Sprache . . . und da nun auch auf die Sprache in derselben Nation eine gleichartige Subjectivitaet einwirkt, *so liegt in jeder Sprache eine eigenthümliche Weltansicht.* Dieser Ausdruck überschreitet auf keine Weise das Mass der einfachen Wahrheit. Denn der Zusammenhang aller Theile der Sprache unter einander, und der ganzen Sprache mit der Nation ist so enge, dass, wenn einmal diese Wechselwirkung eine bestimmte Richtung angiebt, daraus nothwendig durchängige Eigenthümlichkeit hervorgehen muss. *Weltansicht aber ist die Sprache nicht bloss, weil sie, da jeder Begriff soll durch sie erfasst werden können, dem Umfange der Welt gleichkommen muss, sondern aus deswegen, weil erst die Verwandlung, die sie mit den Gegenständen vornimmt, den Geist zur Einsicht des von dem Begriff der Welt unzertrennlichen Zusammenhanges fähig macht . . .* Der Mensch lebt auch hauptsächlich mit den Gegenständen, so wie sie ihm die Sprache zuführt, und da Empfinden und Handeln in ihm von seinen Vorstellungen abhängt, sogar ausschliesslich so. Durch denselben Akt, vermöge welches der Mensch die Sprache aus sich heraus spinnt, spinnt er sich in dieselbe ein, und *jede Sprache zieht um die Nation, welcher sie angehört; einen Kreis, aus dem es nur insofern hinauszugehen möglich ist, als man zugleich in den Kreis einer andern Sprache hinübertritt."* W. von Humboldt [27], pp. 179-180 (italics added).

8. *Ibid.*, p. 119.

9. *Ibid.*, pp. 179-180, as quoted in *note 7.*

10. "Durch diesen heftenden, leitenden und bildenden Einfluss der Sprache wird auch erst der höhere, und oft wohl nicht deutlich genug erkannte Begriff des Wortes *Nation* sichtbar, so wie die Stelle, welche die Vertheilung der Nationen in dem grossen Gange einnimmt, auf dem sich der geistige Bildungstrieb des Menschengeschlechts seine Bahn bricht. Eine Nation in diesem Sinne ist eine durch eine bestimmte Sprache charakterisierte geistige Form der Menschheit, in Beziehung auf idealische Totalitaet individualisiert." *Ibid.*, p. 125.

11. "Die Sprache aber dankt selbst dieser Kraft ihren Ursprung, oder was der richtigere Ausdruck seyn dürfte, die bestimmte nationelle Kraft kann nur in der bestimmten nationellen Sprache . . . innerlich zur Entwicklung, äusserlich zur Mittheilung kommen. Dies ist es, was wir wohl, aber immer uneigentlich, Schaffen der Sprache durch die Nation nennen. Denn der Mensch spricht nicht, weil er so sprechen will, sondern weil er so sprechen muss; die Redeform in ihm ist ein Zwang seiner intellectuellen Natur; sie ist zwar frei, weil diese Natur seine eigne, ursprüngliche ist, aber keine Brücke führt ihn in verknüpfendem Bewusstseyn von der Erscheinung im jedesmaligen Augenblick zu diesem unbekannten Grundwesen hin. *Die Ueberzeugung, dass das individuelle Sprachvermögen . . . nur die sich als Sprache äussernde, den individuellen Charakter der Nationen bestimmende Kraft selbst ist, bildet* den letzten und stärksten Gegensatz gegen die eben . . . gerügte Ansicht der

Sprachen, welche ihre Verschiedenheit nur als eine Verschiedenheit von Schällen und durch Übereinkunft entstandenen Zeichen
betrachtet. *Man begreift nun erst recht, wie die Sprache* . . .
*. . . innig
in den Charakter und die Thatkraft der Nationen verwebt ist, wie
jene Empfindungen und Regungen nicht bloss insofern durch sie
bedingt werden, dass sie nur in ihr auch ihren inneren Ausdruck
finden, sondern dass sie das sie ursprünglich mitgestaltende Wesen
ist." Ibid.,* p. 127 (italics added).

12. Quoted from G. Schmidt-Rohr [46], p. 102 (italics added).
13. *Ibid.*
14. *Cf.* H. Basilius [2]; S. Öhman [38]; S. Ullman [54]; A. A.
Ufimtseva [53]; and M. M. Guchmann [9].
15. J. Trier [49], p. 174.
16. To be found in the works by A. A. Ufimtseva and S. Öhman
referred to in *note 14.*
17. J. Trier [50], pp. 3–6.
18. "Felder sind die zwischen den Einzelworten und dem Wortganzen
lebendigen sprachlichen Wirklichkeiten, die als Teilganze mit dem
Wort das Merkmal gemeinsam haben, dass sie sich ergliedern, und
mit dem Wortschatz hingegen, dass sie sich ausgliedern." J. Trier
[51], p. 430.

". . . die ganze Gruppe ein *Bedeutungsfeld* absteckt, das in sich
gegliedert ist; wie in einem Mosaik fügt sich hier Wort an Wort,
jedes andere umrissen, doch so, dass sie die Konturen aneinander-
passen und alle zusammen in einer Sinneinheit höherer Ord-
nung . . . aufgehen." G. Ipsen [31].

"Ein sprachliches Feld ist also ein Ausschnitt aus der sprachlichen Zwischenwelt, der durch die Ganzheit einer in organischer
Gliederung zusammenwirkenden Gruppe von Sprachzeichen aufge-
baut wird." L. Weisgerber [70]. p. 91.
19. J. Trier [50], pp. 19–20.
20. Quoted from L. Weisgerber [62], p. 171.
21. J. Trier [50], p. 2. The same idea is formulated similarly by L.
Weisgerber in [62], p. 27.
22. L. Weisgerber [70], *Halbband 2,* p. 205.
23. *Ibid.,* p. 242.
24. *Ibid.,* p. 269.
25. *Ibid., Halbband 1,* p. 31, and *Halbband 2,* pp. 206–207.
26. *Ibid., Halbband 1,* p. 67.
27. *Ibid.,* p. 66. See also L. Weisgerber [66], p. 13.
28. L. Weisgerber [70], p. 33.
29. L. Weisgerber [62], p. 51.
30. L. Weisgerber [70], *Halbband 1,* pp. 59–65.
31. *Ibid.,* pp. 35–47.

Chapter 2

1. E. Cassirer [82], p. 18.
2. *Ibid.,* p. 19.
3. "Dass eine solche Vermittlung — sei es durch Lautzeichen, sei es
durch die Bildgestalten des Mythos und der Kunst, sei es durch die
intellektuellen Zeichen und Symbole der reinen Erkenntnis — zum

Wesen des geistigen selbst notwendig gehört, lässt sich leicht einsehen, sobald man nur auf die allgemeinste Form reflektiert, in der er uns gegeben ist. Aller geistige Inhalt ist für uns notwendig an die Form des Bewusstseins und somit an die Form der *Zeit* gebunden . . . Dieser Prozess stellt sich uns überall dort dar, wo das Bewusstsein sich nicht damit begnügt, einen sinnlichen Inhalt einfach zu *haben*, sondern wo es ihn aus sich heraus *erzeugt*." E. Cassirer [*79*], pp. 176–177.

4. E. Cassirer [*84*]; also in [*79*], p. 79.

5. "Wenn es wahr ist, dass alle Objektivität, alles, was wir gegenständliches Anschauen oder Wissen nennen, uns immer nur in bestimmten Formen gegeben und nur durch diese zugänglich ist, so können wir aus dem Umkreis dieser Formen niemals heraustreten, so ist jeder Versuch, sie gewissermassen 'von aussen' zu betrachten von Anfang an hoffnungslos. Wir können nur *in* diesen Formen anschauen, erfahren, vorstellen, denken; wir sind an ihre rein *immanente* Bedeutung und Leistung gebunden. Wenn dem aber so ist, so bleibt es durchaus problematisch, mit welchem Rechte wir überhaupt einen Gegenbegriff und reinen Korrelatbegriff zur reinen Form bilden können. Sprechen wir von einer 'Materie' der Wirklichkeit, die in die Form 'eingeht' und die durch sie gestaltet wird, so scheint dies zunächst nichts anderes als eine blosse Metaphor zu sein. Denn als ein Etwas, das sozusagen nur ein nacktes Dasein hat, ohne schon irgendwie durch eine Form bestimmt zu sein, ist uns ja nichts in unserer Erkenntnis gegeben. Ein solches Etwas ist vielmehr eine blosse Abstraktion -- und eine Abstraktion von sehr fragwürdigem und verdächtigem Charakter. Gibt es denn also überhaupt einen 'Stoff' des Wirklichen, for aller Formung und unabhängig von ihr? Marc-Wogau glaubt mit Recht diese Frage verneinen zu müssen, wenn man die Voraussetzungen annimmt, die ich in meiner *Philosophie der symbolischen Formen* zu Grunde gelegt habe." E. Cassirer [*86*], p. 209.

6. *Cf*. E. Cassirer [*85*], vol. 1, pp. 188–190 and vol. 3, pp. 20–22; and E. Cassirer [*81*], pp. 320–321.

7. "Every authentic function of the human spirit has the decisive characteristic in common with cognition: it does not merely copy but rather embodies an original, formative power. It does not express passively the mere fact that something is present but contains an independent energy of the human spirit through which the simple presence of the phenomena assumes a definite 'meaning', a particular ideational content. This is as true of art as it is of cognition; it is as true of myth as of religion. All live in particular image-words, which do not merely reflect the empirically given, but which rather produce it in accordance with an independent principle. . . .They are not different modes in which an independent reality manifests itself to the human spirit but roads by which the spirit proceeds towards its objectivization, i.e., its self-revelation." E. Cassirer [*85*], p. 78. See also, for instance, [*82*], p. 23, and [*81*], pp. 326–327.

8. E. Cassirer [*85*], vol. 1, p. 80.

9. "Myth and art, language and science, are in this sense configurations *towards* being: they are not simple copies of an existing

reality but represent the main directions of the spiritual movement, of the ideal process by which reality is constituted for us as
one and many—as a diversity of forms which are ultimately held
together by a unity of meaning." *Ibid.*, vol. 1, p. 107.

"Knowledge is described neither as a part of being nor as its
copy. However, its relation to being is by no means taken away
from it but rather is grounded in a new point of view. For it is
now the function of knowledge to build up and constitute the
object, not as an absolute object but as a phenomenal object,
conditioned by this very function. What we call objective being,
what we call the object of experience, is itself only possible if we
presuppose the understanding and its a priori functions of unity."
Ibid., vol. 3, pp. 4–5.

10. "Unter einer 'symbolischen Form' soll jede Energie des Geistes
verstanden werden, durch welche ein geistiger Bedeutungsgehalt an
ein konkretes sinnliches Zeichen geknüpft und diesem Zeichen
innerlich zugeeignet wird. In diesem Sinne tritt uns die Sprache,
tritt uns die mythisch-religiöse Welt und die Kunst als je eine
besondere symbolisch Form entgegen. Denn in ihnen allen prägt
sich das Grundphänomen aus, dass unser Bewusstsein sich nicht
damit begnügt, den Eindruck des Äusseren zu empfangen, sondern
dass es jeden Eindruck mit einer freien Tätigkeit des Ausdrucks
verknüpft und durchdringt. Eine Welt selbstgeschaffener Zeichen
und Bilder tritt dem, was wir die objektive Wirklichkeit der Dinge
nennen, gegenüber und behauptet sich gegen sie in selbständiger
Fülle und ursprünglicher Kraft." E. Cassirer [79], pp. 175-176.

"Die Kraft dieser Erzeugung (des sinnlichen Inhalts durch das
Bewusstsein) ist es, die den blossen Empfindungs- und Wahrneh-
mungsinhalt zum symbolischen Inhalt gestaltet." *Ibid.*, p. 177.

"The symbolic process is like a single stream of life and
thought which flows through consciousness, and which by this
flowing movement produces the diversity and cohesion, the
richness, the continuity and constancy, of consciousness." E.
Cassirer [85], vol. 3, p. 202.

11. *Ibid.*, vol. 1, p. 79.

12. "My protestation too against all charges of idealism is so valid and
clear as even to seem superfluous. . . ." "My idealism concerns not
the existence of things (the doubting of which, however, constitutes idealism in the ordinary sense), since it never came into my
head to doubt it, but it concerns the sensuous representation of
things, to which space and time especially belong." Kant [88], pp.
48–49.

13. "Yet I do not believe an idealistic interpretation of Reality is
necessary to the recognition of art as symbolic form. . . . We need
not assume the presence of a transcendental 'human spirit', if we
recognize, for instance, the function of *symbolic transformation* as
a natural activity, a high form of nervous response, characteristic
of man among the animals. The study of symbol and meaning is a
starting-point of philosophy, not a derivative from Cartesian,
Humean, or Kantian premises; and the recognition of its fecundity
and depth may be reached from various positions, though it is a
historical fact that the idealists reached it first, and have given us

the most illuminating literature on non-discursive symbolisms—myth, ritual, and art." S. K. Langer [91], p. xiv.

14. I shall not go into the details of the theory and the historical evolution of conventionalism; I discussed that issue in my book Schaff [140], chap. 6 of which is concerned with conventionalism. An analysis of conventionalism is also offered in my papers on radical conventionalism: Schaff [139] and [136]. I also refer the reader to the excellent paper by L. Kolakowski [101], which was closely connected with my discussion with Kazimierz Ajdukiewicz, and included a penetrating Marxist analysis of conventionalism.

15. E. Le Roy [104], pp. 529-530.

16. E. Le Roy [103], p. 144.

17. "The fundamental thesis of ordinary conventionalism represented, for instance, by Poincaré, states that there are problems which cannot be solved by reference to experience until a certain convention is adopted, since only that convention combined with empirical data makes it possible to solve a given problem. The judgments which form parts of such a solution are thus not imposed upon us by empirical data alone, but their acceptance depends partly on our choice, since that convention which codetermines the solution of the problem may be altered arbitrarily and may, as a result, obtain other judgments.

"In the present paper it is our intention to present that thesis of ordinary conventionalism in a more general and radical form. We intend to formulate and to justify the theorem that not only some but all judgments which we accept and which form our image of the world are not univocally determined by empirical data, but also depend on the choice of the conceptual apparatus by which we are mapping empirical data. We may choose such or another conceptual apparatus, which will change our entire image of the world. This means: as long as a person is making use of a definite conceptual apparatus, empirical data force him to accept certain judgments. Yet these empirical data alone do not force him to accept those judgments absolutely, since he can choose another conceptual apparatus, in the light of which the same empirical data no longer force him to accept those judgments, since such judgments do not at all occur in the new conceptual apparatus.

"Such is the fundamental thesis of the present paper, formulated briefly and without special concern for precision. We should like to call that thesis 'radical conventionalism' and we think that it is related to the views of the French philosopher Le Roy and possibly also some other thinkers." K. Ajdukiewicz, "The Image of the World and the Conceptual Apparatus," in [109], p. 175. *Ed. note:* See Ajdukiewicz [112].

18. K. Ajdukiewicz [109], pp. 180-181.

19. "The perspective of the world depends on two factors. On the one hand, it depends on the empirical data on which it is built, and on the other, on the conceptual apparatus and the associated rules of language. . . .A change in the conceptual apparatus results in a change in the problems which we solve in the light of the same empirical data." K. Ajdukiewicz, "The Scientific World-Perspective," in [109], p. 217. *Ed. note:* See Ajdukiewicz [113].

20. A more detailed analysis of this problem and also an exposition of the opinions of logical positivists on the problems of language are to be found in my *Introduction to Semantics*, [137], chap. 3, "Semantic Philosophy." In the present work we are interested only in the conclusions pertaining to the role of language in the process of cognition; not in the exposition of the doctrine and an analysis of its general assumptions.
21. R. Carnap [118], pp. xv, 29, 52.
22. C. G. Hempel [125]; B. Russell [134], pp. 148-149.

PART TWO

Chapter 3

1. M. Leenhardt (ed.) [146].
2. See above all: L. Lévy-Bruhl [153].
3. F. Boas [165], pp. 63, 70-71.
4. "It does not seem likely, therefore, that there is any direct relation between the culture of a tribe and the language they speak, except in so far as the form of the language will be molded by the state of culture, but not in so far as a certain state of culture is conditioned by morphological traits of the language." *Ibid.*, p. 67.
5. E. Sapir [250]. We read there, p. 166: "Language is primarily a cultural or social product and must be understood as such."
6. I mean above all "Language and Environment," in E. Sapir [249], pp. 89-103. By way of example I quote a passage from p. 90: ". . . we may expect to find two sets of environmental factors reflected in language, assuming for the moment that language is materially influenced by the environmental background of its speakers. Properly speaking, of course, the physical environment is reflected in language only in so far as it has been influenced by social factors. . . . In other words, so far as language is concerned, all environmental influence reduces at last analysis to the influence of social environment. Nevertheless it is practical to keep apart such social influences as proceed more or less directly from the physical environment, and those that can not be easily connected with it. . . .It is the vocabulary of a language that most clearly reflects the physical and social environment of its speakers."
7. "Everything naturally depends on the point of view as determined by interest. Bearing this in mind, it becomes evident that the presence or absence of general terms is to a large extent dependent on the negative or positive character of the interest in the elements of the environment involved. The more necessary a particular culture finds it to make distinctions within a given range of phenomena, the less likely the existence of a general term covering the range. On the other hand, the more indifferent culturally are the elements, the more likely that they will all be embraced in a single term of general application." *Ibid.*, p. 92.
8. E. Sapir [248], pp. 10-11.
9. "Language is not merely a more or less systematic inventory of the various items of experience which seem relevant to the individual, as is so often naively assumed, but is also a self-contained, creative

symbolic organization, which not only refers to experience largely acquired without its help but actually defines experience for us by reason of its formal completeness and because of our unconscious projection of its implicit expectations into the field of experience. In this respect language is very much like a mathematical system which, also, records experience in the truest sense of the word, only, in its crudest beginnings, but, as time goes on, becomes elaborated into a self-contained conceptual system which previsages all possible experience in accordance with certain accepted formal limitations. . . . [Meanings are] not so much discovered in experience as imposed upon it, because of the tyrannical hold that linguistic form has upon our orientation in the world. Inasmuch as languages differ very widely in their systematization of fundamental concepts, they tend to be only loosely equivalent to each other as symbolic devices and are, as a matter of fact, incommensurable in the sense in which two systems of points in a plane are, on the whole, incommensurable to each other, if they are plotted out with reference to differing systems of coordinates." E. Sapir [246], p. 578.

10.   E. Sapir [250].
11.   B. L. Whorf [275], pp. 135-137.
12.   "Such examples, which could greatly be multiplied, will suffice to show how the cue to a certain line of behavior is often given by analogies of the linguistic formula in which the situation is spoken of, and by which to some degree it is analyzed, classified, and allotted its place in that world which is 'to a large extent unconsciously built upon the language habits of the group'. And we always assume that the linguistic analysis made by our group reflects reality better than it does." *Ibid.*, p. 137.
13.   B. L. Whorf, [276], pp. 213-214.
14.   "We seem, then, perhaps reluctantly, forced to admit that, apart from the reflection of environment in the vocabulary of a language, there is nothing in the language itself that can be shown to be directly associated with environment. . . .If this be true, and there seems every reason to believe that it is, we must conclude that cultural change and linguistic change do not move along parallel lines and hence do not tend to stand in a close causal relation." E. Sapir [249], p. 100.
15.   "It was found that the background linguistic system (in other words the grammar) of each language is not merely a reproducing instrument for voicing ideas but rather is itself the shaper of ideas, the program and guide for the individual's mental activity, for his analysis of impressions, for his synthesis of his mental stock in trade." B. L. Whorf [276], p. 212.
16.   The principle of linguistic relativity was mentioned also by Korzybski, and indeed before Whorf. The representatives of general semantics often refer to what they call the Sapir-Whorf-Korzybski hypothesis (*cf.* Anatol Rapoport and Arnold Horowitz [244], pp. 36-63). Perhaps that is why G. A. Brutjan [171] ascribed to Whorf borrowings from Korzybski. This, however, seems very unlikely, first, because Korzybski's views found some response in public opinion only during World War II; second,

because even then (and now as well) they were not treated in scholarly circles very seriously, in view of the dilettantism of their author and the sectarian character of his school; and third, because, contrary to the opinions prevailing on the subject (especially in Soviet literature), Korzybski in his philosophical interpretations was clearly inclined toward materialism and referred to the category of things, while Whorf, in accordance with his conception of the opinions of the Hopi tribe, declared himself in favor of the category of events. Thus the principle of linguistic relativity is observable in both schools, which, however, differ considerably from one another. That is why it is correct to associate Whorf with Sapir, while it is incorrect to associate him with Korzybski. This mistake has been made not only by Brutjan but also by representatives of general semantics.

17. But in all justice to Whorf, he is not a consistent idealist. W. A. Swegincev also mistook this point, in spite of his well-balanced and objective appraisal of Whorf's theory [259]. As an ethnologist, Whorf occasionally approached a materialistic interpretation of the evolution of the Hopi language and culture. For instance: "In Hopi history, could we read it, we should find a different type of language and different set of cultural and environmental influences working together. A peaceful agricultural society isolated by geographic features and nomad enemies in a land of scanty rainfall, arid agriculture that could be made successful only by the utmost perseverance (hence the value of persistence and repetition), necessity for collaboration (hence emphasis on the psychology of teamwork and on mental factors in general), corn and rain as primary criteria of value, need of extensive *preparations* and precautions to assure crops in the poor soil and precarious climate, keen realization of dependence upon nature favoring prayer and a religious attitude toward the forces of nature, especially prayer and religion directed toward the ever-needed blessing, rain — these things interacted with Hopi linguistic patterns to mold them, to be molded again by them, and so little by little to shape the Hopi world-outlook." B. L. Whorf [275], pp. 157-158.

18. "Actually, thinking is most mysterious, and by far the greatest light upon it that we have is thrown by the study of language. This study shows that the forms of person's thoughts are controlled by inexorable laws of pattern of which he is unconscious. These patterns are the unperceived intricate systematizations of his own language — shown readily enough by a candid comparison and contrast with other languages, especially those of a different linguistic family. His thinking itself is in a language — in English, in Sanskrit, in Chinese. And every language is a vast pattern-system, different from others, in which are culturally ordained the forms and categories by which the personality not only communicates, but also analyzes nature, notices or neglects types of relationship and phenomena, channels his reasoning, and builds the house of his consciousness." B. L. Whorf [269], p. 252.

19. B. L. Whorf [274], pp. 147-148.
20. B. L. Whorf [271], p. 241.

21. *Ibid.*, p. 242.
22. "A linguistic classification like English gender, which has no overt mark actualized along with the words of the class but which operates through an invisible 'central exchange' of linkage bonds in such a way as to determine certain other words which mark the class, I call a *covert* class, in contrast to an *overt* class, such as gender in Latin. Navaho has a covert classification of the whole world of objects based partly on animation and partly on shape. Inanimate bodies fall into two classes which linguists have styled 'round objects' and 'long objects'. These names, of course, misrepresent; they attempt to depict the subtle in terms of the gross, and fail. Navaho itself has no terms which adequately depict the classes. A covert concept like a covert gender is as definable and in its way as definite as a verbal concept like 'female' or feminine, but is of a very different kind. . . .The Navaho so-called 'round' and 'long' nouns are not marked in themselves nor by any pronouns. They are marked only in the use of certain very important verb stems, in that a different verb stem is required for a 'round' or a 'long' subject or object." B. L. Whorf [*272*], pp. 69-70.
23. B. L. Whorf [*267*], pp. 58-59.
24. *Ibid.*, pp. 59 f.
25. "Hopi, as we might expect, is different here too. Verbs have no 'tenses' like ours, but have validity-forms ('assertions'), aspects, and clause-linkage forms (modes), that yield even greater precision of speech. The validity-forms denote that the speaker (not the subject) reports the situation (answering to our past and present) or that he expects it (answering to our future) or that he makes a nomic statement (answering to our nomic present). The aspects denote different degrees of duration and different kinds of tendency 'during duration'. As yet we have noted nothing to indicate whether an event is sooner or later than another when both are *reported*. But need for this does not arise until we have two verbs: i.e., two clauses. In that case the 'modes' denote relations between the clauses, including relations of later to earlier and of simultaneity. Then there are many detached words that express similar relations, supplementing the modes and aspects. The duties of our three-tense system and the tripartite linear objectified 'time' are distributed among various verb categories, all different from our tenses; and there is no more basis for an objectified time in Hopi verbs than in other Hopi patterns; although this does not in the least hinder the verb forms and other patterns from being closely adjusted to the pertinent realities of actual situations." B. L. Whorf [*275*], pp. 144-145.
26. "Any language is more than an instrument for the conveying of ideas, more even than an instrument for working upon the feelings of others and for self-expression. Every language is also a means of categorizing experience. What people think and feel, and how they report what they think and feel, is determined, to be sure, by their individual physiological state, by their personal history, and by what actually happens in the outside world. But it is also determined by a factor which is often overlooked; namely, the

pattern of linguistic habits which people have acquired as members of a particular society. The events of the 'real' world are never felt or reported as a machine would do it. There is a selection process and an interpretation in the very act of response. Some features of the external situation are highlighted; others are ignored or not fully discriminated.

"Every people has its own characteristic classes in which individuals pigeonhole their experience. These classes are established primarily by the language through the types of objects, processes, or qualities which receive special emphasis in the vocabulary and equally, though more subtly, through the types of differentiation or activity which are distinguished in grammatical forms. The language says, as it were, 'Notice this', 'Always consider this separate from that', 'Such and such things belong together'. Since persons are trained from infancy to respond in these ways they take such discriminations for granted, as part of the inescapable stuff of life. But when we see two peoples with different social traditions respond in different ways to what appear to the outsider to be identical stimulus-situations, we realize that experience is much less a 'given', an absolute, than we thought. Every language has an effect upon what the people who use it see, what they feel, how they think, what they can talk about." C. Kluckhohn and D. Leighton [205], p. 197.

27. "While these examples, and many other similar ones, seem clearly to indicate that language habits influence *sensory* perceptions and thought, we must not overestimate this influence... it is perfectly evident that the Navaho, while they denote 'brown' and 'gray' by one term and 'blue' and 'green' by another, are quite able to discern the difference between brown and gray, blue and green. Again this may be done, should ambiguity otherwise result, by circumlocution, just as we can quite simply express in English the difference between the two Navaho words for our 'black'.

"The fact of the matter, then, is not that linguistic patterns inescapably limit sensory perceptions and thought, but simply that, together with other cultural patterns, they direct perception and thinking into certain habitual channels. The Eskimo, who distinguishes in speech several varieties of snow surface (and who lacks a general term corresponding to our 'snow'), is responding to a whole complex of cultural patterns, which require that he make these distinctions, so vital to his physical welfare and that of the group. It is as if the culture as a whole (including the language) selected from the landscape certain features more important than others and so gave to the landscape an organization or structure peculiar to the group. A language, then, as a cultural system, more or less faithfully reflects the structuring of reality, which is peculiar to the group that speaks it." H. Hoijer [195], pp. 559–560.

28. D. Lee [222], p. 82.
29. J. B. Carroll [174]. A detailed analysis of the subject and interests of psycholinguistics can be found in C. E. Osgood and T. A. Sebeok (eds.) [242].
30. "While Cassirer and Whorf made theoretical advances over earlier

work, their approach had a weakness which is common to nearly all of the early investigations into language and cognition. Neither Cassirer nor Whorf was sufficiently explicit in stating the nature of the relationship which they purported to describe. They failed to state in general, yet concrete, terms which types of behavior were supposed to be related. It is true that both of them cited a mass of empirical facts but since they did not at the same time provide a criterion of relevance, we do not know why they selected these particular data, nor do we know whether it would be possible to marshall facts disproving their hypotheses. The empirical material in their writings has an anecdotal character which serves to adumbrate considerations of a basically epistemological nature; it must not be mistaken for corroborative evidence of a hypothesis. In fact, it would be in vain if we were to search their works for *practical* working hypotheses whose verification requires compilation of clearly circumscribed data and which can be accepted or rejected in the light of objective observations." E. H. Lenneberg and J. M. Roberts [228].

A similar appraisal is given by J. B. Carroll in his "Some Psychological Effects of Language Structure" [173], p. 31.

31. R. W. Brown and E. H. Lenneberg [170], pp. 229-263.
32. E. H. Lenneberg, [223]; E. H. Lenneberg and J. M. Roberts [228].
33. J. B. Carroll [174]; J. B. Carroll [173], pp. 28-36; J. B. Carroll and J. B. Casagrande [175].
34. It is worth mentioning that the problem of the relationship between language stimuli (occurrence of appropriate terms) and the distinction and recognition of colors — one of the main experimental problems in psycholinguistics — has been undertaken, though on a different basis, by Soviet psychologists in their detailed and finely documented studies of the languages of the peoples inhabiting the Soviet Union, collected in *Thinking and Speech* [404].
35. The literature of the subject includes such tentative studies as, for instance, H. Nakamura (ed.), [238]. The data contained in such studies can of course be used, but the lack of a uniform research plan, differences in research methods, and differences in the manner of exposition make such studies not quite comparable and hence less useful for our purposes.

PART THREE

Chapter 4

1. L. S. Vygotsky [343].
2. H. Delacroix [285].
3. F. Kainz [299], pp. 111 ff.
4. L. S. Vygotsky [343]. *Ed. note:* Translated from Russian edition.
5. *Ibid.*, in particular pp. 160 ff. and 198 ff.
6. *Ibid.*, p. 161.
7. *Ibid.*, pp. 329-335.
8. *Ibid.*, pp. 331 ff.

9. "Thoughts," Vygotsky says, "are not expressed in words, but acquire existence in them. We might therefore speak about the becoming (the unity of existence and nonexistence) of thoughts in words." *Ibid.*, p. 330 and *cf.* p. 332. I consider this formulation by Vygotsky, so very Hegelian in spirit, to be particularly important and fertile.

10. The research studies of Vygotsky's school are listed by A. R. Luria in A. R. Luria and F. J. Judowich [*314*], pp. 13-22. These studies are also described by Luria in his paper on the role of speech in the formation of psychic processes in children. The most comprehensive data on this subject are given in the same author's article [*308*], pp. 516-577.

11. A.R. Luria [*308*], pp. 556 ff.

12. S. Szuman [*332*], p. 9.

13. *Cf.* A. W. Yarmolenko [*349*].

14. F. Kainz [*299*], pp. 149-156.

15. H. Keller [*301*].

16. W. Jerusalem [*297*], pp. 51-53.

17. L. Arnould [*278*], pp. 41 ff.

18. "In what concerns the potential possibilities of their work in society, blind deaf-mutes are quite normal human beings, but they cannot at all put their possibilities into effect by their own effort; hence, if they are not helped by special pedagogic measures, they will remain all their life on the level of idiocy." I. A. Sokoliansky [*327*], pp. 82-83.

19. "In the blind deaf-mutes touch is the principal means not only of cognition, but of communication as well; speech is tactile ... thought materializes as tactile representations of images of words. The relation between sensory impressions and thoughts is very complicated .... Touch is gradually transformed into a way of acquiring the knowledge of the material world, and next into a way of denoting and generalizing by words ... i.e., it is transformed into the basis of the images of the second system of signals. That transformation and differentiation of touch in blind deaf-mute children is possible only in the process of teaching, since such children, as they cannot convey and receive auditory and visual signals at a distance, cannot spontaneously and continually imitate the people of their milieu, which is one of the principal factors of development of those children who can hear and see." *Ibid.*, pp. 53-55.

20. "The mastering of the first words in their active use means for the blind deaf-mute children the transition to a new, higher, human form of cognition, namely through the intermediary of words, of language .... Speech becomes a means of communication, thinking, acquiring knowledge in the process of school training that follows. A blind deaf-mute child passes from concrete, sensory, individual experience to the formation of representations of the second type, namely the generalized ones." *Ibid.*, p. 120.

21. L. Geppertowa [*289*], pp. 17-31.

22. *Cf.* F. Kainz [*299*], pp. 130-151.

23. *Ibid.*, pp. 136 ff.

24. A. R. Luria [*311*], pp. 132, 137.

25. *Cf.* S. L. Rubinstein [*321*], pp. 369–370. *Ed. note:* Translated from Russian edition.
26. W. N. Kellog and L. A. Kellog [*302*].
27. F. Kainz [*299*], pp. 342–350.
28. *Cf.* K. Goldstein [*356*], p. xii.
29. *Cf.* A. R. Luria [*372*], p. 44.
30. A. R. Luria [*373*].
31. *Cf.* K. Goldstein [*356*], pp. 60–63, and K. Goldstein [*357*], pp. 18–20.
32. K. Goldstein [*357*], pp. 29–30.
33. E. Cassirer [*351*], chap. 6.
34. *Ibid.*, p. 28.
35. K. Goldstein [*357*], p. 40 and K. Goldstein [*354*], p. 496.
36. J. Konorski [*367*], p. 9.
37. *Ibid.* p. 13.
38. O. L. Skorochodowa (ed.) [*324*].
39. K. Marx and F. Engels [*434*], pp. 41–42.
40. *Ibid.*, pp. 491–492.
41. *Cf. G.* Révész [*397*], pp. 124–129, and [*395*], pp. 9–20.
42. B. L. van der Waerden [*406*], p. 166 (italics added).
43. *Ibid.*, p. 173.
44. *Ibid.*, p. 173.
45. The appropriate examples adduced in this connection by the dualists can be found in van der Waerden [*406*], p. 175.
46. A Potebnia [*393*], p. 131.

Chapter 5

1. A still more radical criticism of this standpoint is made by Joergen Joergensen, who refuses mathematical and other symbolism the right to be called a language and reserves that term for the natural languages only. This is the more interesting as Joergensen himself at one time was among the thinkers who came close to logical positivism, and his critical opinions are presented in a paper included in a collection dedicated to Carnap. J. Joergensen [*423*].
2. L. Kolakowski [*427*].
3. H. Eilstein [*416*].
4. *Ibid.*, p. 103.
5. Z. Cačkowski [*412*].
6. A. Schaff [*140*]. *Ed. note:* Pp. 47–65, in Polish edition.
7. K. Marx, " Theses on Feuerbach" [*433*], pp. 82–84.
8. *Ibid.*
9. V. I. Lenin, *Philosophical Notebooks* [*430*]. *Ed. note:* Quoted from a Polish version, Warsaw, 1936, p. 315.
10. K. Marx [*433*].